TECHNIQUE IN DRAMATIC ART

THE MACMILLAN COMPANY
NEW YORK · BOSTON · CHICAGO · DALLAS
ATLANTA · SAN FRANCISCO

MACMILLAN & CO., Limited
LONDON · BOMBAY · CALCUTTA
MELBOURNE

THE MACMILLAN COMPANY
OF CANADA, Limited
TORONTO

ŒDIPUS REX, of Sophocles, presented at Stanford University, California, under the joint direction of Gordon Davis of Stanford University, and Evalyn Thomas, of the University of California, Southern Branch

TECHNIQUE IN
DRAMATIC ART

A DELINEATION OF THE ART OF ACTING BY MEANS OF ITS
UNDERLYING PRINCIPLES AND SCIENTIFIC LAWS, WITH
TECHNICAL INSTRUCTION IN THE ART OF PLAY PRODUCTION
AND PUBLIC SPEAKING

BY HALLIAM BOSWORTH

REVISED EDITION

NEW YORK
THE MACMILLAN COMPANY

PREFACE TO THE NEW EDITION

Many books are revised and for various reasons. Books on scientific subjects are revised generally to place upon the plane of proven fact ideas which have been advanced merely as theories in the original editions. Also, the writers' knowledge of their subjects may have become broader and they desire to present fuller expositions.

When it was proposed to issue a new edition of this book the publishers were assured that this could not be a "revision" in the accepted sense of that term; namely, in the sense of translating into conviction what had been only theory before, or, on the other hand, of deleting statements of theories which had been proved to be false.

Since the first publication of the book in August, 1926, it has been read and examined by many actors of long and seasoned experience. In specific cases the author has asked such actors to criticize freely and to offer complaints as to the accuracy or inaccuracy of the exposition. Such complaints have not been made. The author has frequently asserted in the treatise that the principles outlined are, in his conception, fundamental ones. They are not meant to be a delineation of fashions, styles, and methods of acting, popular in any one period, but are asserted to be in accord with basic laws, both of life and of art. Therefore, it is his conviction that they will be acceptable and proper in the theatre of any time.

With this conviction in mind, then, the author could not remove from a new edition of the book any declaration of principles that had been placed in the original text. Since the principles are true and have never been questioned they must remain as originally stated. He could only incorporate in the new edition whatever new ideas he had gleaned since the first writing and make it an enlargement upon, rather than a correction of, the old.

Writing a textbook on acting out of a personal experience in the theatre is largely a matter of setting down as much as one can think of at the time of writing. Naturally, many principles are overlooked. Very shortly after the book was off the press the author thought of many new principles which might have been incorporated had he thought of them in time. These were immediately written down and kept for future use. They are now included in this edition, besides many others that have come to mind through a thorough perusal of the text.

The student is assured that no attempt has been made to contradict by new material anything that has been previously written. This is especially true in respect to a new paragraph on Moving Backgrounds in the chapter on Directorship. A sufficient explanation has been given in that paragraph of the distinction between the principle of Moving Backgrounds and that of Distraction in another chapter.

In various places verb tenses have had to be changed from present to past, since several people of the theatre have since died.

Many of the plays whose titles have been quoted, and which were fairly well known at the time, have since been largely forgotten. The same titles remain, however, since nothing is gained for the student by substituting the identical principles from new plays. Popular plays pass,

PREFACE TO THE NEW EDITION

but principles are fixed and can be as well illustrated from old plays as from new ones.

The book was originally written with only the amateur actor in mind. Through his activity exclusively in the professional theatre the author can learn of its effect in amateur fields only by hearsay. In the professional field he has had closer touch and has found the book to be welcome to many young professional actors. It is hoped it will continue to be of use to students of the technique of the theatre.

HALLIAM BOSWORTH

NEW YORK CITY,
October, 1934.

PREFACE TO THE FIRST EDITION

During many years on the stage the author of this book has sought to discover the principles underlying good acting and to determine how the various effects sought by the actor are produced. Very little has heretofore been written about the fundamentals of dramatic technique, chiefly because those whose work is in the theatre are artists, and have very little interest in the scientific aspects of acting. An actor commonly chooses his profession because it represents an expression of his emotional nature. In seeking to interpret and convey appropriate emotions to the audience he relies upon his own conception of the emotions rather than upon any scientific principles. For this reason it is difficult for an actor to take an objective view of his own performance, but it is even more difficult for anyone without experience on the stage to understand and to explain the actor's technique.

The author feels that from years of experience in the theatre he has gained an intimate knowledge of professional methods in acting and play producing. With this background he has attempted to step aside from his rôle as actor and has sought to describe and analyze in a scientific manner the various methods which the actor may use to produce the desired emotional effects in the theatre. This is so new an undertaking that appropriate terms and designations have not always been found in use, and it has been necessary, therefore, to devise certain new terms and to define them specifically. Examples of these expressions are: Coöperation, The Law of Attention, Eliminating the Non-essential, The Magnetic Centre, Keeping the Eye on the Ball. These and numerous other expressions are clearly explained in the text and then adopted as standard.

The author's conception of certain principles of dramatic art may differ from that of some of his readers, but it is hoped that in actual practice in the theatre the points will prove definitely useful as they are presented.

Many dramatic selections in the book have been given with accompanying action and business. This is true especially of scenes from Shakespeare's plays. Different actors might interpret these scenes with a wide variety of business and action. Some of the accompanying action has been devised according to the author's conception of how it *may* be done. Much of this business is copied from the traditional business of some of the famous actors in the past.

In respect to make-up, each actor naturally develops his own idiosyncracy. The system outlined is that familiar to the author through his own experience. The student is invited to make use of its general principles, and to develop such additional methods as suit his own individuality and needs.

The whole trend of the work points toward the operation of principles for the acting of plays as a whole, rather than for individual parts. One theory of government is that the individual should live for the state. The theory presented here is that the actor should work for the play.

The author wishes to acknowledge his indebtedness to those who have contributed to the preparation of the book through their encouragement, assistance, and advice.

PREFACE TO THE FIRST EDITION

Mr. John McKee of New York City offered very valuable hints on stage lighting. Mr. Howard Chenery, instructor of Dramatic Art in Central High School, Kalamazoo, Michigan, contributed some useful points and gave helpful advice on the needs of the student, which accrued to a proper elaboration of the work.

Mr. Oliver Hinsdell, director of the Little Theatre at Dallas, Texas, contributed many valuable examples from current plays, which served to illustrate further the principles outlined. The author's work has been exclusively in the professional theatre, and Mr. Hinsdell's experience in the Little Theatre and amateur fields made it possible to incorporate descriptions of many methods in play production for amateur and little theatre groups which apply especially to those branches of the theatre.

It is hoped the book will prove of value to students and teachers working in preparation for either the amateur or the professional stage, and that it will prove to be a convenient handbook for actors and others directly engaged in or interested in the work of the theatre.

HALLIAM BOSWORTH

NEW YORK CITY,
June, 1926.

FOREWORD TO THE FIRST EDITION

Now as never before, America is turning to the theatre. It is not merely that we desire to be entertained. A new and deepening appreciation of the institution of the stage as a cultural factor in any community is making itself felt throughout the country. One has but to note the daily activities of the more representative of nearly two thousand little theatres scattered throughout the United States to be convinced that the theatre, when taken seriously and approached with the dignity worthy of it, has a definite contribution to make to both the individual and the neighborhood.

Alive to these possibilities in the theatre, enthusiastic players and producers everywhere are seeking practical instruction in the ways of appreciating and developing the many forms of art that go into "putting on" a play successfully. In this volume the intelligent lover of the stage will find the answers to such practical questions given in thorough but entertaining fashion.

It seems to me that Mr. Bosworth has achieved an extraordinarily complete manual of acting and play production, and that he has succeeded notably in reducing the technique of acting to certain definite scientific laws which anyone can learn. To be sure, the art of acting can be summed up in a phrase, "getting an effect." But experiencing an emotion and giving a spectator the effect of it are two vastly different things. No matter with what powerful sincerity the would-be actor stirs himself to heights and depths of emotion, if he does not know something of the principles which make it possible to project this emotion over the footlights, he will find his audience cold. The true artist is the one who so stimulates the audience that they become a part of the performance.

The professional actor will recognize in this book the fruits of many years of experience on the professional stage, and that sureness of expression which only a rich knowledge and honest skill in the theatre can bring. The author reveals the tricks of the actor's trade, and he does more. He points the way toward that coördination of spirit with technique which is so essential to the finished and convincing presentation of a play as an artistic whole.

The inexperienced player, will learn from this book how to do many things right the first time, without having to struggle in the dark and learn only through experience. We may profit by our mistakes, it is true, but for those of us who work in the theatre there are inevitably enough of these to keep us humble and there is no need for perilous pioneering where a clear trail has already been blazed.

This book is fused with just the proper background, spirit, and direction to make it a cherished book of reference for the professional, and at the same time an ever ready counsel and training course for the amateur. All of Mr. Bosworth's formulas for staging and stage business have been tried and proven by the gifted leaders of dramatic art on the American stage. His chapter on make-up, with illustrations, tells all the main secrets of that branch of theatrical art, with the result that the beginner can see how and why certain effects are obtained, and can learn to do his own making up, just as the experienced actor always does. The illustrations and diagrams are chosen to meet the needs of actor and director in solving problems of stage business and scenic effect.

Nowhere has the interest in drama been more keen than in our schools and colleges. There is hardly a great educational institution in America which has not its play-writing courses as well as its dramatic clubs, and often the two work together. If these courses are to prove worth while, those at the head of them must not lose sight of the fact that all of the great drama of the world from before the days of Shakespeare down to Ibsen and Eugene O'Neill has been wrought by men who have had an intimate and first-hand knowledge of the stage. True drama has always been the democratic child of a living theatre which has won its livelihood by striving to please a fickle and inclu-sive public.

It is the actual conditions and physical limitations of the theatre which have shaped and developed dramatic form from the days of Sophocles, and today these limita-tions are quite as rigorously compelling as when Athens had her glory. The young playwright of our time cannot hope to succeed if he does not perceive clearly the de-mands which production will make upon his work. The stage and the actors are as inevitably mediums through which he expresses his ideas as pigments of color are for the painter.

The best way to know the theatre, of course, is to see it from the front and to labor in it behind the scenes. In the meantime, Mr. Bosworth's volume will prove an ex-cellent foundation for the understanding which every player must develop for himself day by day. The serious teacher of creative drama should welcome it as thoroughly practical and a most valuable aid in opening up new vistas which he is trying to bring before his pupils.

OLIVER HINSDELL

DALLAS, TEXAS.

CONTENTS

CONTENTS

CONTENTS

ILLUSTRATIONS

ILLUSTRATIONS

TECHNIQUE IN DRAMATIC ART

TECHNIQUE IN DRAMATIC ART

CHAPTER I

THE DRAMATIC SCHOOL

A prominent actor in giving his impressions of the art of acting, its requirements and general nature, said, "Acting is a trade." He could not have meant this in the limited sense that branches of artisanship are trades. We distinguish as trades those manual occupations which require a knowledge of certain technical and mechanical methods. With practice the worker becomes expert in the use of these methods. The sciences are a higher branch of industry; they require a knowledge of the technical methods that apply to each particular science, as well as the higher understanding of natural laws; with the latter the trades deal little or not at all. Still higher in the scale are the arts, in which the technical principles of the trades and the natural laws of the sciences are both included. Therefore, the arts are the highest forms of human expression, since they combine the expressions of artisanship, science, and art itself.

With such a conception, the actor was right in calling acting a trade, but he should have made a more comprehensive statement; because acting is not only a trade, but a science and an art as well. It is a trade in the sense that many technical methods and terms are employed; it is a science in that it requires much knowledge of human nature and the laws of life; and finally, it is an art in that it requires the expression of the highest element of human nature, the emotions of the soul. That ultimate expression is the complement which includes the other two.

The art of acting cannot, therefore, find its most perfect expression without the study of human nature, and the technical methods of expressing it. The three sets of principles stated in the last paragraph are interdependent. In attempting a book of this kind, we cannot suggest ideas to the student without starting at the beginning. The student who would become an expert actor should first learn the elementary technical principles; with these a fair start can be made.

There is a common saying that "actors are born and not made." This is only partly true, and must be understood in the proper sense. The actor without a natural talent for emotional expression is a straw man in art and cannot rise to any great dramatic achievement. With no deep interest in human nature, he will be also deficient. The mere desire for the stage as a life expression presupposes some emotional impulse and talent, else the actor might better be an artisan, a scientist, or a business man. But given sufficient talent, and acquiring through life and experience a knowledge of human nature, then, through a study of the technical laws of acting, the student can bring that talent to its best expression.

There have been many prominent artists who, though not greatly endowed by nature, have, through study and hard work in the technical principles, accomplished much. Assuming, therefore, some original talent in the student, we point to the technique of acting as the field of initial study. A vast number of actors throughout their lives are ignorant of many fundamental principles, whereas with a knowledge of them they might have become far more proficient. As a result, they have grown into habits which have hampered their progress.

We should recognize the value of the dramatic school, if it imparts to the student that instruction which is the most important for his progress. The school should correct primary tendencies toward wrong habits and methods; for a bad habit fixed in youth may be difficult to eradicate later.

A college president said he had forgotten ninety-five per cent of what he had learned in college. That mattered not. Study in his youth had trained his mind to the manner of thought by which he had become what he was. All the expressions of life, whether they lie along lines of art, science, or artisanship, are governed by basic laws. The correct expression of these laws should involve a knowledge of principles, whether that knowledge be intuitional or acquired through experience. The painter, with whatever expression of genius he makes the strokes of his brush, has learned the mechanical methods of preparing and mixing colors, the physical properties of perspective, the primary principles of drawing, and many other rules which are purely elemental. The writer has gone to school and learned his A B C's, and later studied the higher principles of rhetoric and composition. The musician has practiced his scales in early youth, and familiarized himself with the scientific principles of musical art. And yet, while the trades, the sciences, and most of the arts have required preliminary apprenticeship in shops, or study in schools and universities, the drama has been neglected, and has allowed the actor to hit or miss according to his relative merit. He learns what and how he can in a free for all contest for success. Despite her genius, the great Sarah Bernhardt in her youth attended a dramatic school. There she learned the fundamental principles governing the mechanics of dramatic art. Those principles became so engrafted in her expression that, though in time she may have forgotten the scientific methods, her manner was complete and perfect.

The value of the study of principles is not lessened by the fact that many natural geniuses have succeeded without it. They might perhaps have obtained their success more quickly with the aid of guiding minds to teach them the basic laws through a preliminary course of study. They may have ultimately learned these laws; but the process was no doubt the more arduous one of experience and frequent failure, and not the sure knowledge which comes from expert instruction. We learn fundamentals in our schools. We may forget the rules, but their impression has been left upon the mind, and guides us along those lines to which they apply. This is a difference between theory and practice; and theory leads us to correct practice far more readily than practice, through hard experience, finally acquaints us with theory.

By analytical observation of the theatre in America we find on our stage violations of some of the most elementary principles of the art, and oftentimes at the hands of the most experienced players. Art may rise at times above the externals of technique and be its own excuse for the violation of principles. Still, a lack of technique is always a blemish upon art.

The discussions in succeeding chapters have sought to present analysis of fundamental principles. To a finished artist, some of this analysis may seem too minute for precise observance. An actor may be a complete success through his natural talent and inspiration, which enable him to do his work without much thought, or even knowledge, of the underlying principles which he is constantly using. In such a case the actor has instinctive knowledge in the use of these principles. He expresses them through his dramatic sense supplemented by experience. Perhaps, while directing other actors, if he sees faulty places in their technique, he can instinctively find the reasons for their mistakes and suggest the remedies. He knows his own habits in like situations, and judges of their faults through his own expertness. He may not analyze scientifically, but is able to translate the impulses of life into his own expression, and can suggest the manner, if not the method, to those he directs. He can say, "Don't do that, do this," and does not have to give his reasons to the actor.

The professional stage expects competency in those it employs; it tells the actor what it wants done, and resents the necessity of showing him why or how to do it. The expression is often heard, "We are not running a dramatic school." The directors are not always able to impart principles even if they would, and the actor must be largely a "self-made" man in art in order to succeed. The student should therefore learn first the underlying principles of his art in order that he may relate its laws with practice and experience until these laws are expressed as a part of his intuitive impulse.

The last generation or two in the theatre has seen great changes. The theatre of a few generations ago was a theatre of traditions. The manner of acting in those days was distinguished by certain fixed methods of expression which were constant for all situations. The actual derivation of the word *tradition* explains how this was put into practice. The word comes from the Latin, *tradere* to transmit, or hand over. In the theatre, it referred to rules and methods which were transmitted from one to another by word of mouth from generation to generation.

There were two distinct sets of these traditions. One set referred to established bits of stage business in various rôles which had been originated by the more talented players and accepted as the best business by subsequent portrayers of these rôles; the other set referred to certain fixed methods of technique. The first-mentioned set of traditions had relation to what is now known as the "classic drama." The term "legitimate drama" now distinguishes all spoken drama from the motion pictures. Legitimate drama is composed of the classic and the modern.

Today we understand as the classic drama, the plays of Shakespeare, which stand at the head in this class, and a few other plays which have survived from the past and have gained the right to be called dramatic classics. These plays, unlike the modern pieces, were played year after year, and were thus kept constantly before the public; even today, they have their periodical presentations. The same public saw them performed by successive casts of actors, and their leading parts were played by famous stars. There was ample opportunity for comparison of the methods and stage business with which they were performed. For example, each star who played a leading Shakespearean rôle originated for that rôle the stage business which appealed to him, and being a prominent, or even a great, actor, the business was often illuminating and striking. These fine performances were copied as closely as possible by less prominent actors, who did the same business in certain situations that their great predecessors had done before them.

One or two examples will show the student what is meant by "stage business." When Edwin Booth, as Hamlet, followed the ghost off the stage, after the ghost had commanded Hamlet's presence for the interview at another part of the platform, Mr. Booth elevated the handle of his sword. The sword handle formed the sign of the cross, a symbol of divine protection. Again, in the banquet scene of *Macbeth*, Edwin Forrest, after the second appearance of the ghost of Banquo, dashed his goblet at the retreating figure. In the New York Public Library there is a volume containing an account by an eye witness of the stage business done by the great Sarah Siddons in her wonderful performance as Lady Macbeth. It was natural that these and other noteworthy bits of business, since they were the best that had been devised in any age, should have been handed down and copied by most of the succeeding actors. These bits of business came to be known as "traditional business," and are done by many actors of classic rôles today. In modern plays, the business is preserved in the scripts while the pieces are performed; the lives of these plays are short, and this type of tradition has no relation to them.

In this discussion we are mostly concerned with the second set of traditions. An example or two will show the nature of these traditional methods. A character passing another character from one side to the other must always pass between that character and the footlights, never behind him. Again, a character standing with another in the centre of the stage and wishing to turn up stage toward the back, must turn outward with his face toward the footlights, never inward toward his companion; it made no difference which happened to be the easier way to reach his objective point. These and many other methods became traditional. We are not concerned with them for present study.

By reason of these fixed traditional methods, the stage of the past was a school in itself. There is an added sense therefore, when we hear it spoken of as "the old school." The directors and older actors stood in the relation of teachers to the newcomers, to instruct them in the principles. Today we consider these principles stereotyped and "old-timey." Life itself is responsible for the change; for as our expressions of life change, the theatre changes with them, because it reflects life as it finds it in any age.

The style of our modern drama has rendered some of these old methods undesirable, and others almost impossible. They had their place and utility in the theatre of their time and served their purpose well, because they were natural to the style of plays and acting in which they were used. In this school of acting, knowledge and proficiency resulted because the rules were absolute and fixed. Like any artisan, the actor had fixed methods of securing his effects. Like the artisan, however, he attained only to varying degrees of expertness in the performance of his work.

Today, the old stereotyped methods of past eras have been nearly all cast aside. This is necessary because of the nature of our modern plays. The spirit of the old plays was that of idealism, while realism is the moving principle of the new. Realism argues that any practice may be true to life, and no fixed methods need apply to all situations and conditions. If an actor is awkward in his gesture, that is real, because many people are; if he speaks with his back to the audience, that is real; if his elocution is faulty, that is true to life; and if he walks in front or behind another on the stage, or turns about in any way that suits his convenience, these things are done in real life and no criticism is offered. We use methods of acting which suit us in this modern day; and between the two methods lies the difference between the Real and the Ideal.

As a result of this change, the fundamental principles of tradition are not found to a large extent in the modern theatre. Still, since fundamental principles underlie the expressions of life itself, our stage, in depicting life, must put many of them into practice. When this is done, it is done instinctively and without set rules. The modern theatre does not present a school of acting in the sense that the old theatre functioned in that respect. This, however, is still possible. Admitting that the old methods are archaic, we can still teach new methods which, though elastic, are subject to rule. If, for example, a person may cross behind another as well as in front, then that becomes a rule and the rule is fixed.

Russian dramatic art is thought by many to be the greatest in the world. It is true, at least, that in Russia the drama is studied with more intense seriousness than perhaps in any other country. Dramatic schools exist in which a distinctly Russian method is used for developing the actor. The greatest of these schools, or methods of development, is that presided over by Stanislavsky, of the Moscow Art Theatre.

In the opinions of many, the drama can be expressed ideally and still seem real. This, after all, should be its essential purpose. We believe that in presenting a series of discussions on dramatic technique, practices can be suggested which do not dissociate realism from idealism. Perfect diction, for example, is ideal, but no one can deny that it is real as well. Fixed systems of technique can be taught theoretically in the modern theatre, as they were imparted by the laboratory method in the old. After the student's initial instruction through books and dramatic schools, the systems can be worked out and assimilated in practice. The technical methods will vary in kind as manners and customs change. Nevertheless, the fundamentals are constant for all times.

INTELLECTUAL PLAYS

The principal theme of drama has been the conflict of good and evil, with the ultimate triumph of good over evil, thus following a law of life. Plays with this central theme contain characters of distinctly evil tendencies who are ultimately triumphed over by those of heroic or virtuous nature. In the past generation the theatre has shown a tendency to depart from this more or less conventional type, and there has sprung up a new style of drama which we may call "the drama of ideas." Henrik Ibsen is said to have been the pioneer in this field.

These plays of ideas are constructed around central themes which reflect some of the social problems or conditions of our modern life. The central themes serve as social backgrounds for the unfoldment of the plots. Our intensive civilization, with its acute struggle for existence, gives birth to many social, or sociological, problems. These problems naturally find their way into the theatre and are discussed upon the stage. The public welcomes the opportunity to hear them discussed, and the authors seek to combine that discussion with enjoyable entertainment.

When the background idea of a play presents a social problem which is not of a very serious nature, or has a central theme which is not a problem at all, but merely the reflection of some harmless social condition, then these plays can be made to have a distinct popular appeal, and are usually presented in the form of comedies. One play may be written on the theme of the extravagance and freedom of the daughters of the rich; another may have for its central idea the tyranny of children over parents; still another may dramatize the idleness of some wealthy wives.

The more serious aspects of our social life, however, are often presented. This work is done by the more literary and cultured of the playwrights, and there is not so much attempt to make merely a "popular appeal." The plays are largely sociological discussions and endeavor to present to the attention and thresh out our social difficulties. These plays are intended for the cultured and intelligent minds, and for those who support what is called the "new movement" in the theatre. There is probably no set term by which to classify these plays unless we speak of them indefinitely as sociological, or intellectual, plays.

A stock company which changed its program from week to week, and offered to its public a wide variety of entertainment ranging from the classic drama to farce, one week presented one of these intellectual social problem plays. The manager considered that the company had given the best performance thus far that season. The next week the company, pursuing its policy of variety, presented our American classic, *Uncle Tom's Cabin*. With as much sincerity as he had praised the previous week's performance, the manager condemned this one, and said that in *Uncle Tom's Cabin* the company had given the poorest performance of its engagement.

There was a reason for this. *Uncle Tom's Cabin* is about seventy years old. It was written in the romantic and emotional style of the theatre which has, for the most part, passed away. The actors of that day were trained for the style of acting of their time, of which *Uncle Tom's Cabin* is a fair example. This play gives a correct reflection of the conditions of its day, and the actors of that period merely imitated the conditions in which they lived. Conditions of life have changed in the past seventy years, and the actors of today can better present the plays which deal with their times. They are more expert in reflecting conditions which they see about them from day to day; and the stock company consequently could not do justice to *Uncle Tom's Cabin*.

But it had done justice to the modern intellectual play. There was another reason for this besides that already mentioned. The modern sociological, or intellectual, play is the easiest to act in all dramatic literature. At the opposite extreme stand the plays of Shakespeare. The plays of today have been stripped more and more of the bombastic methods of the past; their language is more colloquial, and their emotions more suppressed. The intellectual play is a good example of this. It is made up largely of colloquial discussions of our social problems, and we are accustomed to such dialogue and arguments in our everyday life. In the old dramas, the actor assumed a stage manner and method for his work, and was required to "act" in the sense of that term. In the modern play of which we speak, the actor merely uses on the stage the kind of language, and expresses the kind of thought, which he may indulge in every day. Therefore in many scenes very little acting is required. A part of acting is to learn not to act; nevertheless, the suppressed, or negative, acting of this modern play is easier than the positive emotionalism of the old. Performances of these plays often gain credit for being especially artistic and the individual acting remarkable; but the reason is that audiences hear questions discussed and language used which they indulge in themselves, and are impressed with the fine literary, though colloquial, style in which the plays are written. They then give credit to the actors for their work when the ideas expressed have held their attention, but the author deserves most of the credit. In these plays, more than in the old, the lines themselves, rather than the way in which they are acted, arouse most of the attention.

Since it is comparatively easy to perform, the intellectual play is admirably suited to performances by amateurs. Even in professional stock companies an occasional play of this character has been found to be of value, in that it not only lends variety to the weekly program, but elevates it to a higher standard of excellence.

While the new edition of this book is being prepared, a new form of drama has made its appearance. Though the future cannot be foretold, it is possible that in view of present unrest in economic affairs (1934) this form of drama may gain much prominence. It may be termed the drama of class struggle. Much of it has been presented in Russia; and in New York City a drama of this nature has been performed with much success. It is called *Peace on Earth* and concerns a strike by workers in a munitions factory in protest against war. This piece cannot be classed among romantic and domestic dramas, so must take its place therefore among intellectual plays. Such plays are distinctly dramas of ideas.

The intellectual play has achieved increased prominence as the result of the little theatre movement throughout the country. Modern drama is becoming increasingly colloquial, and so practical for the amateur or semi-professional that he may act any type of plays he desires. He will need to learn only the fundamental technique of acting in order to give acceptable presentations. The following chapters are written to instruct him in the technical principles of the art of acting. With a knowledge of these he may develop his own style.

EXERCISES

1. What do we understand by the legitimate drama?
2. What are "traditions" in the theatre? What two kinds can you mention?
3. What is understood by "the old school"?
4. Explain the "drama of ideas."
5. What do you understand by the "intellectual drama"?
6. Give your conception of the difference between idealism and realism in the theatre.

CHAPTER II

ELEMENTARY PRINCIPLES

In the present chapter we shall explain some of the
A B C principles of acting. The student should start at
the beginning, so in this chapter he will be given some of
the simplest details. Many principles can be picked up
with very little practice; still, at the risk of seeming too
minute, we give them here that the student may quickly
acquire them.

Several of these discussions were suggested by an
observation of some rehearsals by a company of young amateurs. Most of them had never taken part in any dramatic performance before. Their treatment was, therefore, purely elemental. We shall point out the faults
which they committed. From comparison, sharp contrast can be shown between the wrong and the right way,
and the right way more firmly impressed upon the mind.

On the following page is a diagram of a plain interior
setting showing entrances from all possible directions,
and some of the positions. A scene indoors is called an
interior; one out of doors, an exterior. Abbreviations of
the terms used in the diagram are given below:

C	Centre
R C	Right centre
R	Right
L C	Left centre
L	Left

R 1 E	Right first entrance
R 2 E	Right second entrance
R 3 (or U) E	Right third (or upper) entrance
L 1 E	Left first entrance
L 2 E	Left second entrance
L 3 (or U) E	Left third (or upper) entrance
C D	Centre door
D in R flat	Door in right flat
D in L flat	Door in left flat

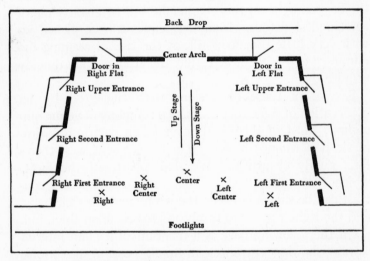

PLAIN INTERIOR WITH ALL POSSIBLE ENTRANCES

The other terms on the diagram have no technical abbreviations, and, excepting up and down stage, are not needed for the direction of the actor.

Right and left relate to the actor as he stands facing the audience. The right is then on his right hand, and the left on his left hand.

In this chapter many directions will be given regarding

movements. As the student reads the directions he can rehearse the movements for himself. If he will copy the diagram and move little bits of paper about on it according to the directions, he can readily visualize the movements. An arrow marked on each bit of paper will indicate the direction in which the actor is facing.

HOW TO STAND

The marks shown above give the relative positions of the body, when two persons are standing together in conversation. It is seen that they face partly toward the audience and partly toward each other. These relative positions are variable, but the actor assumes them as the general positions for ordinary conversation. He must not face squarely toward the audience because he is supposed to be talking to his companion; he must not face his companion squarely because his audience must be considered and they desire to see the expression of his face as much as possible. From these general positions the actors can turn squarely toward the audience when the sentiment in the lines or the action so demand, or squarely toward each other.

When they are sitting on either side of a table they may observe the same rule; they may turn their chairs in the same positions as their bodies in order to be comfortable. The actor should be comfortable at all times. When seated in this way, if they desire to cross their legs, they can do so without disturbing their positions. The actor at the right of the table may cross his right knee over the left, and the one at the left the left knee over the right. These positions may be called standard, and are varied in respect to the action. For example, in shaking hands the actors would face each other squarely, but in expressing some special sentiment or emotion they would turn squarely toward the audience. Discretion in the matter of position is part of the more developed art of acting and will be discussed later.

DISTANCE

When two actors stand in conversation they should be at a certain distance from each other. This principle may have had its origin in the old days of the classic drama. In those days gesture was an important element in acting—more so than it is considered today. The actor had to have room for the full-length swing of his arms. When a beginner came too close to an experienced actor, the latter would exclaim, "Keep away from me, my boy." Because of the need for freedom of gesture the actors stood some four or five feet apart. Actors today are guilty of crowding at times. The amateurs at the rehearsals mentioned above were observed facing squarely toward each other, or with their backs turned partly toward the audience, and standing too close together. The actor should as a rule stand off at a comfortable distance.

There is another reason for maintaining the proper distance. The line of vision of those sitting in the front rows at the extreme right or left is disturbed when the actors stand too close together. The actor on the right may be hidden from spectators sitting at the extreme left, and vice versa. Lovers, however, especially in modern plays, stand close together in similar situations. This is particularly noticeable in motion pictures; but this art is not the highest form.

This principle is sometimes difficult to observe in the motion pictures. The playing space is often cramped, especially when a number of people have to be caught by the camera. There is then little room for unhampered movement. The motion pictures do not furnish the best of training in the ideal art of acting, and therefore we are not concerned with them here.

There are many situations in which the actors must close up their distance. They must come close when they shake hands or embrace, and in many other situations. After the action they need to get back to their distance. To do this they do not turn deliberately and walk back. The distance is only a few feet and they simply back away. This movement is imperceptible and comes easily with a little practice. Some directors might call this "working back," while others would use any arbitrary term to express the principle. More will be said about such movements shortly.

THE CENTRE OF THE STAGE

If the student will look at the diagram, he will see that the point marked centre is not, strictly speaking, in the centre of the stage. It is in the middle of an imaginary line drawn from side to side, and is nearer to the footlights than to the back wall of the "set." The actor, when standing at "centre," must be down near the footlights in the middle, as shown by the mark.

If we pour a small amount of liquid into a bowl, the force of gravity magnetizes the liquid to the exact centre of the bowl. The centre of the stage is a magnetic point which attracts all action. Action tends to converge toward this point and radiates from it as required. The magnetic centre refers to the work of the actors when in a standing position. When seated they must, of course, be wherever the furniture is placed.

Let us see how the principle of convergence and radiation operates. A person is standing at a window at the right upper corner of the stage. Another comes on at a door at left first entrance and says, "Hello, John." John, at the window, comes down to the centre, or just a little right of it, and the one who has entered comes forward to meet him there. They then stand in conversation on either side of the exact central point. After a short scene in these positions, John goes off the stage at the centre door, and his companion makes his exit whence he came. Their action has converged toward the central point for their scene, and has radiated from it when required by the action of the play as a whole.

We will take another example, where only one person is concerned, and will use Hamlet's first soliloquy which occurs in the first act. On the exeunt of the king, queen, and courtiers at right first entrance, Hamlet is left standing alone by the throne, which is over at the left. He comes into the centre as he says,

O, that this too, too, solid flesh would melt,
Thaw and resolve itself into a dew!
Or that the everlasting had not fixed
His canon 'gainst self slaughter! O God! God!
    (*He goes over to a chair at the right.*)
How weary, stale, flat and unprofitable,
Seem to me all the uses of this world! (*He sits.*)
Fie on't! ah fie! 'tis an unweeded garden,

That grows to seed; things rank and gross in nature
Possess it merely. That it should come to this!
But two months dead; nay, not so much, not two;
　　(He looks at a picture of his father in a medallion about
　　his neck.)
So excellent a king; that was, to this,
　　(He looks off right after the King, or at the opposite
　　picture in the medallion.)
Hyperion to a satyr; so loving to my mother
That he might not beteem the winds of heaven
Visit her face too roughly. Heaven and earth
Must I remember?
　　(He rises and comes again into the centre.)
　　　　　　　　　Why, she would hang on him,
As if increase of appetite had grown
By what it fed on; and yet within a month—
Frailty, thy name is woman!
　　(He advances a few steps toward right first entrance
　　where the queen has gone off.)
A little month, or ere those shoes were old
With which she followed my poor father's body,
Like Niobe, all tears;—why she, even she—
O God! a beast that wants discourse of reason
　　(He goes back to the centre.)
Would have mourned longer—married with my uncle,
My father's brother, but no more like my father
Than I to Hercules!
　　(The next few lines are cut here with most actors.)
It is not nor it cannot come to good:
But break my heart; for I must hold my tongue.
　　(He goes a little to the left, leaving the centre open for
　　Horatio, who enters with Marcellus and Bernardo.)

It will be seen that Hamlet, in this soliloquy, plays in
or near the centre while standing, and goes out of it only

to sit down, or to make some other definite action. The actor must play in the centre of the stage *unless he has some definite reason to be somewhere else.* The amateurs spoken of above, instead of grouping themselves evenly about the central point, frequently shifted off it and had to be shifted back again. The actor easily gains a sense of the magnetic centre, and the beginner should acquire it early.

Two or More Persons at Centre

When two persons play at centre, the central point is just between them; when three persons play in this manner, the middle one is at the exact centre, while the other two are at right centre and left centre respectively. If two more are added, they are at right and left respectively; all the five have the positions marked in the diagram. When standing in these positions, they are arranged symmetrically with the set. By the word "set" is meant the scenic setting, whether it be an interior or an exterior. These positions are standard, but vary greatly with the action; they are used when the characters stand on the stage and carry on the story of the play, and at times when there is no definite action requiring that the symmetrical arrangement be disturbed. The actors should not huddle over at one side or the other when there is no definite reason why they should not be "playing at centre." In general, the stage director attends to the positions of the actors, and tells them where they shall be. At the same time, the actor's sense of symmetry must teach him to use his own instinct in keeping the groupings balanced. This is called "dressing the stage." For this purpose, he must instinctively move into many new positions without being told to do so.

TAKING STAGE

Suppose two persons are conversing at centre. A third comes on at the right-hand door down stage. This is marked on the diagram as right first entrance. The person crosses to centre between the two persons standing, to speak to the one at the left. When he does so, they must make room for him between them. To do this, the one on the left backs away a few steps with the imperceptible movement we have described; the one at the right takes a few steps to the right and turns back into the conversation. This leaves the actor who has entered at exact centre, and the other two at the proper distances from him on either side.

In his action the person at the right may commit a fault of which many professional actors are guilty. When the actor on the left moves, he can easily back away a step or two; but when the one at the right moves, he must *walk* away. In this action, some professional actors select the spot to which they shall move, go to it deliberately, and face back toward the others with the precision of soldiers. This is wrong, as these actions are indefinite; they have no value in the telling of the story; they are not a part of stage direction, and the actors should do them instinctively, just as we instinctively move aside when people come too close to us, but always easily and naturally.

Instead of making a definite, positive movement to a spot and turning definitely about, the actor at the right should make his movement as imperceptible as possible.

If he does not, he attracts the attention of the audience to an action which has nothing to do with the story. He should move over quietly with the idea of attracting no attention to himself whatever. This leads us to the consideration of definite and indefinite action.

DEFINITE ACTION

Definite action is practically all action which relates to the story of the play; it is a part of stage direction and is outlined for the actor by the stage director. The actor, also, may create some of it in the development of his performance. It must be done in a positive way, so as to show direct intention on his part. If the actor makes an entrance or an exit, if he goes to a chair and sits, or does any other bit of business connected with the story of the play, this is definite, and he must do it with sureness of method.

In the amateur rehearsals we are using for illustration, one actress had a speech something like the following: She was standing at centre talking to her husband in the play. She said, "Oh dear, I must sit down and rest. I've been shopping all day, and I'm worn out." On this speech she was to go to a sofa, which was behind her at the right, and sit. As she began her speech, she backed off a couple of steps, looked about in two directions, finally located the sofa, went to it gingerly while talking over her shoulder, and dropped into it at the wrong time.

Two principles were involved in this simple business. The first was definiteness. She should have known just where the sofa was. She should then have turned toward it with her face to the audience, walked deliberately to it, and sat down. There should have been no uncertainty in her movement. She was in her own home, and familiar with her surroundings. Had she been in a strange house, there would have been some logic in her first locating the sofa before she went to it. Even then, she should have located it in a definite way.

The second principle is "suiting the action to the word"; this will be discussed more fully later. As she spoke the first words of her speech, which were, "Oh dear," she should have turned away, and she should have been seated completely just as the last words left her lips. These were, "I'm worn out." Moreover, she could have secured a good effect, because of the nature of this particular speech, by expressing fatigue on, "I'm worn out," just as she sat down. She should have timed her movement to the sofa so as to begin and end it simultaneously with the first and last words.

When a performance has not been sufficiently rehearsed, much of the action which should be definite is indefinite, because the actors are not sure of what they are to do. No argument need be offered for thorough rehearsal. Whatever the actor has to do he should anticipate with exactness so that when the time comes to do it he is ready, and can do it in a definite, positive way.

At this point we must mention two faults which were committed by one of the amateurs. He was to go to a door, speak a certain line from that position, and then make his exit. The first fault may be termed, Reverse Physical Action. As he started for the door he protruded one foot, at the same time throwing his head and shoulders back slightly in order to make his first step. This was the reverse of the proper method, and in real life he would not have done it. The brain is the seat of thought.

Intention originates there. With the intention of going to the door, the physical action should have started where the intention was born, namely the head. When we start into a walk from a standing position, we throw the head and shoulders slightly forward, and the body and other members naturally follow.

When the actor had finished his speech at the door he committed the second fault. While he spoke the line, his gaze naturally traveled on a level with his head to the person addressed, who was also standing. When he turned to go out, he looked down at the floor as if seeking a foothold for his steps. The stage was level, and it was not as if he were walking on stepping stones over a brook. He should have turned and made his exit with his gaze on the same level as it was while he delivered his speech. It is, of course, permissible for an actor to watch his step on the stage, as in real life, in any place where that is necessary.

The perfect physical technique of turning to the right would be to turn the eyes, head, and shoulders to the right, and to start off with the right, not the left, foot. In turning to the left, the left foot would be the first to move.

INDEFINITE ACTION

This has to do with all business which is not necessarily a part of stage direction, has no special, or in fact any, relation to the story, and is necessary for various reasons connected with stagecraft. At rehearsals, when a stage director lays out the relative positions of the actors, he should place them in certain positions to be ready to speak certain lines from those positions. In general, the director gives each actor a definite reason for each change of position that he makes. Through expert direction, the necessity for indefinite action is largely avoided. Still, much indefinite action is necessary in every performance. We have already given one example, where the actor takes stage to make room for another.

When the players are spread across the stage in the positions shown on the diagram, other players may join the group, and they cannot all remain down stage across the front. Those that are not immediately concerned in the dialogue must make room for the others. It is the director's duty to tell them where to move. These movements are not necessary to the story, and are put in to get certain actors out of the way for the time being. One may be told to move up behind the table and talk to another who is already there; another must go up behind the sofa to be for the moment out of the way. The movements must be done quietly and unobtrusively, and not with that soldier-like precision we have mentioned.

To give a concrete example: Mr. X is standing down in the left corner. A scene is going on at the centre between a man and a woman standing. In a few minutes she is going to faint, and must do so in Mr. X's arms. He must be there to catch her. If the director has found no definite impulse for Mr. X, on one of his lines, to move into a convenient position, or if Mr. X has no lines in that scene to give him an impulse, then the director tells him to move over quietly to the position in time to be ready. Mr. X must not march to the position; it would attract attention to himself, and attention is on the couple at centre. To use a common expression, Mr. X must "work" into the position so that the attention of the audience is not attracted to his movements. He must move rather slowly and complete his action as easily as possible. All indefinite action should be done rather slowly, as having no definite purpose.

A scene in Eugene O'Neill's *Beyond the Horizon* further illustrates this principle. The family group are sitting about the table reading, and discussing the departure of a son. The mother sits at the right of the table knitting. At a cue she rises and crosses the stage for a definite purpose. The director found it necessary, with no impulse of lines, to get her back to her original position. As she rose to cross the stage, he had her drop her knitting. After her business, then, for an impulse to return, he had her notice the knitting on the floor near her chair, and she went back under the pretense of winding up the ball which she still held in her hands.

Much indefinite action is necessary in what is called "drawing-room deportment." It is the easy familiarity of people in their own homes or in familiar surroundings. Here is an example from Mary Roberts Rinehart's play, *The Breaking Point*. Doctor David is seated at the left in his office. Dr. Harrison Miller enters at right upper, says, "Well, David, how's everything?" and comes into the centre.

DOCTOR DAVID: Fine, Harrison, Dick does all the work.
DOCTOR MILLER: Great boy, that nephew of yours. Looks like he and my daughter Elizabeth are getting pretty friendly. I'm for it, you know.
DOCTOR DAVID: He's got character, Harrison.
DOCTOR MILLER: He's got a mind. I know a mind when I see it; minds are my business. (*Here the actor was given no business by the director, but to seem comfortable*

and natural he strolled over to the table at the right, and smelled of the flowers which were on it.)

DOCTOR DAVID: Used to be, when a man was sick he came to me to find out what ailed his stomach. Now—

DOCTOR MILLER: He comes to *me* and I ask him what he's hiding. (*Miller is a psychiatrist. During this speech he strolls back into the centre.*)

DOCTOR DAVID: Yes, they go about it in different ways today.

DOCTOR MILLER: Well, times change. I suppose the good Samaritan wouldn't pour oil on the What's his Name's wounds today, he'd pour iodine. (*During this speech he strolls to the back of Doctor David's desk and helps himself to a cigarette.*)

It will be noted that he "strolls"; he does not go to any position deliberately, but easily and quietly so as not to distract attention from the substance in the lines. This action is not at all artificial, but is quite true to life.

English actors are masters of this form of technique, but American actors are not as expert in this respect. The American actor sometimes shows stiffness in situations in which the English actor is quite at home. The latter is probably the best drawing-room actor in the world. It is bred in the bone with him, for the Englishman through a national custom has practice in drawing-room deportment every day. This is the custom of afternoon tea, in which pure sociability and exchange of ideas are brought into constant practice. Where the American actor might look awkward with a tea cup and saucer on his knee, the English actor handles them with perfect ease.

An amusing incident is told of an American director

who went to London to produce an American play. One day when the director was supervising the building of the scenery, the stage hands, on some mysterious signal, laid down their tools and started for the regions under the stage. The director called out, "What's the matter, boys, is there a strike on?" Just as one of the men disappeared, he answered over his shoulder, "No strike, sir, just afternoon tea, sir."

Since afternoon tea is a feature of drawing-room life in England, the Englishman is intimately familiar with the drawing-room manner from his childhood. The English actor is therefore quite at home in the familiar, indefinite movements of the stage. Let us devise a scene which might take place during afternoon tea in an English family and try to illustrate the indefinite action.

The tea is being poured, when the young son of the family enters flushed from a game of tennis. He says, "Hullo, family, I see I'm just in time. I'm deuced thirsty, too." He places his tennis racquet in a corner, and comes down to his mother, who hands him a cup of tea while he says, "I got even with Wetherbee for yesterday; I won every set." With his tea he strolls into the centre. The conversation of the others goes on while the young man strolls over to the left and sits on a tabouret against the wall. In a few moments, when he has finished his tea, his mother says, "More tea, Bertie?" "No, thanks, mater," says Bertie, and rises to go up to the back and talk to his cousin Emily and her brother. The brother is called away, and Bertie and Emily stroll down to the sofa and sit, ready for some lines between them in a few moments. These movements are given to Bertie to dispose of him until he is wanted, and since they have little value in the story, but are only to create "atmosphere" and serve the purposes of the director, they are to be done in that easy, graceful manner in which the English actor is so adept.

"What Shall I Do with My Hands?"

This question was asked by one of the amateur actors. The beginner, and many an actor of greater experience, has asked himself the same question. The answer was, "Do anything, but by all means be comfortable." In this particular case, the young actor was told to put his hands behind him. He might also have resorted to some definite use of them, such as handling his watch-chain, the string of an eye-glass, or something in the hands, but never in such a way as to make the action distracting.

One of the first things the actor should try to learn is to be comfortable when the hands are at the sides, an accomplishment which is not as easy as it may appear. Whether a person can or cannot stand at ease with his hands hanging loosely at his sides depends upon the poise of the body. Some actors' bodies are naturally well poised, and they have little trouble with their hands even as beginners, while others have to give the principle much attention.

Actors, as a rule, stand straight and acquire "presence" in their attitudes. This may be due to the fact that early in their experience they were bothered with their hands. If the shoulders are thrown back and the chest out, the weight of the body becomes equally divided on either side of a vertical axis. The arms then fall naturally by the sides. When the young actor feels that every person in the house is looking at his hands, or thinking he looks as awkward as he himself feels, his body is out of poise. The vertical axis, instead of extending from the top of his cranium to the balls of his feet like a plumb line, strikes the ground some inches in front of him. If he straightens up, draws back his chin, puts out his chest, and draws his feet fairly well together so that he stands squarely on *both* of them, he should quickly forget his hands. If he cannot do this, and is still uncomfortable, he should put the unruly members out of the way somewhere. If the actor is over-conscious of his hands, the audience is likely to be conscious of them also. Actresses seem to have less difficulty with their hands than actors, for women become actresses more instinctively than men, and begin the art of make-believe with their dolls.

People in Oriental countries who carry burdens on their heads are noted for their erect figures. The habit of distributing a weight equally on a vertical axis has given their bodies poise. It is well for the actor to practice walking as if, in like manner, he were balancing a weight on his head. In walking the arms may swing a little, but only from the shoulders, not the elbows; in standing, the elbows should not extend outward with angularity, but should be held fairly well at the sides.

Some actors resort too frequently to the side pockets. In a former generation, side pockets by some companies were taboo, and actors sewed them up in their stage clothes. Today the side pocket is in favor, and placing one hand in a pocket helps to relieve awkwardness. It also relieves the monotony of seeing an actor with his hands constantly at his sides just because he thinks they ought to be there, when he has not the expertness to vary their positions. It looks better to place only one hand in a pocket at a time than both at the same time.

Placing the hands behind the back is a good refuge for awkwardness, and folding the arms is permissible. English actors have a peculiar mannerism. This is to stand with the hands holding the coat lapels. It is not ungraceful and helps the actor to appear at ease. Stage detectives like to put their thumbs in their vests; it seems characteristic of certain classes of people, and is popular with actors to express pomposity. Placing the hands on the hips is also a possible position, with the fingers either front or back. A graceful position for a man is to hold one hand by his side and the other in the region of his watch pocket.

Hands held at the sides for long at a time in most cases look awkward. Whether they do or not depends upon the poise of the body. To hold them gracefully in this manner requires an erect posture. In *Peace on Earth* an actor held his hands at his sides during an entire scene and looked perfectly natural in so doing. A woman may clasp her hands in front at her waist, or let one arm hang while the other rests on her hip. The last position, however, is somewhat theatrical, and often looks affected. There are many poses which would be affectation if repeated as a habit, such as a constant habit of placing one hand on the hip and the other against the cheek. This is a practice with Ethel Barrymore; but while it is natural to her distinctive style, it might not always look graceful in one of lesser artistry. In female character parts, or on some comedy lines, arms akimbo are often used.

Some of the positions for the hands are more suited to eccentric, or character, parts than to "straight" ones. Character parts are those showing characteristics which are foreign to the real person, such as dialects of all kinds, unusual eccentricities, or physical mannerisms. Lisping, stuttering, limping, and so forth, all belong to character parts. In general, all parts portraying persons no longer young are classed as character parts. Straight parts are those, generally, of young people, in which the actor uses his own personality, and, as it is expressed, "plays himself."

In the straight parts of heroes and lovers, some of the more ungraceful positions of the hands should not be used, while for character parts, these positions may be employed according to the nature of the part. Of all the positions, that which is most difficult is none at all, namely, to let the hands hang and forget them. The actor should train himself in this from the beginning of his career.

Crossing in Front and Behind

The student will recall what was said in the first chapter, of an old traditional method by which an actor should always cross in front of another and never behind, and that today either way is allowed. Still, there are rules to be observed. When one crosses in front, he must not do so while the person he crosses is speaking. The reason is obvious. If he crosses in front while the other is speaking, the action blurs the other's effect during his line; if he crosses behind while he himself speaks, his own speech suffers in like manner. He may cross in front while speaking.

The director gives him a reason to cross; it is upon some impulse of his own, or upon a command or suggestion from one of the other characters. If he crosses behind, he must finish what he is saying before doing so; if he has another speech to follow, he must wait before speaking it until he

is again in full view of the audience on the other side.
Example: A character standing at the left of another
says, "I'll tell Madame you're here." She then crosses
behind the other. When she is on the other side she says,
"She's lying down at present." If the maid crosses in
front, she may say the whole speech as she is crossing.

Whether to cross in front or behind depends upon which
happens to be the shortest line to the objective point.
Two persons are standing at centre down stage. If the
one on the left crosses in front, she is probably going to
the door down right, and to cross in front is the shortest
way to the door. If she crosses behind, she is probably
going to the right upper door. If she crossed in front to
go to that door she would have to go around her companion, and thus describe a curved line to her objective.

In one production, the director made a point of having
the characters cross behind, even at times when it did not
appear necessary. They did this, of course, when they
were not speaking. Much of this action was employed,
and his idea may have been to keep some of the characters
in view as much as possible. This is a point in directorship, and does not logically belong here.

How to Turn

In the section on Indefinite Action, during the scene
between Dr. David and Dr. Miller, the latter strolled over
to the table at the right and smelled of the flowers. In
doing so, he went in front of the table and smelled of them
with his back partly toward the audience. When he turned
back to Dr. David, he had made a complete turn of the
body to the right. This suited the actor's convenience and
was quite permissible. He could have done it in another

way. He could have gone only to the left side of the table to smell the flowers. Then, in turning back to Dr. David, he should have turned to the left with his face toward the audience. Either way is comfortable and natural.

In the section on Taking Stage, two actors make room for another who crosses between them. The one at the right takes a few steps to the right and turns back into the conversation. When he turns back, it must be to the left with his face toward the audience.

The principle of turning outward from another actor, or inward toward him, which was mentioned in Chapter I, depends on the nearest route to the objective. Two persons may be at centre. One wishes to go to the centre door at the back. As he is partly facing his companion, and the centre door is just behind the pair, the most convenient way for him to turn is inward toward his companion. If the actor at the left wanted to go to the left upper door, or to the one down left, it would be more convenient for him to turn outward toward the audience. If he wanted to go to the right first door, he would cross in front of his companion, and if to the right upper door, he would cross behind him. For the actor on the right, the directions are just reversed but the principle the same.

Suppose an actor goes over to the right and, as he does so, turns to listen to another who is speaking at the right upper door. He continues to turn in the same direction, namely to the right, until his back is to the audience. He may then remain in that position listening until his attention is directed elsewhere. If, after going toward the right, he turns to listen to a person at the left upper door, or to any person on the left, it is more convenient for him to turn back to the left with his face toward the audience.

If he is standing at right with his back toward the audience and his attention is called from the left, the easier way to turn is the nearer way; that is, to turn the body to the right to face the person over at left.

Sometimes an actor appears awkward by starting to walk with the wrong foot. In the modern theatre less attention seems to be paid than formerly to certain rules of technique, so we cannot be too rigid. Still, exact principles of the correct, or ideal, technique are always worth while. The preferable foot with which to start into motion is always the one nearer to the objective point. For example, if the actor is talking to another at the centre and is facing toward the right, his right foot is nearer to the right side of the stage. Therefore, to go toward the right he should start with the right foot. The same is true if he starts to go up to the back from this position. If he is facing toward the left he should start with his left foot. It looks awkward when an actor, facing, for example, toward the right, throws his right foot across his body to go to the left. In general, he should not back away when he is supposed to go definitely. Sometimes, in order to reach an objective point, to turn to the left or the right is equally convenient. Actors on the Russian and Yiddish stages give the preference in such cases to turning to the right.

On paper some of these directions may seem at first confusing, and a little too minute. However, they are very simple in practice, and the student will grasp them easily. At the same time, there are no set laws to govern them. An actor who played Mr. Pim in A. A. Milne's charming play, *Mr. Pim Passes By*, made his performance most effective by turning in the wrong way at every opportunity. This business was part of the actor's characterization. The only fixed rule for standard purposes is to be governed by comfort and convenience, and to do that which seems most natural.

ENTRANCES AND EXITS

A person comes into a room through a door as he does in real life; there is little or no difference. A glance at the diagram shows that the doors all open down stage. If the hinges and handles were reversed, entering would be awkward for the actor. As a rule, doors swing off stage as shown; but those which lead to out of doors usually open inward. Sometimes, but not often, a door in an interior set is made to open inward. This occurs when some special business is to be done with it, as when a character must hide behind it while it is open. In real life, of course, a door between two rooms in a house may open into either of the two rooms; but on the stage the business is usu-ally rendered more convenient by the outward opening door.

The standard method of entering through a door at the left is to open it from the outside with the right hand, pass through it, turn toward the audience, and close it with the left hand. To go off by the same door, open it with the left hand, pass through and close it with the right hand. If this door is opened with the right hand, the action turns the body away from the audience and looks awkward; the same principle, with the other hand employed, applies to the right hand door.

At times these standard methods must be varied, as when one comes on with a heavy bundle, or wishes to produce some comic or eccentric effect. The absent-minded Mr. Pim might do it in any awkward way. If a character came in quickly and locked the door against pursuit, he would no doubt not change hands, but would swing about with his back toward the audience and close the door in the quickest and most convenient way.

If an actor precedes another through a door, he may wait with his hand on the knob until the other has entered and then close it in the standard manner described. In ushering him out, he reverses the process, following instead of preceding him. As exterior sets have no doors, nothing need be said about entrances and exits in respect to them. Actors should always close doors after them, unless there is special direction to leave them open.

SPEAKING OFF STAGE

When an actor has to speak off stage, the scenery which intervenes between him and the audience tends to drown the sound of his voice. In speaking off stage, therefore, he must raise his voice. The degree depends upon what he is saying. If he says, "Madeline, where are you?" he need not use a much higher tone than on the stage. If he speaks in anger, he naturally speaks in a higher key, even as he would on the stage, or in real life. He must also speak louder when his back is to the audience. If he is supposed to call from a distance, he must give the effect of being really far off. To do this, he may go to the back corner of the stage proper, and cup his mouth in his hands to muffle the sound. Then, if he calls again, to give the effect of coming nearer he may walk closer to his entrance. In *Julius Cæsar*, preceding the Forum scene, the supers are often placed in the cellar for the shouts, as the mob is coming to the Forum from the distance.

In speaking off stage, the actor should always speak distinctly.

ANTICIPATING CUES

The expression "anticipating cues" means that an actor must take a cue ahead of the actual cue on which he begins some action or speech; he must anticipate his real cue. To do this he must be familiar with the dialogue that precedes his actual cue. With a little practice, he develops a sense of anticipation; he knows when his cue is coming, and when necessary can act before the cue is actually delivered. A lack of this sense is one of the greatest faults in many amateur performances, and is a primary evidence of inexperience. This, above all, causes many amateur performances to drag, and to lack the brightness and vigor of professional acting.

The actor should sense the approach of each cue, though he may not actually know the preceding lines. He is familiar with the story, and that is sufficient. He is then ready on his cue to "pick it up" promptly and without causing a wait.

Since amateur actors are sometimes inexpert in this principle, directors of amateur performances need to resort to various expedients to gain results. One director told the actors to imagine that a ball was being tossed from one to another, and that they must always keep it on the move excepting at times when the dialogue was to be spaced with pauses or business. Any illustration from a director will do in order to achieve the result desired.

Anticipation of cues applies to entrances perhaps more than to any other business. In the scene between Dr. David and Dr. Miller already referred to, Dr. Miller

entered and said, "Well, David, how's everything?"
He had to open the door from the outside, and get well
into the room before speaking. The cue for this speech
was given from the stage. If Dr. Miller had waited outside until he heard the cue before opening the door, and
had opened and closed it before speaking, there would
have been an uncomfortable break in the thread of the
performance. This is called a "wait." The actor on the
stage would have been uncomfortable because Dr. Miller
was late by several seconds; and on the stage that is a
long time. Dr. Miller knew just when his cue was coming,
and he used the line preceding it to open the door. He
timed the line so that he had already closed the door and
come "into the picture" ready to speak when his cue was
given.

The anticipation of cues is very necessary in the parts
of butlers and other servants. These people have to come
on and announce the arrival of visitors, or that dinner is
served, and so forth. The work of the butler is formal;
he usually has to get into a certain fixed position before
speaking, and does not speak until he is "set." Therefore,
he must start ahead of time to get to his position.

Suppose a husband and wife are conversing at a table
down stage. The butler comes on at the back with a card
and presents it to the wife with the line, "A visitor to see
you, ma'am." The dialogue of the man and wife may be
something like this:

THE WIFE: You know Henry, the boy is infatuated with
the girl. What can I do?

THE HUSBAND: I'll give the young cub a good talking to.
Marriage at his age? Nonsense!

THE WIFE: Well, I hope you can reason with him, I can't.

At that time the butler must be at the wife's side, but has had to make his entrance and walk some distance down stage, and, moreover, with the measured, unhurried tread of ideal butlers. The only cue the butler has in his part is the "speaking cue." He must therefore be familiar with the dialogue ahead of it, and must select what is called an "advanced cue" to enter on. This must be far enough ahead to give him just enough time to reach the wife's side for his speech, and neither too late nor too soon. If he is too late a wait occurs, and if he is too soon he has to wait at her side until his cue is spoken, to his own discomfort and that of the audience, perhaps. In either case, the rhythm of the performance is jarred. If the butler takes for his entrance cue, "What can I do?" from the wife, he can arrive at the proper moment to speak; and he should time his movement in order to do so.

When a butler comes on at the centre door to announce the arrival of a visitor, he anticipates his entrance, and goes to the *opposite* side of the centre opening. If his entrance is from the left, he then goes in front of the *right* side of the opening; he does not circle around and stand in front of the left side of it, as many a professional actor butler is known to do. He waits for the visitor to pass into the room before making his exit. If he comes on at a door at right upper, he stands above it and allows the person to pass in front of him. In announcing visitors or dinner, he faces the audience squarely. Such announcements are meant for all persons in the room, and are therefore directed to no particular person. He always anticipates his entrance, to be in his position for the line.

To cite still another example of the importance of anticipating cues: The father of the house is reading his evening paper. His young daughter, at a certain cue, must come on and place her hands over his eyes. Only one cue is written in her part, before which she must make her entrance and tiptoe down to her father's chair, ready to do the business. She naturally must anticipate the cue to be there when the business is called for.

We have discussed this principle at some length because it is very important. A slow butler, or other actor for that matter, can do much damage to a performance; many a professional performance has suffered when the butler was not properly rehearsed. In general, a performance is held together through a continuous series of anticipations. This suggests the subject of the right moment for speech or action.

"THE PSYCHOLOGICAL MOMENT"

The word psychology has been much used in the theatre of late, and is probably much abused. Nowadays, however, when the expression "the psychological moment" is employed, its meaning is understood. We will use it here to indicate that moment when each character shall begin to speak, or shall start upon some action.

This moment can be hurried, or it can be delayed. When it is hurried, its effect, to use an expression of the theatre, is often that of "stepping on the cue." The actor speaks so quickly on the speech preceding his own that his speech comes almost simultaneously with the last words of the other character. This not only contributes to an imperfect performance, but is not true to life. It is not true to life because many of the thoughts expressed by one character are dependent upon those expressed by another; therefore, the actor should hear completely what the other says before he answers. The audience should hear as well. The jumbling of lines when, figuratively speaking, the actors "tread on one another's toes," is confusing and unsatisfactory to an audience.

One director has suggested that this law need not operate in the case of "broken speeches." These are speeches which are interrupted by some one else speaking before the line is brought to its period and the completion of its thought. However, the rule operates just the same. The actor should know the last word which the other actor has to speak, and should take up his own speech immediately, with the same regard to the principle. If the broken speech is, "I saw him speak to the ———," the other actor should not "tread on his toes" by speaking after the word "him," for example, nor should he leave the actor perhaps saying, "to the -er-er," and waiting for his broken speech to be interrupted when he really has nothing more to say. Many plays, like *The Famous Mrs. Fair, Mary the Third*, and *Dancing Mothers*, are replete with broken speeches, and the actors need to know their parts well in order to deal properly with the "psychological moment."

The "psychological moment" should not be delayed. If it is, the performance drags, and the action is slow. A performance moves with a regular beat and rhythm, and the "psychological moment" is employed in a performance in such a way as not to disturb the evenness of this measure.

Just when, therefore, does this moment for picking up a cue take place? When a character has a speech of several sentences, he takes a breath before starting a new sentence, or in places where, in writing, a comma would occur. The "psychological moment" between the speeches of two characters is just long enough for the second character to take a breath. There are, of course, many exceptions to this rule. These are cases of intervening business, or pauses made to project some special thought or idea. A performance is made up of something more than words, but there must be something going on all the time. If there is a pause, that pause must be filled with an idea toward which the attention of the audience is directed, or with some definite piece of business which they see. If there is a pause with nothing in it, the actors have widened the gap between speeches, and the "psychological moment" for speaking has not been put into operation. Practice imparts to the actor a proper sense of how to speak neither too soon nor too late.

DICTION

Little need be said about diction. Every one knows that audiences want to hear what the actors say. Though the fault of incoherence can be laid at the door of many a recognized artist, he is no better by reason of it. Pure and distinct utterance is a joy to the auditor, and does not fail to gain his appreciation. Young actors will do well early in their careers to practice distinct speech, and to study the correct enunciation of words in order to attain it. There is perhaps no better practice for this purpose than the reading of poetry and blank verse drama aloud. In this, besides the exercise for the tongue in the framing of syllables, there is excellent practice in the development of tone, and the use of the voice in general. One of the most important principles all singers have to practice is the habit of singing out on the lips. When they produce the sound too far back in the throat, its effect becomes guttural and also lacks that distinctness of utterance which belongs to good diction. When the words are formed and the tones produced in the *forward* position, they become resonant by means of the sounding box just above the tongue, and are produced with much less effort. A person can talk much longer, with better effect, and without fatigue if this principle is followed. Many actors do not know how to use their voices in this way, but speak from the back of the throat. Thus they suffer at times from chord rasping, and often have to resort to medical treatment. The student should remember that speaking is closely allied to singing, and should endeavor to cultivate the correct method. In the case of an unpleasant voice, its systematic culture with the aid of a competent elocutionist is worth while.

FINDING THE OBJECTIVE

In the amateur rehearsals we are using for illustration, one of the characters had to make an entrance at centre door and come down stage exclaiming, "Oh, Mother, see the lovely present which Uncle brought me." She was looking down at a necklace about her neck. She then exclaimed, "Why, where is she?" Her mother was not on the stage, and she had not first ascertained that fact. Simultaneously with looking up she said, "Why, where is she?" without learning first that her mother was not in the room. This required a definite action *preceding* the speech, and not simultaneous with it. She could not have known her mother was gone without first looking about to learn it. What she had done was bad technique. She should have entered and come down stage on, "Oh,

Mother, see the lovely present which Uncle brought me."
She should then have looked about on both sides, and
after noting the absence of her mother, said, "Why,
where is she?" to the other character on the stage.

Here is another example: A character who has just
committed a crime is skulking through the dark. As he
stops at a certain point, a confederate taps him on the
shoulder and says, "Well, Joe." The criminal turns
quickly, and as he does so, says, "Where have you been
all this time?" This is illogical. The criminal would
first turn about to see who had tapped him on the shoulder
before addressing any line to that person. He would first
locate his objective for the line. If the second person had
been a policeman, and the criminal's line had been, "I
didn't do anything," then in the excess of fear he might
assume that he was arrested, and would speak immediately. His fear would be the idea to be projected, and this
could be shown more effectively by his not locating his
objective first. The latter instance is an exception to the
rule.

William Faversham once gave an excellent example of
this principle. He was alone on the stage, and at a call
from off stage he desired to conceal an umbrella before
the off stage character entered. He looked about in all
directions for a suitable place. He looked toward the
sofa, and thinking it a likely place, he approached it.
Changing his mind, he looked toward the open door, and
went partly toward that to put the umbrella behind it.
Changing his mind again, he looked nervously about, and
finally located a niche beside the fireplace. He went to it
and concealed the umbrella there. In each piece of business he punctuated his action by first looking toward

his objective before going toward it, and the series of actions was absolutely clear cut.

There are many instances for the observance of this principle. They must be governed by reason. We cannot find a thing without first looking about for it, nor do we generally speak to a person whose presence we were not aware of without first learning who it is. If a person speaks to another who is absorbed in a newspaper, the reader first looks up to see who is speaking before he says, "Why, hello, John." In real life, every one does these things naturally, but on the stage, when the actor knows beforehand what he shall say, he often omits intermediate steps. In this last instance, the reader has two definite things to do; one is to look up and recognize his friend, and the other is to speak. Again, if a character says to another, "Hide me somewhere," the other, before he says, "Hide over here," first looks about and locates the objective place before directing his companion to it.

All this looks simple, and the student may at first see no reason why it need be explained. In practice the principle is not always adhered to, because the actor often forgets to make the pretense of not knowing what he actually *does* know. The amateur actress knew that her mother was not on the stage, and Mr. Faversham knew just where he was going to hide the umbrella. The observance of the proper technique gives the correct illusion. To do otherwise gives the audience the impression that the actor *seems* to know beforehand.

WHERE TO DIRECT SPEECH

In the section on Definiteness, the amateur actress was mentioned who, in turning to go to the sofa and sit, talked back over her shoulder. She said she was tired and must sit down and rest. This speech was not direct and might have been spoken to any number of people in the room. It was not necessary to speak the line directly to the character on the stage with her.

Whether an actor shall speak directly to the person for whom a speech is intended, or whether he may deliver the speech while engaged in some action which accompanies it, and without looking directly at the person, depends upon the nature of the speech. This is true to life, and the student will easily recognize it. Still, discrimination on this point requires judgment. An actor may deliver many speeches in a direct or indirect manner according to his preference and technique; their effectiveness is great or small according to his skill in discrimination.

In 1923 The Moscow Art Players, the famous dramatic company of Russia, played their first engagement in New York. Among other fine qualities in their art they proved to be adept in this principle.

Here are some speeches which might have been delivered directly to the person addressed, but were not. A father, whose son has become engaged to a woman much out of favor with the parent, sits reading, and awaiting his son's return. When the son enters the room, the father looks up to note the boy's arrival, and then looks back at his book.

THE SON: Good evening, Dad.

THE FATHER (*without looking up*): Where have you been, with that woman again?

THE SON: Yes, I have, Dad, what of it?

THE FATHER (*still looking down at his book*): You know I don't approve of her.

THE SON: Well, Dad, my life's my own, and I love her. (*Here the father wishes to make his speeches more direct; he places his book on the table, rises, and advances toward the boy.*)

THE FATHER: Listen to me, my boy. You're all I have, and I'm deeply concerned for your future.

(*From here on their speeches are direct.*)

To revert again to the amateur actress who said she must sit down and rest. We said she should have gone to the sofa without looking back, for the speech was too indirect to require such an action. But suppose that on her walk to the sofa the other character says something like this: "Young Loomis was killed by an automobile today." She says, "What?" As she does so, she turns directly to the person who has made this startling statement. Such a direct speech as this can be accompanied with no other action.

One character says, "Where are you going?" and the other answers, "Into the garden." As he does so he walks toward the door. The speech is indirect, and he does not turn to the questioner to deliver it. At the door, however, he wishes to make a more pointed speech. He turns to the other and says, "You have heard my proposition; tomorrow I shall expect an answer." One of the commonest uses of the indirect speech is made when a character is absorbed in a book or newspaper; he may deliver many of his speeches without looking up.

There are no set technical rules to govern directness or indirectness in the delivery of lines. The choice of method must be left to the artistry and judgment of the player. The stage director may have much to say about it, especially when the actor commits elementary faults in this respect. As a general rule, the beginner needs to bear in mind the fact that we do not always have to look at people when we address them.

"Oh," "Ah," and "Well"

These little interjections are often great nuisances. When an author writes a play he spends months, perhaps, in working out his story and writing the dialogue. He goes over the latter repeatedly to be sure he has expressed it in a terse and comprehensive way. Every "Oh," "Ah," and "Well" has its purpose and value. Where these do not occur, there is a reason for their omission. They occur at the beginnings of lines which do not require a pointed and direct delivery. Speeches without them are more direct. For example, a character says, "Oh, no." That answer is less direct than if he said, "No." He would say the latter when he wished to make a more positive statement. "Oh, no" is weaker and less positive in most cases than just, "No." When a person precedes a speech with "Well, I'll tell you," what he is going to say is more casual than if he began with, "I'll tell you." In the latter case he may be going to make some important statement. In some dramatic scene a character may say to another, "How do you know that what you say is true?" The other character answers, "I'll tell you. I was concealed in the summer house and overheard every word." This is a pointed statement; to insert "Well" before it weakens its force. In a farce, a wife may ask her husband to explain his absence over night. He cudgels his brains for an excuse and then says, "Well, I'll tell you." The "Well" here better indicates evasion on his part, than if he had omitted it.

When a play has been running for some time it is often found necessary to call a rehearsal. The performance has lost some of the exactness of technique with which it had been "set" at the original rehearsals. Actors have a prevalent tendency to introduce foreign matter into lines and business after the monotony of a play's run has begun to have effect. In this way the "Oh's," "Ah's," and "Well's" often creep in where they do not belong.

Another little interjection also is a great intruder. This is, "er." It is often heard in performances which have not had sufficient time for preparation, such as those of stock companies, when only a week is given. When the actor introduces a speech with "Er," he is generally trying to think of his lines, and wants to give the semblance of continuing the dialogue without a wait. An actor had the habit of putting in this interjection even when quite sure of what he had to say. It was a bad habit, and gave the impression that he was stumbling in his lines. If one needs to think for his next line he should check any tendency toward audible utterance until the line comes to him; a pause is better than the subterfuge of saying, "Er-er" to hold the attention of the audience. We except, of course, the cases in which these interjections are written in a part for a purpose. The actor should not allow unnecessary "Oh's," "Ah's," and "Well's," to creep into his performance. They indicate careless treatment on his part; and since they pervert definiteness into indefiniteness, they only tend to weaken the author's effects.

REPOSE

This subject does not logically fall within the category of elementary principles. We desire to introduce it here, nevertheless, because the young actor cannot begin too early in his career to endeavor to gain it.

Perfect repose is a valuable asset in the art of acting. It comes to some actors only after years of experience, when advancing age has made them sparing of action, and their movements slow. This is a somewhat false repose, since it is less the result of art than of senility. To some actors repose comes not at all. When a young actor acquires repose it is of the true quality, in view of his active youth and vigor.

Repose can be given several definitions. If we seek for a concrete one which will satisfy the average question, we may say, in the first simple definition of Webster's dictionary, that repose is "a lying at rest." The dictionary also says, "Opposed to anything which is overstrained or violent." In relation to acting, repose is the art of doing absolutely nothing.

When we say "doing absolutely nothing," the sense must be taken in two ways. When the actor is in perfect repose, he is doing nothing in relation to the play, and, moreover, he is doing nothing in relation to himself. When he is doing nothing in relation to the play, he is out of the play for the time being, just as the baseball player is out of the game while he waits for his turn at the bat. At such times, the actor is more effective when he expresses that nothing by remaining in a state of repose. To be "out of the game" for the time being, and not in repose at that time, is distracting to the audience. Baseball players practice and are active before the game, but while out of the game awaiting their turns, they are, figuratively, in repose on the benches.

Repose in relation to the play is an easy matter if the

actor is master of repose in relation to himself. The "art of doing nothing" means here doing nothing of a useless nature, and unnecessary to the work in hand. An actor may be in repose while speaking; and this form of repose is the more important to discuss in this section. The force of vocal effort often causes various members of the body to move when that movement has no value in the effect of the lines, and, moreover, disturbs the poise of the body. This is a violation of repose.

Actors have different habits by which they disturb their repose—habits, which, with long and unrestrained practice, become actual mannerisms. One well-known actor had the habit of twitching his fingers. Many actors, when they raise their vocal efforts above colloquialism, cannot refrain from shifting on the feet. Young actors often have the idea that acting means "to act," when in many situations it means not to act at all. The young actor has some lines to speak, and he feels that he must do something in the way of action to accompany those lines. Not knowing what to do, when there is really nothing, but feeling that if he does nothing he falls short of the artistic requirements of his rôle, he shifts on his feet, moves his hands, and strolls about in vague indefinite ways, when all he needs is absolute repose.

An amateur actor had a speech as colloquial and reposeful as the following: "I met Wilson on the street today. He told me you had rung him up, and said he would see about the matter right away." No acting is required in this speech; it is entirely colloquial. Acting can be divided broadly into two classes—acting with action, and acting without. The former cannot employ repose in its performance; the latter requires repose.

When the young actor spoke the lines like those above he committed the faults which have been cited. A variation of this speech, of a more positive character, would have been an example of poor acting if delivered in a state of repose. Suppose the speech had been, "But I tell you I *saw* Wilson on the street. He told me you had rung him up, and said he would see about the matter right away. Now please don't bother me further." In this variation there is emphasis and the emotion of impatience. The speech cannot be reposeful. The emphasis of the first sentence justifies a gesture with the hand and the impatience of the last sentence, a movement away. The actor learns with practice and experience to discriminate between speeches that require repose and those that require action. The true artist learns to eliminate useless movements of the body which have no meaning, and which only lessen his effectiveness.

There are what may be termed "live repose" and "dead repose." In live repose the actor may sit or stand in a reposeful though attentive attitude and appear to be listening to what is said around him. He is then "alive" to the situation going forward. In dead repose he may be either lying unconscious on a sofa or may be slumped in a chair with his head and arms on a table expressing grief or despair and seem thus to be oblivious to his surroundings.

Of all violations of repose, movement of the head is the most common. The next time the reader goes to the theatre, if he will watch the heads of the actors, he will no doubt discover some one at least of the company who punctuates his speeches with meaningless movements of his head. This fault is not confined to mediocre members of the profession. A leading actress in a big New York success had this habit to a marked degree. Her competence in other features of her work glossed over this fault, and to those absorbed in her story it was not distracting. To an acute observer, however, it detracted from the interest of her work. In the last analysis, she was not a finished artist; no fine artist is ever guilty of this meaningless movement.

There are times, of course, when the movement of the head can be made eloquent. Acting uses not only the voice, but every member of the body as well. We nod the head for Yes, and shake it for No. We throw it back in laughter or surprise, and move it in various ways in various situations. All movements of the head must have a definite meaning, or accompany some emotion which tends to embellish the actor's work. A general law can be set down as follows: When the actor uses any member of his body in action, he should give that movement a definite purpose, or make it express a meaning which enhances the value of his words. When no significance can be made to accompany physical action, that action should be eliminated, and the body should remain in repose.

How to Commit Lines to Memory

The study of a part requires two mental processes. One is to study the character and the method of interpreting it; the other is to commit the lines to memory. The first process is entirely artistic and will be discussed elsewhere; the second is a purely mechanical one. Since this chapter is designed for the amateur and the young beginner, it is advisable to give them a few suggestions as to how they may the more easily learn their parts.

Amateur performances often suffer because the actors have not been able to learn their parts with sureness of method.

Actors in single productions of plays have three or four weeks of rehearsal, and the task of committing the lines to memory is therefore comparatively easy. In stock companies the actors must accomplish this within a week's time. For them the commitment of lines is the prime essential, and all other considerations must be subordinated to it. The stock actor, therefore, acquires the quickest and surest method for his purpose.

The actor today rarely studies from a printed book of the play. The parts of a play are written out in typewritten form, with only the speeches of the individual part, and the cues belonging to them. In the old days the parts were written in longhand on both sides of the paper; there were then two "sides" to a page. The typewritten parts are now copied on only one side of the paper, but the pages are still called "sides."

An inexperienced actor at first is likely in studying his part to learn completely one speech after another. This is not a good method. Some actors in stock companies learn the first page, or side, and "cue" themselves on it. They then learn the second page and test themselves on that, after which they start at the beginning and cue themselves on both pages, proceeding thence to the third page, and so on. This, also, might not be considered the best method. It may not give the actor the flow of the story which the part is telling.

The following is probably the best system: The actor naturally reads the entire part first. This acquaints him with the entire story which his part has to tell. He then starts his study. As a rule, ten sides are enough to take at a time, or the whole first act if this does not include more than twelve or fifteen sides. Some actors study while pacing up and down, but a state of physical repose is probably more effective. The actor reads to himself the first cue and the first speech, always reading the cue with the speech to establish the connection in his mind, then the next cue and the next speech, and so on. He reads these only once, and proceeds in this way through the entire section he has laid out for himself. Repetition in reading the speeches is apt to disturb the flow of the story in the part. When he has read through the entire ten or fifteen sides in this steady manner, he goes back to the beginning and does it again in the same way.

He does this six or seven times. He then judges whether he is sufficiently familiar with his part to test himself. For this purpose some actors write their cues on the opposite blank sheet of their parts, and as they read over these cues, try to remember the speeches that belong to them. A simpler method and, to some actors, the more effective, is to hold a piece of paper over the speech while disclosing the cue, and gradually to move the paper down the page from cue to cue with a glance at the lines when required. This is a more effective method with some actors because they learn largely by "photographing" the pages in their mind, and often remember a line by seeing it mentally at the top or the bottom of the page, as the case may be.

Every part has "hard spots," and these may be read twice each time through the section. As a general rule, the actor should not stop in his reading but continue steadily in order to produce as nearly as possible the smooth flow in which he shall actually deliver his lines. When he thinks he is "room perfect" in his first assignment, he may proceed to the next. The following day at rehearsal he will probably find that the business and physical movement tend to drive many of his speeches out of his head, and he must look them over again to get them to "soak in" more surely.

When an actor studies from a printed book, he should place a mark before each of his speeches to locate it on the page, and underline the few last words of each speech preceding his own to serve as a cue. He can then proceed in the same way as described above.

As actors use different methods in committing their lines to memory, a method which might be useful to one might not do for another. One actor found the following method effective: He read his part over three times to himself and three times aloud. He then put the part away for about half an hour, after which time he read it again three times aloud. He generally knew the part after this ninth reading. He had a "quick study," for most actors require, with any method, much more of what is termed "pounding," or "grinding."

It should be borne in mind always that the most artistic way of learning a part is not to learn the lines only and trust to inspiration at performance to supply correct expression of them. During his study the actor should seek to learn his lines through their ideas, not to receive the ideas through first learning the lines. The finest actors always have the former habit; the latter is employed only by careless actors.

Committing to memory is purely a mechanical process, and has no relation to the artistry of a performance. The methods just described are suggested for those who must learn a part in the shortest possible time. The study of a character should not be hampered by a slavery to memory if the best results are to be achieved. This touches upon principles which will have their proper places in following chapters.

EXERCISES

1. Make a simple diagram showing the relative positions of two actors standing at centre in conversation.
2. How far apart should two actors stand while talking at centre, and why?
3. Where is "the centre of the stage"?
4. What is "taking stage"?
5. Describe definite action. Indefinite action.
6. What are "character parts"? "Straight parts"?
7. What is the standard technique for entering through a door on the right? On the left?
8. What is "anticipating" an entrance cue?
9. What is meant by the expression, "the psychological moment," as used in these discussions?
10. What kind of movements may violate repose?
11. What are the two mental processes required in the study of a part?
12. What is meant by "timing a movement"?
13. What is "repose"?
14 How should doors usually open in interior sets? Exterior sets?
15. What is meant by "dressing the stage"?

CHAPTER III

ACTING MAGNIFIED IN THE THEATRE

William Faversham once said at a rehearsal, "The stage is like life, only bigger." We play in a much larger space than that in which similar scenes would be enacted in real life, and the actor meant that we must magnify our work in order that its effects may reach to the limits of that space. A magnifying glass placed above an insect magnifies the insect to the eye, so that its minute parts are distinguishable. The glass does not, however, distort any of those parts to our sight, or place them out of focus. When we magnify our work to fill the larger space, if we overstrain our voices or expression we distort the effect, and this is not true art. True art is seen in effects which seem natural to the audience, however near or far away they may be. The audience do not notice that the actor has magnified his work for their benefit, in voice, expression, and gesture. The same magnification is seen in paintings, when the true effect must be caught from a certain distance.

When people first speak lines on the professional stage they rarely speak loud enough. More experience teaches them the true pitch for the voice; but only seasoned and expert actors learn the exact degrees of magnification in all the variations of volume, shading, inflection, emphasis, and gesture.

The ancient Greek actors had tremendous voices. Their words had to reach audiences composed of thousands of people in the open air. Their gesture was broad and their style declamatory. They could magnify all these but not their faces. Therefore they wore masks on which were painted expressions characteristic of the parts they played. These expressions might be the scowl of villainy, the grin of comedy, and so on.

Some critics make the claim that dramatic art is waning. Certainly definite change has come about in the matter of declamation and volume of speech. In recent years much complaint has been made that the actors in many instances could not be heard "beyond the tenth row." Our theatre today is one of "naturalism" and "realism." To secure this it is a question whether the actors do not go to extremes and speak in such low tones that, though this might be natural in real life, in the theatre it is not art. It is a part of the art of the theatre that the actor at all times shall so magnify his voice as to fill the necessary space and at the same time seem natural in the quietest of tones.

At this point it may be well to dwell for a moment on the voice in relation to magnification. Singers, it is well known, seek to develop clearness and resonance in their tones and to eliminate all effects of rasping. They practice also entering upon all initial notes in their musical phrases smoothly and without muscular hindrance by the vocal chords. Comparatively few actors are free from muscular tonal obstruction. It was said of Edwin Forrest, the celebrated American tragedian, that though he often "bellowed like a bull," he could speak with the tenderness of a child. The young actor will do well to practice clarity of tone, through which the most subdued of tones will be possible and at the same time sufficient

Model of the Oropus Theatre based on excavations by the Greek
Archæological Society

Set for the Roman Senate scene in Eugene O'Neill's LAZARUS LAUGHED

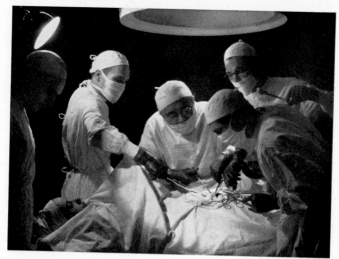

The operation scene from MEN IN WHITE; Pulitzer Prize play
in New York City

Scene from the production of RICHARD OF BORDEAUX in New York City

magnification to be audible. Not to be heard can have no excuse.

The broader and more declamatory acting of the past has been replaced by a more colloquial method, as modern plays do not require the declamatory and romantic methods of former times. For presentations of these plays, therefore, theatres are smaller and more intimate. Actors who have been playing a piece in one of these intimate theatres, if they are suddenly moved into one of the larger ones with the same piece, have to adjust themselves to a new pitch of tone. As a result of this, their voices may become strained and their general effects thrown out of focus. An actor playing Antonio in *The Merchant of Venice* in a very large theatre came on to the stage and almost shouted his opening line. It was, "In sooth I know not why I am so sad." This line required an easy, natural tone in the middle register. Because of the large space to be filled, he was not able to magnify his effect and still retain it in a seemingly natural tone; the effect was harsh and out of key. The company had been playing in smaller theatres, and this one was too large for any modern presentation of drama. Conversely, a company playing a bombastic play which required much melodrama and broad dramatic effect, was moved from its original theatre into an intimate, or "little," theatre. The smaller space tended to constrict the effect, and the whole performance seemed too broad for the space which inclosed it. Today, managers seek theatres that are suited to the styles of their plays.

The student may expect to be given rules and laws which will assist him in acquiring the habit of true pitch in his work. There are no methods of exact technique to govern this principle. The proper pitch for the voice can come only through practice and experience. When actors are mediocre, failure in this principle is often found among their deficiencies. Their voices may always be too loud and their actions too extravagant. On the other hand, actors of the finest quality sometimes speak too low, and pay too little regard to the rights of an audience to hear. They seldom, if ever, commit breaches of this principle in anything but speech, for the true artist is always careful to temper to the limit of his ability that part of his performance which appeals to the eye.

When one person speaks to another at a distance he magnifies his voice and broadens his gesture. He does this through instinct and not with any acquired technical knowledge. The expressions which show upon the faces of people in private conversation, and the tones they employ, would not register in the larger space of the theatre. The actor learns to sense this, and with experience gets the pitch of tone and the exaggeration of gesture and action necessary for that space, and in the proper degree. Stage whispers especially require the use of this principle. They cannot be in any way true to life, for they must be spoken so loud that the audience can hear, and others on the stage also, though as characters in the play the others are not supposed to hear.

Since the first edition of this book, radio has been developed and much has been accomplished in respect to amplification in motion picture theatres. Some of these theatres seat several thousand people. When speaking occurs, it is now possible to amplify the voice so that it can be heard in the farthest parts of the house and still permit the actor to speak in a natural stage tone. This amplification is even regulated in relation to various positions of the actor on the stage. If, for example, he turns up stage and speaks with his back to the audience, a man at a switchboard off stage amplifies the actor's voice more than the normal medium and reduces the amplification as the actor turns again toward the audience. This practice applies only to picture theatres, where "presentations" are made to supplement the motion picture program.

During the final rehearsals of a play, the director sometimes sits in the empty auditorium; and if the voices are too loud, or not loud enough, and the projection of various actions and stage business not sufficiently marked, he informs the actors of their faults. In practice, then, actors develop expertness in magnifying their effects. Dramatic schools endeavor to teach the technique of acting where that can be imparted through instruction. In the final analysis, if the actor possesses the original talent necessary for success, proficiency in technique will come naturally in the course of his experience.

EXERCISES

1. What is meant by "magnification"?
2. What is the principal fault of non-professional actors in respect to magnification?

CHAPTER IV

THE LAW OF ATTENTION

Audiences naturally pay attention to the story of the play, and actors must simulate that attention as well. In this they assist the audience's attention. In real life, intercourse among people consists in talking on the one hand, and listening on the other; or action on the one hand, and attention to that action on the other. So in real life, we are interchangeably actors and audience. In so far as is possible the theatre must reflect life as it is; and acting, therefore, must seek to be exact in that reflection.

The theatre may be like real life in one respect and unlike it in another. Where it is unlike real life we must fill in that deficiency with artificial means. Suppose two persons in real life are holding a conversation, and suppose that they are alone. In whatever way the conversation is conducted, it is true to life because it *is* life. This situation is unlike any in the theatre because, though there are two actors, there is no audience. Suppose, again, that these two persons are holding a conversation and several others are listening, but taking no part in this conversation. Here we have a situation similar to a duologue in the theatre, because there are actors and an audience. In such a situation, however, there may be this difference between real life and the theatre: In real life one of the parties to the conversation may pay little or no attention to what his companion says. He may gaze into space, shuffle his feet on the ground, toy with his cane, or be occupied with any other action. The interest of the listeners is not considered, though by his inattentive actions he may distract their attention from the words of the speaker. Still it is true to life. In the theatre, however, the requirements of drama must be considered; the interest of the audience must be taken into account. Therefore, the actor who is supposed to listen must *seem* to do so. He must be completely attentive to the points which are to be brought out.

But at times there may be a situation in which he is *supposed* to be inattentive. Then he may engage in any of the distractions mentioned above. The other character may then exclaim, "But you are not listening." In that case, the subject matter of the speaker is not vital to the story, and the inattention of the other character is the point to be brought out. If no such point is involved, and it is necessary that the audience get the full import of the speaker's words, then the second actor must give his attention.

The purpose of this is focus. Each character who speaks is entitled to the attention of the audience. A story is to be told, and the audience comes to hear it. Attention on the part of the actors telegraphs to the audience that their attention also must be focused on the speaker.

The eyes of an audience travel from one speaker to another as the dialogue proceeds. If the actor does not properly focus his attention on the central points of interest, the eyes of the audience may be led to places where they do not belong. In such cases, the actor is not observing the law of attention in places where it should be observed. A director will often discover that this inattention is not true to life in any circumstance. For example, if an actor is inattentive in places where, obviously, every character in real life would be vitally interested, the situation cannot be true to even the artificial representation of the theatre. Actors then must also play the part of audience.

When we observe the principle of attention, the eye is the most important feature of the body which we must bring into play. Thought is expressed principally in the eyes, and therefore, if the attention of the mind is directed toward the words of another, the eyes must be properly focused on that person and be at rest there. Perfect attention requires a motionless posture of the entire body. If the body is motionless, but the eyes rove away from the focal point of attention, the illusion is spoiled. It is better that any other member of the body express inattention rather than the eyes, for it is through them that the thought of another is reflected in the mind.

In a performance given in German, a household were discussing domestic affairs. During the discussion, the young son of the family practiced strokes with his golf club. He was presumably paying no attention to the conversation. This seemed a distraction from the interest of the scene, as the attention of the audience was disposed to follow his movements and thus be led away from the subject matter of the dialogue. One who did not understand the language could not tell to what extent this was a violation of the law we are discussing. However, if the stage direction was expert, then, at vital points of interest, the young man no doubt ceased his action and gave attention to the dialogue. Such should, at any rate, have been the case. There is a tendency in continental productions to be somewhat unobservant of the law of attention. Each character may engage in whatever action seems natural to his particular impulse. But the law still holds. The actors and the director must decide when attention may be withdrawn for independent action, and when it must be focused on the central points of interest. At all times, they must give the story of the play first consideration. Any character not concerned in the dialogue, though his part at any one point may not call for attention, must not introduce such actions as will withdraw the audience's attention from the story. This suggests the subjects of "side line action," and "moving backgrounds" which will be discussed in other sections.

A well-known actor played an engagement with a leading actress. She complained that he was difficult to play with. He gave an individual performance of his own part, with no attention to the work around him. As she expressed it, "he carried a frame about with him in which he appeared alone." He should have been merely a part of the dramatic structure, but was, instead, an independent unit. He failed to coöperate. The actor played his own part in a thoroughly artistic way, but he did not assist in the playing of the piece as a whole. The principle of coöperation will be discussed in a later chapter.

In the Metropolitan Museum of Art in New York there is a painting by Raphael entitled The Madonna Enthroned with Saints. In the centre of the picture sits the Madonna holding the nude form of the baby Christ. Various apostles surround these figures. Aside from the beauty of its execution, the picture has one remarkable feature. The attention of every other figure is focused on the central one, which is the Christ child. That figure occupies the centre of the picture, not only in position, but in idea. The attention of the observer is directed to this central figure through the postures of the surrounding figures. The Madonna looks down at the child. Several of the Saints look toward him. One apostle holds a book in such a position that a line from the elbow through the book would extend directly to the Infant's face. Moreover, the ray of light with which the painting is illumined shines directly on the Saviour's countenance. Nothing can more fully illustrate the law of attention as applied in the theatre than does this beautiful painting. In this picture the Christ child corresponds to the actor who requires the attention of the audience; the surrounding figures to the other actors who assist in directing that attention, while, of course, the observer corresponds to the audience whose attention is required. The law can operate in other lines of art as well as in the theatre. An interest in the painter's art, as in all others should be of profit to the actor.

A further illustration of the principle of attention may be given here. In a play one actress had to listen to a long emotional speech by another and, of course, should have given close attention. She provided herself, how-ever, with a handful of stage coins, which she concealed in her purse. Just preceding a dramatic point in the speech, she unclasped her purse and allowed the coins to fall out and roll in various directions about the stage. The noise of the falling coins attracted the attention of the audience, and she then occupied herself in looking about for them under the table and chairs. Of course, this thoroughly shattered the attention and interest of the audience in the focal point, since it was diverted by this act to an incident which had nothing to do with the play. A cat walking on to the stage could have produced a like effect. Such an incident as the one just cited has happened more than once and bespeaks the value of harmony in a company. Inharmony has disrupted many a dramatic organization.

Some actors have a habit of looking into the audience, recognizing friends, or estimating the size of the house. This may not interfere with the work of the other actors, but if noticed by the audience, distracts their attention. Sometimes an article falls on to the stage by accident. For a moment this draws the attention of the audience away. The professional actor easily adjusts such a mishap by picking the article up. It would be natural in real life to do so. Non-professional actors, not being so much at ease on the stage, often make the mistake of leaving an article where it has fallen. This prolongs the distraction in the audience's attention. A story is told of one amateur group of actors who repeatedly walked around a sofa pillow which had fallen, because no one had the courage to pick it up. The sofa pillow, and not the actors, received the focus of attention throughout the act.

One night E. H. Sothern, while playing Shylock, became furious at a super who, in the courtroom scene during one of Mr. Sothern's dramatic speeches, brushed a fly off his nose. The super had been instructed to keep perfectly still. Such little things as this can violate the important principle of attention, and attention must always be given first consideration. A fly lighting on the nose is true enough to life, but the theatre must be true to life in semblance rather than actuality. And much of the truth of life is not art.

The actor may pay attention in numerous ways. One of these, and the most simple, is to look directly at the person speaking. He may then remain still, whether sitting or standing. He does not move until his own turn comes to speak.

But the actor can pay attention to another's words when he is himself occupied with action. For instance, he may turn the pages of a magazine or smoke a cigar. He must show to the audience that he is listening, nevertheless, and may glance up occasionally as he himself speaks. In this way he becomes actor and audience alternately. When action is combined with listening, the action must not be so broad or definite that it distracts attention.

Again, while another speaks, an actor may be pacing up and down the stage under the stress of emotion. At times he may stop to listen more intently to some pointed remark of the speaker, and may then resume his action. In such a scene, the stress of emotion on the part of the listener may be the point to be brought out. While he paces up and down he occupies the focal point of interest rather than the speaker. That focal point is transferred to the speaker only when the walker stops to listen more intently. The jealousy scene between Iago and Othello is an ideal example of this.

From this scene, one of the greatest in dramatic classic literature, an excerpt is given. Well along in the scene Othello says:

OTHELLO: Give me a living reason she's disloyal.
    (*He stops and listens to Iago's next speech.*)
IAGO: I do not like the office;
    But sith I am entered in this cause so far,

Pricked to't by foolish honesty and love,
I will go on. I lay with Cassio lately,
And being troubled with a raging tooth,
I could not sleep.
There are a kind of men so loose of soul,
That in their sleeps will mutter their affairs:
One of this kind is Cassio.
In sleep I heard him say, Sweet Desdemona,
Let us be wary, let us hide our loves,
And then, sir, would he gripe and wring my hand,
Cry, O sweet creature! and then,
Cursed fate that gave thee to the Moor!

OTHELLO (*rushing across to the left*):
O monstrous! monstrous!

IAGO: Nay, this was but his dream.

OTHELLO (*stopping for his speech*): But this denoted a
foregone conclusion;
'Tis a shrewd doubt, though it be but a dream.
(*He then paces up the stage and down during Iago's
next speech.*)

IAGO: And this may help to thicken other proofs
That do demonstrate thinly.

OTHELLO (*now down stage*): I'll tear her all to pieces.
(*He crosses to the other side, and up the stage again
and down during the following speech of Iago.*)

IAGO: Nay but be wise: yet we see nothing done.
She may be honest yet;
(*Othello, as he paces about, exclaims, "Ah!"*)
                          Tell me but this,
Have you not sometimes seen a handkerchief
Spotted with strawberries in your wife's hand?
(*Othello stops suddenly and says:*)

OTHELLO: I gave her such a one; 'twas my first gift.
(*Iago continues with his lie, and a moment later:*)

[73]

OTHELLO: Arise, black vengeance, from thy hollow cell!
Yield up, oh love, thy crown and hearted throne
To tyrannous hate! Swell bosom with thy fraught,
For 'tis of aspics' tongues!
  (*He again paces up stage.*)
IAGO: Yet be content.
OTHELLO (*still moving*): O blood, Iago, blood!
  (*and continuing while Iago says:*)
IAGO: Patience, I say: Your mind may change.

The principle of attention we are describing ends here, and the scene is direct to the end.

Another example of this principle was shown in John Drinkwater's play of *Abraham Lincoln*. In one scene, Lincoln stood with his back to the audience and his hands behind him. As he listened to the verbal blows of his military staff, he punctuated his feelings by unclenching and clenching his fists. In this way he directed strong attention to himself at certain points.

These few examples serve to illustrate the general principle. At the same time, no hide-bound rules can be set down to govern all cases. There may be times when no rules at all need be observed. Such cases may occur when crowds and mobs are staged, scenes of general confusion and dramatic turmoil, and various situations which do not require the finer and more exact technique. The idea must be borne in mind that there is always a true focal point at which the attention of the audience should be directed. That focal point may consist of only one person and his action or speech, or even an inanimate object. It may be the hand of a clock on the stroke of twelve; it may consist of two or more persons or things; and it may be, for the moment, a stage full of actors, like the mob at the opening of *Julius Cæsar*. Whatever it is, however, the actor should try through conscientious training to keep the attention of the audience where it belongs.

EXERCISES

1. What is "the law of attention"? What is its purpose?
2. What is one bad result of not observing the law of attention?
3. What is one common way of paying attention?

CHAPTER V

"KEEPING THE EYE ON THE BALL"

Every golf player knows that in driving off from the tee there are several things he must do. First, he must plant his feet firmly on the ground a foot or two apart and opposite the ball. Next, he must grasp the club firmly with the proper grip. He must then poise the base of the club against the ball itself to get the right distance for the stroke, and after raising the club over the right shoulder for the swing, and after the swing itself, he must "keep his eye on the ball." If he does not do this, but, instead, is too anxious to see the effect of his stroke and raises his eyes too soon, the stroke is impaired, and its effect is probably spoiled as well. He may not strike the ball squarely, or at all, may strike the ground, or else send the ball a shorter distance than he would have done with a perfect stroke.

Still, the expression "keeping the eye on the ball" is not, strictly speaking, correct, and the expert golfer does it only in part. Trying to keep the eye on the ball from the instant it leaves the tee causes the mistakes mentioned. The golfer really fixes his eye on the ball during the whole process of poising, raising his club for the swing, and swinging downward. When the ball has left the tee, the golfer's eye remains on the tee itself and not on the ball, until the swing is entirely finished and the club is extended downward over the left shoulder. Not until the golfer recovers does he raise his eyes to follow the flight of the ball.

This principle has an exact analogy in acting, and refers to effects which the actor desires to produce, either in the delivery of certain lines, or the performance of various bits of stage business. Suppose there is a line to be delivered. The principle must be observed whether the line calls for laughter or applause, or an effect founded merely in the interest of the story. To use the golf simile, the ball corresponds to the line to be delivered; the position and attitude of the golfer correspond to the relative position and attitude of the actor while delivering the line; the golf club and the expertness of the swing correspond to the method with which the line is delivered; and keeping the eye on the ball corresponds to the player's act of holding his position and sustaining his tone and delivery until he has completely delivered the line and its effect is registered upon the audience. The flight of the ball, of course, corresponds to that effect. This can be impaired in the same way that a faulty stroke impairs the work of the golfer. It is best to do one thing at a time, and to do it thoroughly before we pass on to the next.

Let us see how this principle can be applied in acting. Examples will best illustrate it. In Frederic and Fanny Hatton's comedy, *Lombardi Ltd.*, a character stands down stage close to the footlights. At a certain point in the dialogue he exclaims, "Thank the Lord! I'll go right down and write some checks." Through certain incidents in the play and the motif of that particular character, this line is funny and, in the expression of the theatre, is "good for a laugh." After speaking the line the character moves up stage. In this situation, the complete effect to be registered lies in the line alone; the movement up stage has no relation to that effect, and is merely put in because the stage direction requires that the actor remove to another position. After the actor has delivered his line and its effect has been registered on the audience, he simply gets "out of the picture" and leaves the rest of the characters to continue the dialogue.

When this play was rehearsed, the director noticed one day that the actor turned to move up stage while still speaking the last two or three words of the speech. The line was to be directed toward the audience. This is called "speaking front." The actor was then not "keeping his eye on the ball," in this case toward the audience, until he had, figuratively speaking, finished his stroke.

We will cite another case and then make comparisons. In *Six Cylinder Love*, a visitor comes to the house and is received by the husband, who invites him to dinner. The husband calls to his wife, who is off stage, "Oh, Lucy, here's a visitor, and I have invited him to dinner." The wife, off stage, says, "Who is it?" and the husband answers, "Come and see." The wife then enters and sees the visitor. Through previous incidents in the piece, the visitor has become very distasteful to the wife, and at sight of him she exclaims, "Oh my God!" and strides in disgust out of the room. The play is a comedy, and this line registers a substantial laugh.

These two cases have much similarity. In both, the lines are spoken front. After the line in both cases, the character moves up stage. There is, however, a difference between the two cases. In the former, the only effect to be registered lies in the line alone, while in the latter, it lies not alone in the line, but in the action accompanying the line as well. That action is one of disgust. The actress, therefore, must produce a double effect in order to make the laugh register its fullest value. She procures the double effect through the proper delivery of the line, combined with the proper action of disgust in walking off the stage.

A difference in treatment is necessary between these two cases. It is very slight, but is worthy of mention. It has been said that in the first case the actor's movement up stage after speaking the line had no value in producing comedy effect; it was merely a part of stage direction. Therefore, the actor needed to hold his position until he had registered the line and the laugh had actually started. Not until he *heard* it start should he have turned up stage. Then he could go up while it was still in progress.

In the second case the movement away was part of the value in producing the effect, for the actress needed to register her disgust, not only in the line, but in the action as well. Therefore, she needed to move off stage immediately after speaking the line, and *without* waiting for the laugh to start. She needed to be careful, nevertheless, to speak the full line directly toward the audience before turning. In the theatre this is called, "landing," or "planting," the line. Then, as she walked in disgust off the stage, the laugh came as a result of the two actions, the one of speech and the other of movement. The movement increased the laugh, provided, of course, she "kept her eye on the ball" and did not turn too soon.

The following case involves a difference only in positions: A religious old Scotchman has a lady visitor at his cottage late at night. She is much disheveled and he thinks her a shameless woman who has come to flirt with him. She asks him to go on an errand for her, and he starts out leaving her alone with his cat. At the door he has the exit line, "Put Tammas oot please, he's a respectable cat." He then goes out and slams the door. He naturally speaks the line to her and not "out front," as in the cases mentioned above, and holds the position until he has delivered it completely; his angry exit and slam of the door increase the laugh which the line has started.

This principle applies in other ways than in comedy lines. It also governs lines that are not meant for comedy effect, as well as particular bits of stage business. Such lines may often be delivered while a character stands at a door ready to make his exit. The lines may contain some dramatic effect which convey a salient point in the unfolding of the story, and must be given the same treatment as the examples in comedy already cited. Suppose a line is, "The man who stole the necklace was Lord Lovell himself," and the plot calls for consternation from the others at this statement. This line is obviously directed to some character, or characters, on the stage. The treatment here is the same as in the other cases. The actor holds his position, probably with his hand on the door knob, until the last syllable has left his lips before he turns to go.

As in the first example, an actor often turns to leave the stage, or turns up stage, while still speaking, and the effect of his final words is lost. This is a common fault in acting. There are times, however, when this is just what he *should* do. For example, during the dialogue he may have gone to the door, and he speaks his remaining speeches from that place. He says, "Well, I'm going into the garden." In this case he turns to go while he is still speaking the line. He must only be careful to deliver in full his line before he disappears. This speech has no special point, perhaps, and even if it should have and be good for a laugh, the natural action for anyone in real life on such a line would be to suit his action to his words. A line of such nature would naturally be accompanied with the action. This relates to another principle. The present discussion concerns only speeches that carry ideas meant to register special dramatic or comic effects, when actual truth to life would demand that they be treated in the way herein described.

These "points" may also carry the effect of applause, and the treatment is just the same. Certain bits of action, also, which are called "stage business," must be made to register in the same way; sometimes on the stage action is more effective than words. Action registers on the eye instead of the ear. In speech, the actor should be careful of his "stroke" in enunciation, direction, and completion; in "business" he should regard the definiteness of his action, and should give it the necessary breadth of execution to make it completely visible to the audience. He should also finish it entirely before passing on to something else. Several actions may be combined in this way, all of which are concerned in the one general effect to be registered. Expert acting is often seen in the clear-cut precision and completeness with which these things are done. Examples of stage business need not be given, for the governing principle is the same as in speech.

The reason that, when improperly executed, the points we are discussing do not gain the right effects, is that the audience do not catch all the words or action. In the case of words, the action of turning away too soon throws the actor's voice away from the audience. Physical movement, also, while the actor is still speaking, tends to interfere with the clearest possible enunciation. This is just as if a man were to aim a gun at a target, and then, an instant before the shot, were to swerve the muzzle to one side.

In *Pollyanna* the line occurs, "How dare she say I'm a cripple, I only limp." The actor then hobbles up stage. Some man in the back of the house, hearing some of the audience laugh, may turn to his wife and say, "What did he say, Mary?" and she replies, "I don't know, I didn't get it." Perhaps the actor has been too anxious to get his laugh, and, being inexpert in the production of his technique, he bungles his "stroke" by turning up stage too soon. In speech and action, passing on to another thing too quickly blurs the execution of the thing in hand, so that in the case of speech it may not be spoken properly and therefore not understood, and in the case of action not properly seen. On the other hand, in these examples, if speech is followed too late by action, the fault is just as great in the opposite extreme. In respect to the whole principle, we should warn the actor that he must not make his practice of it too precise, lest his treatment be mechanical and fixed. If this happens, his acting will lack that spirit and spontaneity which are so necessary to the illusion. Feeling the spirit of the lines and practicing the principles will make the actor's work definite and clear cut, and enable him to feel the psychological moments for following one part of his work with another.

Different treatments of the same principle will be discussed in other chapters.

"KEEPING THE EYE ON THE BALL"

EXERCISES

1. Explain what is meant by "keeping the eye on the ball."
2. Devise some line and situation in which you should "keep your eye on the ball," and illustrate the action.
3. What is one bad result of turning away before finishing some important speech?
4. What three things should an actor be careful of in his speech?
5. What two things should an actor be careful of in his "business"?
6. How can an actor make his work appear spontaneous and clear cut?

CHAPTER VI

THE FOURTH WALL

A stage setting has one, two, or three general dimensions. The setting may run straight across from right to left first entrance, in which case it has one dimension only and is called a front scene, or scene in 1; it may present only one corner of a room and have two dimensions; or it may show the full interior of a room, in which case it has three dimensions. These are the back and the two sides. It can never have the fourth dimension, for that must be left open to the audience. The fourth dimension is therefore imaginary, and is called the fourth wall.

The actor is separated from the audience by a platform along the front of which is a row of strong lights; and this separation isolates him in a little world of his own. He bends his effort toward expressing what seems, on analysis, to be actually true to life. The fourth wall, however, constantly intervenes to defeat this purpose.

If acting were done with no calculation for the audience, it would be done much differently. The actor could act as if the fourth wall were really present. He could place his back to it at will, as he does in any real room. He could stand in any position, and face in any direction. Because of the fourth wall principle he must conform to certain laws regarding it.

When several characters stand in or near the centre, they arrange themselves somewhat in a row and face toward the audience. This is necessary, for the audience needs to look in on their action. In real life these people would hold their conversation in some grouping approximating a circle. Their grouping is natural only when they move out of the action and group themselves at the back.

In the productions of the old days a banquet table was filled on only three sides. The famous painting, The Last Supper, shows this arrangement. Today, those characters who have least to do in a scene are placed on the down stage side of a table, for in real life people occupy all four sides. Still, in many situations there is an open formation of character groupings, when in real life the formation would be closed.

Formerly, inasmuch as a conscious effort was made toward idealism and romanticism, the fourth wall principle was frankly admitted. The actor then left himself "open" to the audience by fixed rules. Never to turn his back to the audience was a common example; but the rules gradually became less fixed. We find Mark Antony in an old prompt book of *Julius Cæsar* going in front of the corpse of Cæsar, turning his back to the audience, and saying to the conspirators, "Let each man render me his bloody hand."

In the same prompt book use is made of the fourth wall in stage business. In Brutus' garden, the conspirators group themselves over at the right. Decius says, "Here lies the east: doth not the day break here?" At the same time he points with his sword directly toward the audience. In the melodrama, *Sherlock Holmes*, one of the thieves in the underground den raises his lantern to examine a window in this fourth wall; while in *Treasure Island*, a dramatization of the book of that name, Black

Dog sneaks into the inn, peers about on all sides, and takes in the fourth wall in his scrutiny.

The above examples refer to observance of the fourth wall in respect to stage business. This belongs to the art of stage direction, and is occasionally used in the production of plays.

The actor finds the fourth wall principle more difficult to treat in his individual performance. He must give the illusion of being unconscious of the presence of an audience, while at the same time he must act in conformity with that knowledge. The audience must see his full face occasionally in order to note its expression, and are irritated if they can seldom see more than his profile. Some of the best artists can bring the full face into view very often without seeming consciously to do so. Sarah Bernhardt was able to play with her full face in view most of the time, and at the same time be completely related to those about her.

In one of the dramatic schools the use of the fourth wall principle is called the "abstract" and the "concrete." The former refers to looking toward the audience and the latter to looking at the person speaking or addressed. False judgment in this respect often makes actors fall short of the right effects. What conditions then permit an actor to turn his full face to the audience, and what situations permit it to be seen in other postures?

The actor may look toward the audience but never at it, and must not focus his gaze on any person there. The inexperienced actor does not always have the right discrimination in this principle. He knows the value of the full face, and often stands looking squarely toward the audience without the art to conceal his intention, or the judgment to select the opportune times. Young actors often assume such postures. This causes them to talk to their companions across their right or left shoulder, and the principle of the three-quarter positions, as mentioned in Chapter II, is therefore violated.

Not all performances are meant "to hold the mirror up to nature"; and in certain branches of the theatre acting is openly directed toward the audience. This practice prevails principally in burlesque and vaudeville, and there is a strong tendency toward it in musical comedy. A modern term calls this "getting it over." In burlesque, to "land" his laughs, the actor usually advances a few steps toward the footlights, describes a half-circle, and speaks his lines directly at the audience. The exaggerated methods of vaudeville, also, find the actors facing directly toward the audience in order to more surely register their points when they should be facing partly toward each other in the three-quarter position.

The above cases are mentioned in order to point out a contrast. The actor as a rule, however, should give the illusion of being inclosed within his own little world without being conscious of that occupied by the audience. In whatever he does he must not destroy that illusion.

An actor played the part of an irate father. He was introduced to his son's new wife whom he had to snub, passing from one side of the stage to the other with his nose in the air. As the actor crossed over, he could not refrain from looking out at the audience. The director said, "Pay no attention to the audience; imagine there is a brick wall along the footlights." The action was false, as the actor looked "out front" when there was no reason to do so.

Three sides of any room correspond to the three dimensions of a full stage setting, and the fourth to the position of the audience. Let a person sit in a room facing squarely toward one wall. Let him look at an object on the right-hand wall, and then divert his gaze to some object on the left-hand wall. If the student will try this, he will find that in the change of gaze from right to left he has seen nothing on the wall in front of him. The eye can convey intelligence to the brain only when it is focused on things within its range. The person does not see the things within his sweep of vision because his mind is not centred on them; he is not thinking of objects on the "fourth wall," but only of those on the right and left.

This should be true in the theatre. The actor should begin early to think of the audience as a wall which rises before him, and give it no attention other than knowing it is there and that it requires good acting. Anyone can perform the above experiment perfectly; yet many actors, when, instead of this fourth wall, there is a large auditorium of people, are noticeably conscious of the fact. In looking from one side to the other they allow their gaze to focus for an instant on the audience. The beginner should guard against this tendency at the outset and learn to shut out the audience at will. If he does not do so, his mistake takes him from his own world into their's, which would not happen if there were actually a wall between them.

When may the actor look toward the audience, and when must he direct his attention toward persons and things on the stage? There is great elasticity in the license to be allowed. It is impossible to set down any fixed rules; different actors give different treatment to any section of dialogue. We can only offer examples which may serve as general suggestions; the actor proves his discretion and skill in so far as he makes himself effective.

As a general rule, all parts of soliloquies not accompanied with action are directed "front." Hamlet gazes toward the audience, or into the footlights, when he begins his soliloquy on death with the words, "To be or not to be."

Here is an example of the "out front" speech interspersed with action in a soliloquy from the famous old comedy, *A Scrap of Paper.* Prosper invites Suzanne to search for a scrap of paper which he has hidden, and leaves her alone on the stage.

> SUZANNE (*after watching him off she turns front and says*):
> He's actually gone. Hang the man. (*Again turning toward his exit.*) His impertinence is perfectly delightful. (*Imitating him.*) "Search, search—everything is open for your inspection—everything but this casket." (*Turning to look at it.*) My dear sir, (*turning toward his exit*) the stress you lay upon the casket convinces me that the letter is *not* there—But it *is here*—somewhere. Where can he have concealed it? (*Looking front and then about. There is a knock at the door. She looks front.*) Has he returned? No—it is at this little door (*looking at it*) leading down into the park. (*Knocking again.*) Who can it be? (*She looks front.*) I don't want to be found in a strange gentleman's room—one's never too old for scandal—a pretty mess I've let myself into—that comes of meddling with other people's affairs. (*Knocking again, and she opens the door.*)

There were many "aside" speeches in these old plays where the actor uttered aloud the thoughts that were in his mind and which the others on the stage were not supposed to hear. In these speeches he turned away from the person he was addressing and delivered the "aside" toward the audience. A great mistake can be made in delivering "aside" speeches. An early American play called *Fashion* was performed at the Provincetown Playhouse in New York. It abounded in "asides." To show the obsolete method of a former day in respect to "aside" speeches, and to burlesque the method, the actors stepped down toward the footlights to deliver them. This ludicrously showed the methods of burlesque actors, who do this to register their comedy points. For the most part, an actor should deliver his "aside" speech by merely turning toward the audience, but not moving out of his position. If he does so it is very likely an evidence of lack of repose. There are exceptions to the rule, however.

A revolutionary exception was made in Eugene O'Neill's *Strange Interlude*. For the first time in many years the aside speech was brought boldly back into use. There was a great difference, however. In this play the characters, instead of turning toward the audience to deliver the "asides," looked directly at the persons about whom the mental comments were made. In real life their thoughts would not have turned their bodies away, so on the stage this restraint from physical action was really more natural. The method was used to indicate their secret thoughts. On many lines the effect was made clear by the character commented on turning away instead of the speaker. In another play of O'Neill's, *Days Without End*, one character's secret thoughts were represented by another actor made up to closely resemble him, who sat or stood just behind him and spoke the asides. Such methods are of course not in general use. Though the aside speech is practically out of use, short soliloquies are often allowed and are sometimes effective. People frequently speak aloud to themselves in real life.

Aside speeches, when other characters are on the stage, are in general considered too unreal for modern plays, but are conceded in the old plays to have had great power in unfolding the story.

We will give a few examples from *A Scrap of Paper*.

PROSPER: The greatest curiosity? Woman, of course.

SUZANNE: It seems you have studied the animal.

PROSPER: Sometimes, and generally they are the fairest to the eye. (*He turns to look at the Baroness and sees her take down a little statue where a letter is hidden. Aside, turning front.*) She's at it again. (*Aloud, and to them.*) I was just making that identical remark to Madame de la Glacière.

A little later:—

PROSPER: Oh, the merest trifle, sometimes, is enough—a mere scrap of paper, perhaps—a morsel of handwriting.

SUZANNE (*aside, front*): He means some letter. Hm! Hm! What is all this? (*A moment later he takes down the statue with the letter concealed in it.*)

LOUISE (*aside to him*): Stop, sir!

PROSPER: Don't be alarmed, madam! . . . (*Aside, front.*) I feel the letter.

SUZANNE (*aside to Louise. In this case she speaks directly to her, but in a low tone*): Your husband's eyes are on you.

LOUISE (*aside to Suzanne*): Oh, did you but know! (*The letter falls, and Prosper puts his foot on it.*)

SUZANNE (*aside, front*): A letter! I was sure of it!

The following example from the same play shows how the posture can be varied to turn the face front when the speech is neither a soliloquy nor an aside:

ZENOBIA: Madame de la Glacière, indeed! The greatest flirt that ever existed! (*With that feminine petulance which is so expressive in women, she may then turn front.*) I'm sure she got herself prettily talked of before her marriage. (*Then turning back to her companion.*) Only ask that absurd friend of yours, Prosper Couramont.

BRISEMONT: Well, if she *did* flirt with Prosper . . . before she was married . . . what of that?

ZENOBIA: What of that? (*Looking at him.*) Flirting is flirting before or after, and she and her flighty Parisian friend, Mademoiselle Susanne, who is old enough to know better (*she may then settle back in her chair and look front*), are not fit associates for an innocent boy like that.

It will be noticed that the parts of speeches which she delivers front are not as direct as those she delivers toward the other character, as, for example: "What of that?" This should never be spoken front.

In the melodrama, *Within the Law*, an inspector cross-examines a young woman. She sits tense on the other side of his desk and stares straight before her. She answers most of his questions in this position. She turns to him only when she says something as positive and direct as, "But I tell you I was not in the house," and may turn front again as she says, "I know nothing about the whole affair." The business of butlers, when they look front on the announcements of visitors or dinner, because these announcements are for the general ear, is included under this principle.

THE FOURTH WALL

Almost without exception, an apostrophe to God is delivered front, and, of course, with the eyes raised upward. During a conversation, all parts of the dialogue delivered in a state of revery may be directed toward the front. In this state the actor would be likely also to look downward. The revery of persons sitting before a fire would be delivered into the fireplace. In such situations the fireplace would correspond to the fourth wall. As spoken of here, the fourth wall need not always be in the position of the audience. It may be understood as a line parallel to the general line of the grouping, as in the case of people sitting before a fire.

In Arthur Hopkins' production of *The Gypsy Trail* an important love scene was played by characters who kept their backs to the audience throughout the entire scene. In this instance the fourth wall was the fence and gate in front of a house.

It should not be necessary to mention further examples. The occasions for the use of this principle are countless. The actor should be careful that in looking toward the fourth wall, he does not look beyond it into the world where his action does not belong—namely, the audience. He must stay within his boundaries. When he has acquired a finished technique, he knows where to direct his gaze to be most effective.

EXERCISES

1. What is "the fourth wall"?
2. What is an "aside" speech? Where is it directed?
3. What other kind of speech may be directed "front"?
4. Name a situation in which the fourth wall principle is used.
5. What is one wrong way of delivering an "aside" speech?

CHAPTER VII

GESTURE

The romantic school of the past and the ways in which it differed from that of the present have already been mentioned. It was natural that the broad method of former times should involve a great difference in gesture from the present. The modern school pays little attention to gesture, allows all mannerism to be considered natural and to pass without complaint. We lay great stress today upon the value of personality. The actor with a distinctive personality and method in his work commands attention thereby. The manner of his gesture, whatever it may be, is held to be a part of that method, and tends to accentuate his personality rather than detract from it. In the old days, people considered studied grace of gesture of distinct value to the actor, but today little or nothing is said in its favor as necessary to the better elements of his art.

If we admit that art should strive to attain the ideal, then grace and beauty of gesture are of value even in our modern theatre. Art is graceful, and the actor should try to express it as gracefully as possible. He cannot do this if he neglects the principles of gesture more than other phases of his work.

The reader easily remembers some of the great artists he has seen. He may not have given special attention to their hands, but he will admit there was nothing in the actor's use of these members that marred his appreciation of their work. No really great artist is deficient in the use of his hands; and it is safe to say that graceful gesture can be considered one of the ultimate tests of a great artist. Whoever saw the great Sarah Bernhardt will not forget the grace and beauty with which she used her hands, and with what perfect expression they accompanied her moods. Jean Coquelin, also, the great French comedian, who spent his career in the old romantic school, illuminated his acting with a wonderful expressiveness of gesture, which emphasized the perfections of his art.

The part of Othello contains the most violent of passions. When the mind is moved by emotion, the body reacts to that emotion, and expresses it physically in gesture. Therefore, to be moved by strong passion without expressing at least some phases of gesture is not true to life. Yet an actor played Othello with his hands nearly always at his sides. This fact alone was ample proof that he was not a great artist.

Though polished and graceful gesture is always attractive in a performance, it is quite possible to overdo it. A star actress in a Continental theatre was observed using a great deal of it. Her rôle was a sprightly one in high comedy; and much gesture was not only permissible, but suggested in her part. Still to our Anglo-Saxon coolness, it might have seemed too abundant and not always necessary. Sometimes, also, it seemed to distract attention from more pertinent things. We can safely lay down a rule that though we can often embellish a performance by employing some gesture in it when that is permissible, we should avoid employing too much.

The poetic drama of a former period allowed greater scope for the practice of gesture, and therefore the actors of that time gave it greater attention. Our modern plays contain diversified types which illustrate every phase of human character and eccentricity, and do not call for the use of polished gesture in the same degree.

This is as it should be. We do not expect an actor, when he plays a peasant, a tramp, or a beggar to delight us with the grace and polish of a Coquelin or a Bernhardt. In these parts he is justified in portraying the real and subordinating the ideal. The style of gesture used in any part should be natural to the character portrayed, and actors inspirationally use different styles of gesture in different parts. Some of these characters may require great fullness of gesture in accordance with the emotions expressed and the characteristics of the person portrayed, while others must be played with little or no gesture at all.

There is ample reason why gesture should conform to the actor's characterization. But parts which contain idealistic traits and sentiments, and especially those which carry the romance and sentiment of a play, should be embellished with as much grace as possible in all their aspects. In such parts, namely, heroes, lovers, and the like, grace of gesture proves a decided asset.

Amateur actors naturally have less skill in gesture than professional ones. Especially is this true in "costume" plays. A director of an amateur group who were producing a classic costume play hit upon the device of pinning lace into the sleeves of the actors' coats at rehearsals. This enabled them to develop some degree of ease in their gesture, as the hands unconsciously followed the graceful movements of the lace.

We shall not attempt to give more than a few suggestions regarding gesture, and endeavor to explain some of its standard principles. There are countless mannerisms in its use, which may all be characteristic of the actor's own personality. In gesture, however, as in all the other principles of acting, every actor should observe certain fundamental rules. The section on Distance in Chapter I relates to gesture. The actor needs room for the full-length action of his arms. In many gestures he should extend his arm to its full length. The next time the student goes to the theatre he may notice, if he bears this principle in mind, that many of the actors use cramped gestures. The best art expresses itself to the full, and the best actors, when the need arises, express their gestures fully and to the limit of length.

Any emotion must be preceded by a thought or idea, and this has its seat in the mind. When the idea has produced an emotion, that emotion is related to the heart. Some scientists believe that it is expressed in close association with the solar plexus. Therefore, physical reaction to feeling is expressed through the solar plexus and travels outward along the limbs to the extremities.

When a physical impulse has been properly started from the solar plexus, and sufficient impetus has been given to carry it the full distance, it travels all the way to the extremities, and a correct gesture is made. The first physical sensation of gesture, after its impulse has left the solar plexus, is felt in the shoulder, whence it proceeds through the elbow to the hands, and ends at the tips of the fingers. Gesture which is expressed in the cramped, unfinished manner so often seen, has not received this perfect impulse. Motion picture actors, when a number of them are crowded together in a scene which occupies a small space, often make this cramped style of gesture because they have not enough room for freedom of movement.

The first principle to observe regarding gesture, therefore, is the full-length movement. This should be the governing principle of very many gestures, but not of all. We make exception of the thousand and one little gestures of character and eccentricity, besides those indefinite and casual movements of the hands which are made with little effort in expressing a mood. We will deal only with those gestures which can be called standard. They are to be seen more often in the legitimate and poetic drama, but may be used in any style of play.

The commonest of the full-length gestures is perhaps the index. This is made by extending the arm with all fingers closed on the palm except the index. It is often seen in the familiar figures on sign posts. Some actors are careless in this simple gesture, and make it with the fingers spread out loosely. To produce the gesture thus, weakens its force. The actor should see that the fingers are completely closed; the common crossroads sign is the best teacher.

It would be a mistake to make the gesture by extending the arm stiffly from the side. The correct treatment might be likened to the cracking of a black-snake whip. The impulse travels from the arm and hand of the wielder along the whip; and as the whip uncurls it straightens out as the impulse reaches the tip. So, in the gesture, the impulse travels from the solar plexus through the shoulder to the elbow, which it raises, and the hand naturally follows. This brings the hand up opposite the chest, and the impulse then throws the hand forward and out and ends at the tip of the index finger. Unless intentionally pointing down or up the actor extends the arm on a level with his shoulder. This standard method may be generally used in all of the full-length gestures, with one or both arms, when they are to be definite and positive.

This gesture should never be made across the body. That is, if the actor is facing the audience and desires to point to the right, he should do so with the right hand, and vice versa. The gesture is made when pointing directly at single objects. An actor points directly at some object in the landscape with the index finger, but if he wishes to indicate the entire landscape, he does so with a swing of the arm and the palm open.

The index gesture is used in command. If a person points to a door and says, "Go," it is with the index. On the other hand, if the emotion, when he says this, is that of repulsion, the gesture may be made with a wave of the hand away from the body and the palm down. There is probably no time when the index gesture does not show more complete artistry through use of the full-length movement, the individual habit of the actor notwithstanding, if the mental impulse is more than casual, is definite, and expresses direct purpose.

A prominent dramatic school teaches that the index gesture should be made differently from that of command. The index gesture, they say, is made with the palm outward and the fingers closed over it, while that of command is made showing only the side of the hand and the closed fingers downward. This distinction may have been suggested by sign posts, which often show a figure of the hand with the folded fingers outward, and the thumb and index finger above. Sign-post figures are made in both ways. As a matter of fact, the gesture of command and the index gesture may be made in the same way. In respect to the gesture of command, the command is registered in the words, while the gesture itself merely indicates where the command shall be obeyed.

A mother welcomes the return of her prodigal son. She extends her arms to their full length, palms upward, to take him to her. When asking for mercy or pity, or expressing entreaty, the same gesture may be used. When the arms are flung wide open, with palms open and fingers extended, the gesture may express an excess of emotion, either despair, entreaty, remorse, or some other strong passion, as if all the feeling of the soul were laid bare. The gesture expresses complete abandonment to the emotion. A familiar gesture used in greeting or farewell from a little distance is made by throwing the arm and hand out with the palm in.

When the arm is extended with the palm open, it may indicate a chair to sit on, or it may call attention to a litter of objects on the floor. A person may point to something with the index finger and say, "Do you see that rubbish?" He may then say, "It was left for me to pick up," and he indicates it again with the palm open.

Entreaties to Heaven are made with the arms extended upward and palms out. A supplication to God for a gift or benefit can be made with the palms upward horizontally. We are familiar with the gesture which responds to the highwayman's command of "Hands up!" The ancient Roman's gesture of Hail or Farewell was made with one hand in the same manner. A gesture of despair can be made by throwing both arms upward with the palms out, as when one exclaims, "Oh, what's the use?"

Gestures of repulsion are made with the arms forward and palms out, as when one says, "Keep off," or, "Don't touch me." They are made with one or both arms, as the emotion requires.

An actor may express finality of refusal by swinging one or both arms downward, palms toward the floor. The same gesture may be employed when he says, for example, "It is all debasing and horrible." When he bows and says, "I am your humble servant," he may extend the arms downward and outward with the palms out.

All of the gestures thus far mentioned are more effective with the full arm movement; there are many others in practice which the actor finds necessary.

A gesture of horror or physical revulsion is effectively made with the palms raised upward and outward over the face. The gesture with which a person beckons to another is a familiar one, and is made by throwing the hand outward and bringing the fingers toward the body. A gesture of supplication to a person may be made by clasping the hands, and the attitude of prayer by placing the palms together and elevating the eyes. A gesture of reproval is made by shaking the index finger, and one of contempt by snapping the fingers; the latter serves, also, for emphasis in various ways.

When Mark Antony says to the mob, "Nay, press not so upon me, stand far off," he swings his arms inward and out, if he does not actually push the mob aside. A gesture of negation may be made by swinging the hand from side to side with the palm out. A gesture which seems to be characteristic with the Germans, and which is used to express disdain or disgust, is made by throwing the hands forward and away from the body with the palms out.

There is a gesture which is made by throwing the arms away from the sides laterally with the palms out and accompanying it with a shrug of the shoulders. It expresses a mystified or troubled state of mind. This gesture is distinctly continental, and is much used by actors in the German, French, and Yiddish theatres.

A common gesture is made with the fingers half closed and the thumb out. The person points backward with the thumb. Some teachers call this a "physical" gesture. It is used only by those impersonating uncouth characters. Spreading the fingers wide with a gesture generally indicates excitement or fright. These emotions tend to lift the arms up; therefore gestures expressing them should be made above the waist line.

Besides the gestures mentioned, there are various movements of the hands which cannot properly be called gesture, but rather illustrative action, such as are used in pantomime, or when an actor substitutes action for speech. It should be understood that the action we call gesture is not meant for illustration, but is the impulsive and inspirational accompaniment of emotion and mood.

The actor should use no gestures unless they have a meaning and a purpose. A recognized law in acting is that gestures should be used as little as possible. We may state this principle in another way by saying that the purpose of gesture is only to accentuate an emotion. When there is no emotion which needs pointing or emphasis, gesture is superfluous and should be eliminated. Therefore the less acting scope there is in a part, the less gesture is required, and vice versa. Gesture is not compulsory at any time; but when it is used the actor should be careful that it fits the emotions expressed.

GESTURE

The effect of many parts is greatly heightened by embellishing them with gesture as much as possible, never, however, overlooking the principle of appropriateness and purpose. For example, excitable foreign characters such as irascible Frenchmen, vengeful Italians, and so on, may use the gestures natural to their race. Gesture is, however, used less in the modern theatre than it was in the old.

Gesture of whatever kind should never be so spasmodic as to get beyond nerve control. Wringing the hands, for example, should not be so violent as to make it apparent to the audience that the actor is really being physically racked. He should make all gestures easily and without nerve tension. Acting is only a semblance and a suggestion, after all. No physical movement, whether it be the individual action of one person, or a struggle between two, should get beyond the limit of reserve. To struggle actually on the stage with the same force that persons would use in real life would lack that perfect illusion which an artistically simulated action would accomplish. Shakespeare said of gesture to "use all gently," and showed in this another evidence of his wisdom as a director and showman.

Again, when he said, "suit the action to the word, the word to the action," he proved that he understood the laws of acting. Suiting the action of gesture to the word is done by making gesture end simultaneously with the speech, or the central idea in the speech. For example, if an actor says, "I tell you to go," and points to the door, he should make his gesture end with the word, "go." To point on the word, "tell," would be wrong. Again, if a character waves his hand toward a chair and says, "Won't you be seated?" the gesture should end on the last word. In respect to the central idea in a speech, when a mother says, "I implore you to save my boy," the central idea is contained in the word "implore," and she must make whatever gesture she uses on that word. She may clasp her hands simultaneously with the word or place them on the person's shoulders.

Suiting the action to the word is done when gesture accompanies some word in a speech. There is an exception which seems to disprove the law, but does not really do so. This is when gesture is made to precede speech. A person may point to the door before speaking and then say, "go," which is equally correct. The mother mentioned above may advance to another character and place her hands on his shoulders first, after which she may say, "I implore you to save my boy!" The choice of method depends on the discretion of the actor. In many cases, the latter method is better when a quiet effect is desired.

The use of gesture *before* the word has sometimes an added value in that it telegraphs to the audience what is coming. Audiences at times like to be taken into the actor's confidence; they like to get ahead with the story, as it were, as quickly as possible, and this method allows them to anticipate the lines and the events before they actually happen. There are many other occasions for the use of both these principles, but these examples serve to illustrate them.

Finally, to classify gesture broadly, we may understand it as all movements of the members of the body, whether the hands, the feet, the head, or other parts, when used to accompany and emphasize the emotions.

GESTURE

EXERCISES

1. What kind of parts require the most graceful gestures?
2. What would you understand to be an important consideration in respect to gesture?
3. How is the index gesture made? With what hand would you make this gesture when pointing to the right? The left?
4. What is the general purpose of gesture?
5. On what word in a speech should a gesture be made? Give an example.

CHAPTER VIII

COMEDY

Actors generally concede that it is harder to act in comedies than in serious plays. This is true because comedy effects depend largely upon the methods used by the actor, and these he must constantly watch. Besides the use of technical methods, the playing of comedy depends also upon personality. Any actor of average ability is able to "get laughs," if there is material for them in the lines, but some actors are better fitted for comedy than for serious work; and the personalities of some actors are so distinctly comical that they are funny in any situation. Still, every actor should learn the technical principles which produce humorous effects.

An actor in a musical company was dissatisfied with his part and decided to give notice that he was leaving the company. The star, a comedian, learned of this intention and asked the actor to call at his hotel the following morning. The actor did so, and, being asked his reasons for wanting to leave, informed the star that his part was so poor he could get nothing out of it and therefore was dissatisfied to remain in it. The star took down the telephone book and began to read from it. The actor was soon laughing heartily. The comedian said to him, "My boy, it is not so much the thing you say as how you say it that counts. It has taken me twenty-five years to do it, but now I can make even the telephone book funny. Your part can be funny if you know how to make it so."

The comedian had two advantages. First, he had a naturally humorous personality, and second, he had studied all the laws for the production of comedy effects. Some comedians have asserted that they could get a laugh on any line whatsoever if they so desired.

This delineation of methods in comedy technique refers to the performance as a whole, and not to the work of one person alone. Thus, the methods explained will be those which the actors must use for mutual assistance. The best effects in comedy often require more than one person if they are to be entirely true to life. This point touches strongly upon a principle which will be explained in the chapter on Coöperation.

The actor, then, should devote himself in comedy, as in other phases of his work, to the good of the performance as a whole, and not to his own self-interest. Comedy allows much opportunity for the actor to make himself prominent in a play, but if he does so it is often to the detriment of his fellow actors' work and ultimately of the box office, for too much prominence in one part may injure the general performance.

In comedy, especially, the work of the theatre cannot be entirely true to life on account of the audience. In this branch of acting, the audience plays a very important part with their laughter. In folklore there is a legend of a sleeping palace, the main theme of which follows: A prince wanders in search of a princess whom he has been directed to seek out, and after much travel he comes to her father's palace. Bad Genii have put all the people in the palace to sleep for a hundred years. Each person remains motionless in the attitude he was in when the spell was cast and does not awaken until the prince arrives and kisses the princess. When he does so, they all start into life as if nothing had happened and with no knowledge of the lapse of time.

Upon certain comedy lines, while the audience is laughing, those upon the stage must perform the act of "the sleeping palace." The audience's laughter has caused a lapse in the action and the actors must wait without motion until the laughter subsides and enables them to be heard, when they may resume the play.

This is called "holding the picture." Audiences wish to have their laugh out, and at the same time do not want to miss anything that goes on. The actors should respect this desire. They should not break the picture, for so doing distracts the audience's attention and interferes with their full enjoyment of the situation in hand.

In an effort to "keep the performance going" some directors with the more recent modern training go to extremes. In directing a serious drama, which, nevertheless, had many opportunities for laughs, the director said to the actors, "Don't wait for any laughs; speak right through them and go on." The leading actor immediately protested, "I won't speak through my laughs if I get any; I'll wait." The actor was right. People come to the theatre to enjoy themselves; the more laughter they can have in comedy scenes the more they appreciate the entertainment. Just as an actor might resent some disturbance in the audience which would interrupt his work, so the audience resents interference by the actors which interrupts their laughter.

Holding the picture can be carried to extremes. This is done if the actors prolong it to a point beyond that at which the laughter has subsided and thus seem to strain self-consciously for the effect. When we say "until the laughter subsides," we do not mean until it ends completely, but merely until the actor can again be clearly heard without effort. This keeps up the tempo of the play. A monologist in vaudeville made a diagram like the following ⌐✕ to illustrate the nature of laugh-

ter and the point at which he always resumed his speech. The laughter rose suddenly to an apex of volume, as indicated by the highest point in the figure above, and then subsided less suddenly, as illustrated by the down stroke. He resumed his speech just before it had completely died away, as illustrated by the cross mark.

Sometimes an actor may hold the picture with his body, but foster the laugh to greater volume with some slight gesture, such as a lift of the eyebrows or some gesture with the hand. The late Nat Goodwin in *Why Marry?* did this successfully, when he wished to coax laughs, by flicking the ash from his cigar, or biting viciously upon it.

It is probably necessary without exception to hold the picture when the line that provokes the laugh is a question. Here is an example: In *Adam and Eva*, an old bachelor has been living in idleness on the bounty of his rich relatives. News comes that the head of the house has become financially ruined. The family straightway turn to the help wanted columns in search of work. While they are all busy with their papers, the old man suddenly looks up, peers across the stage over the rim of his spectacles and inquires of the others, "Say, how long does it take to learn to tune pianos?" This brings a generous laugh. The old man naturally waits for a reply, and in so doing holds his position while gazing over his spectacles until the laugh subsides and the answer is given. His posture of inquiry also helps to prolong the laugh.

In the above situation, all the actors should remain motionless, the others as well as the speaker. On such lines, the laughter is provoked by the ideas contained in them, and there is nothing more anyone needs to do; the actors merely wait for the laughter to subside.

In some cases, the actor who has spoken a comedy line may elaborate the effect with action to prolong the laugh, depending, of course, upon the nature of the line, while the other characters remain motionless as before; but he must always remain in the picture. Here, again, the law of attention operates, which, as a concrete principle, we have already mentioned. In the comedy, *It's a Boy*, two young men are playing with a mechanical dancing doll dressed as a ballet dancer. A minister arrives unseen by them, and the audience receive from his entrance a suggestion for laughter. One of the young men, who has been dancing to the motions of the doll, turns and sees the minister. The two hold their positions, the minister with a shocked expression and the other with a look of alarm, while the third actor works up the laugh. He fumbles with his clothing, grins sheepishly, sits and picks up a basket of knitting, and so on, until the laugh subsides. In this case the actor who has been dancing is the centre of attention and has "fed" his own laugh in this way.

In many cases, when a line is spoken by one character,

or when he does some bit of comical business, the "feeding" is done by the other character or characters. This may be done through some reaction on their part to the line or business. Whether they shall react or not depends on the nature of the line. If it is a remark having no relation to those on the stage, no reaction may be necessary; but if it is personal,—some impudent allusion to another, for example, a reaction from the person to whom the line is directed is natural and true to life. The reaction will help the laugh to register with better effect. The difference between lines with or without reaction is that in the latter case the laughs pass from the actor who speaks directly to the audience, while in the former they pass from the actor who speaks, through another character, or characters, as well, to the audience. Brilliant and impersonal wit has direct transmission and does not require reaction from the others. Here is an example: "If a man sits on an American easy chair before a Flemish table covered with an Algerian table cloth, and smokes Turkish tobacco in a German pipe, drinks a Chinese beverage out of Dresden porcelain, and asks for Italian music, can he call himself a Frenchman?" This is good for a laugh. It does not require any reaction from the others, and gets its laugh on its own humorous merit. It should be borne in mind that during such a laugh there should be no action from any of the other characters, lest it distract the attention of the audience. They do not want to be disturbed in their laughter; and the actors should wait for them to finish it.

The following is an example opposite to the foregoing: A hypocritical and unwelcome character comes to a house and inquires of the maid for her mistress. He says, "Good morning, Nora, you're as blooming as ever. Is your mistress at home?" With arms akimbo Nora answers, "She's not at home to the likes of you, and you may keep your blarney for your grandmother's cat." In real life anyone would react to such a rebuff, and the actor does so by showing it has affected him. He may lower his head and arch his eyebrows, or use some other action natural to the actor himself.

There was a danger in the dancing doll situation. The actor might be over-anxious to prolong his laugh and might resort to tricks for that purpose which would be out of keeping with the logic of his portrayal. Comedians sometimes do this and thereby merge from the natural into the grotesque. Their effects are overdone.

Zou Zou, in the old play of *Trilby*, had several occasions to say, "Oh, la, la, la, la, la," which was written in certain places in the part and always got a laugh. Willie Baxter, also, in Booth Tarkington's *Seventeen*, had often to say, "Ye gods!" If the actors had taken liberties and increased the number of times for speaking these phrases in order to elaborate their performance, they would have grown monotonous and their freshness been lost. In burlesque this sort of thing is permissible, and we may see the man "with the funny slide" or the man "with the humorous squeak," and so on, introducing his trick at every opportunity, for that is consistent with this form of entertainment. In legitimate drama, however, the actor should learn that moderation is better than overdoing. The element of suggestion is of value; it permits the audience to do some of the acting.

Oftentimes, when a director rehearses a play which he has directed before, he tells the actors that such and such lines are "good for laughs" or for applause. This is not always wise, for it is likely to create self-consciousness on the part of the actors, and they may overstrain for their effects. It is better to leave the actor in ignorance of the probable response on any speech so that he may preserve and crystallize the natural spontaneity he had when he was unaware of where his responses lay.

We may often wonder why the characters themselves do not laugh at a witticism, when in real life people would be very likely to do so. This is stage license as well as stage law, which demands that the amusement shall be for the audience and not the actors. Still, there are exceptions. Here is a case from *The Acquittal:*

DOCTOR: Do you think it's a case of guessing when a man's life is at stake?
YOUNG MAN: You ought to know, you're a doctor.
DOCTOR (*laughing*): Oh, come now!

In this case the laughter from the doctor is natural; besides, he assists the audience to grasp the point and thus greatly increases the laugh.

Burlesque is an entertainment of comedy and music. Aside from the music, its sole purpose is to get laughs, and it presents any travesty on life for that purpose. Vaudeville is a slightly higher form of art. In the comedy features of this entertainment, three main scientific principles are employed. These are tempo, climax, and laugh getting. The last is produced with the aid of the other two. Vaudeville largely sacrifices other principles to these three; but in comedy, as in other kinds of drama, truth to life must be maintained, and the principles which underlie this rule should not be neglected.

Two heads are oftentimes better than one, and this expression applies in drama as in other things. Comedy situations that require more than one person to develop them as a rule get the biggest laughs. While one person, who delivers some impersonal witticism, can only start a laugh on its way and let it die out naturally, two or more persons, when the situation permits, can keep it alive with reaction and feeding. The old play of *Charley's Aunt* is full of examples in which comedy situations are prolonged in this way.

As an example, Fancourt Babberly, dressed as the Aunt, has a scene with Deacon Spettigue. As Spettigue turns to go Babberly hurls a magazine at him and knocks his hat off. Spettigue turns, and seeing, as he supposes, only a dignified old lady quietly fanning herself, is mystified as to where the missile came from. He stares at Babberly, looks about the room, and so on. The combined actions of these two prolong the laugh. In the same play, also, when the boys force Babberly to put his dress on again after he has refused to go on with the deception, their fumbling with the female attire causes prolonged laughter that usually continues until the actors grow tired and discontinue the business. At the same time, they must not continue the business beyond that point where the laughter ceases to be fresh and spontaneous on the part of the audience.

Comedy moves with a quicker pace than serious drama. It is light and airy and too slow a tempo tends to destroy the effects. This is especially true of farce. A play of this nature is usually started at a bright and fairly rapid pace in order that the actors may get the swing of it and continue the pace throughout the play. In vaudeville

COMEDY

comedy acts the actors observe great care in this principle. In this class of entertainment, however, they often carry it to extremes. They are made to speak and move so rapidly that they have not enough time for the proper delineation of their characters. On this account, drama in vaudeville is not entirely true to life, for there is no time to develop light and shade.

The student is asked to recall what was said in a previous chapter concerning the solar plexus and the relation it is supposed to bear to the production of all physical movements pertaining to gesture. The proper action of the solar plexus has great influence in the abatement of tension. Tension may be of a distinctly physical nature and therefore may be a prime factor in hindering the correct production of tone. In comedy, quite as much as in the serious elements of drama, physical tension may restrict tone and be a serious handicap.

Anything that is done well is usually done easily. This fact applies strongly to the production of comedy effects. Tension is an enemy to ease in the execution of a comedy effect which should be produced naturally.

Some actors suffer from self-consciousness in their comedy work. As a result of this, they often "go stale" in their effects. Laughs, which at first they were able to register with natural spontaneity, gradually become more forced until at times they lose the effects entirely. The actors then work hard to recover the lost laughs, and in so doing over-exert themselves. This develops a physical tension and distorts their comedy effects. Tempo, also, is reduced and the "pace" of the lines becomes much slower. It can be made a fixed rule that in acting one must never work too hard. This over-exertion is generally due to conscientiousness, through which the actor tries to do his very best. He should be generally conscientious, of course, but in the principle we are considering conscientiousness is misplaced. In such a case the actor should relax in order to relieve physical tension and should seek to quicken his tempo. The latter automatically coordinates itself with physical relaxation. Singers understand the principles, and know they cannot sing effectively if the muscles of the diaphragm, and the body in general, are rigid and tense. More is said of tempo in Chapter XIV.

Though it is well to understand the scientific principles of acting, the actor should not analyze himself too closely in respect to the scientific facts which underlie his work, for his inspiration must have free play if he is to present that spontaneity which his work demands. Still, if the actor finds himself troubled with self-consciousness and the bad results which it often produces, it is well for him to understand the conditions which cause the mistakes and the means he may use to correct them. When he finds himself forcing his effects, he will discover through study that the solar plexus has tightened up when it should be open to allow free passage for his vocal expression and the regular action of the diaphragm. The diaphragm is of more importance in the art of acting than is usually realized. In all cases of tension, the actor should relax and see that he is breathing naturally and easily before speaking any line which requires a comedy effect. Otherwise, he hits his tones too hard and his delivery lacks the smoothness which comedy, above all, requires. Comedy lines must be easily spoken if they are to result in a spontaneous laugh. This easy, natural delivery also gives the actor sufficient reserve force, without which all acting is ineffective.

"Going stale," which was mentioned a while back, is not always the result of self-consciousness alone. One of the most frequent reasons is the monotony which results from long runs of plays. When an actor has played one part for many weeks or months, he is likely to become careless in his reading and action. This carelessness produces effects which are more or less mechanical, and the mechanical delivery does not ring true. In the theatre, the actor should present the illusion that he is saying and doing everything for the first time. If he has gone stale, his work is mechanical, has lost its spontaneity, and the illusion which must be delivered is destroyed. There is a term used in the professional theatre to designate this principle. It is "The Illusion of the First Time." Professional actors know that what they say should give the illusion of never having been said before.

Sometimes plays are rehearsed too long, and the actors tend to "go stale" before the first performance. It is then better to omit a few days of rehearsal in order that just before the opening they may recover their enthusiasm and spontaneity.

"The illusion of the first time" relates more to words than to actions, for the latter may be done indefinitely and not result in a mechanical process on the part of the actor, whereas words, which carry the thought of the play, are more likely to suffer from a lack of spontaneity in their delivery.

When the loss of "the illusion of the first time" is due principally to self-consciousness, the staleness is more marked in that part of the performance which calls for response from the audience, either in laughter or applause. As comedy especially contains a large number of lines evoking laughter the actor should guard particularly against "going stale." There are no technical laws to govern the principle. In a treatise on dramatic technique, therefore, it can scarcely be said to have a place. It is mentioned only because we are trying here to cover the dramatic subject as comprehensively as possible. The actor must present "the illusion of the first time" through his inspirational feeling, and should endeavor to keep his work always keyed to a point where it is spontaneous and natural. He can often do this through conscientiousness and enthusiasm. Mechanical means for preventing the ill effects of going stale are suggested in the chapter on Breathing.

The two most important physical effects produced in an audience are laughter and applause, while the moving of an audience to tears, does not occur so frequently. In certain situations the actor gains applause in a different way from that in which he provokes laughter; it is mentioned here in order to point a contrast between the two. In comedy lines, as already explained, the general rule is to hold the position until the laughter has subsided. To win applause in a similar situation requires an opposite treatment. The actor gains his effect more easily if he breaks his position at the end of his speech and moves up stage, or to some other position. In the opinion of some this may be looked upon as a trick, and so it appears to be if the actor does not perform it so naturally that the audience cannot perceive its mechanics.

The actor's technique, or the "tricks of his trade," should not be allowed to show through his work, although technique is the mechanical structure upon which his art is built. A veteran Shakespearean actor was known to use obviously certain tricks to start his applause. In *Othello*, for example, when at a certain point he buried his face in his hands upon a table, he would strike the table a resounding blow with his fists. At another time he might strike his thigh with his hand. The noise of the blows would telegraph the suggestion for response to the audience. Actors often start applause in the audience by a single clap of their hands off stage. These tricks are not recommended.

Whether the actor may logically break his position at the end of a speech calling for applause depends on the nature of the speech. On some speeches it is quite natural to do so, and the actor is then performing the correct action. To do so as a constant habit, when it is not at all times logical, discloses the trick in many cases.

Breaking the position generally telegraphs to the audience that the thought is finished and they may then offer the response called for by the speech. It may have caused a tension or suspense, and the movement acts as a signal to the audience.

It is scarcely necessary to give examples of comedy lines to illustrate this principle regarding them. Holding the position is necessary in most cases. There are various exceptions, however, in which the actor may break his position after delivering a comedy line, and move away in order to elaborate and feed his own laugh. For instance, the actor might have the line, "My wife has gone off to that ball without me. But two can play at that game; I'll go to the same ball without her." He then breaks his position and dances a few steps up stage. This action carries out the idea expressed in the line and increases the laugh.

In the case of a line calling for applause, no idea of elaboration is contained in the movement away, but is merely the signal to the audience, which we have mentioned. Such a speech might be, "You have had the upper hand in this matter far too long. They don't know yet of your trickery and deceit; but I shall secure proofs and will show you to them for what you are." The actor then moves away, and the signal telegraphed to the audience through this movement starts the applause. The psychology behind this movement lies in the fact that to remain motionless at the end of the speech might cause the audience to think that there were more lines to come. If the actor made an exit on this speech the effect would be doubly sure.

To all rules there are exceptions, and there is one to this. As in so many previous examples, whether to move or not depends on whether or not there is a logical impulse to do so on the line spoken. A line expressing defiance or strong emotion might have better effect if the actor held his position at the end of it. As a general rule, the actor may rely mostly upon his inspiration to determine whether he shall move or not. In many cases the character, stirred to an excess of emotion by what he has said, does the logical thing in changing his position, such as in the speech just given, or, again, if he said, "I shall disclose the whole infamous plot and be damned to you," he would move away. If, on the other hand, the line were some startling disclosure such as, "The man who committed the crime stands there," the only logical thing to do would be to hold the position. In all cases, discretion, aided by his inspiration and feeling, must be the actor's guide.

On curtain speeches, whether they evoke laughter or applause, the actor with rare exceptions holds his position. A curtain speech is the last speech spoken in an act; the "tag" of the play is the last line, and is delivered at the final curtain.

Here is an example of a comedy line delivered as a curtain speech. In Mary Roberts Rinehart's *The Breaking Point*, during a dramatic scene, a sheriff draws his gun on one of the cowboys and says, "Stick 'em up, Jack, I ain't trustin' you any tonight." In the final line of this act, which brings down the curtain, the cowboy retaliates on the sheriff with the same command and says, "Stick 'em up, Sheriff. I ain't trustin' *you* any tonight." This line, through the nature of the contrasted situation, gets a laugh and the cowboy holds his position. The "curtains" of a play generally make "a picture," and all members on the stage hold their positions, unless there is some business which requires movement.

Another example of holding the position may be cited in Mary Turner's speech at the end of Act II in the melodrama, *Within the Law*. She confronts the man who sent her to prison. She tells him she has married his son and then says, "Four years ago you took away my name and gave me a number. Now I've given up that number and I've got your name." They stare at each other, motionless, as the curtain falls. To move would ruin the melodramatic effect.

In Chapter I we spoke of finding the objective. This principle applies to comedy in a marked degree. Comedy requires the same treatment as lines of any other nature in respect to naturalness and avoidance of mechanical tricks; but there are special points to observe regarding these principles in order that their effects may be assured. These points should be observed both in the matter of action and reaction. When the actor has a comedy line to deliver, he must find the objective for it. This objective may be some other character if he is speaking directly to that person, or the line may be impersonal or indefinite and require delivery toward the front. Here is a line which employs both these objectives: A strange man and a woman intrude upon an old bachelor in his cottage late at night. They are searching for something they have lost and go into his bedroom together. Their friends arrive in search of them and the old man is asked as to their whereabouts. He points mysteriously to his bedroom door and says, "In there." Then, shaking his head sadly, he says, "And no female has ever profaned it before." On the words, "and no female" he looks front and directs his gaze at the door as he says, "profaned it before." The technique used in this speech calls the attention of the audience to the central ideas in the completest way. The actor may be likened to a guide for tourists in foreign countries. He should show them all the points of interest. The proficient actor is a guide to the audience, revealing to them all the thought of the author, and his work should be devoted to that end. More is to be said in this connection later.

Let us now consider reaction through another person. The objective in this case must be found by the person to whom the line is directed or by the person upon whom the line has some effect, and who may be the next to speak. In this case, also, the reaction of the second person helps to feed the laugh. The following example will illustrate this point: In *The Breaking Point*, a cowboy, who acts as a temporary servant in a household, puts his head through a doorway and announces dinner in these words: "Grub pile, come and git it." The next speech comes from a character on the stage and is a comment on this unusual announcement. With an expression of amusement, he looks toward the door after the retreating head, and holds his position until the laugh has subsided. This action is logical on his part as an introduction to the comment he is about to make. As a general rule, the actor does the logical thing in looking at the person who speaks a comedy line, both while it is being spoken and during the course of the laugh, unless at the end of the line he finds some opportunity to react to it and in that way work up the laugh.

No branch of acting can be controlled more accurately by sheer scientific method than comedy. In the hands of an accomplished artist, as in the case of the comedian with the telephone book, his methods have become so inspirational and natural that the mechanics are not apparent. All of these methods need not be touched upon here, but some will be explained later in connection with other subjects. One more, however, should be mentioned. It is the practice of breaking a line somewhere in its delivery with a slight pause. This practice has the effect of causing a laugh to register with better effect, providing, of course, there is comedy value in the line.

The break is placed just before that part of the speech which contains the comedy idea. The actor should be careful to make the pause in the right place; sometimes, when he relies more upon his inspiration than upon scientific analysis, he finds it without thought.

This method should be put into practice only when the nature of the speech renders it necessary or permissible. An actor had learned the beneficial effect of this principle upon comedy points and made use of it at every opportunity, but without discrimination. As a result, his performances acquired monotony of method and did not ring true, since they showed a mechanical effort to get laughs and not true delineations of character.

This technical treatment should be worked into the actor's interpretation of a part so as always to appear natural. When people stop to think of what they shall say they naturally pause. Therefore, with few exceptions, the principle is used only when a character gives the semblance of thinking of a way to express himself. For example, the ingénue in a play, in a fit of comedy temper, says to her young beau, "I think you're a horrid————— spifficus." Not knowing what to call him she thinks for an appropriate word and finally utters this meaningless term. Again, a character is recommended to another as of kindly disposition and ready to grant any request. The second character has grave doubt of this and says, "Have you seen him? His face looks as if he were— smelling an onion." Again, he pauses to find the proper words of description. The break in this case, as in the case of breaking the position after a line calling for applause, telegraphs to the audience that something is coming for which they must listen. No doubt the psychology of their amusement is involved in this expectancy and suspense.

In these two lines the break occurs in the proper places. If the ingénue had said, "I think——you're a horrid spifficus," the treatment would have been wrong. In the other speech the comedy idea is contained in the phrase, "smelling an onion," and the break should be placed just preceding these words.

Many lines are written thus by the author, who himself devises this method for their delivery, but others do not contain any suggestion of this nature and the actor may often heighten their effects with a free treatment of this principle. In these cases his own discretion is his guide. The long speech given in this chapter beginning with, "If a man sits on an American easy chair before a Flemish table," etc., is not written with a break in it; but, according to her method and discretion, the actress might enhance its effect with a slight pause just before she said, "can he call himself a Frenchman?"

The mechanics used by some actors in their technical methods are often apparent. The late Nat Goodwin employed more or less fixed technique in his comedy. His acting was so artistic, however, and he possessed to such a degree the "art which conceals art," that his effects always seemed natural.

Actors commit many faults in comedy which destroy the desired effects. The ideas contained in comedy lines are usually cumulative. That is, these ideas occur at the ends of lines or speeches. Therefore, the register and tone must be sustained until the end. Nat Goodwin was a master of this form of technique. When he wished to deliver certain lines with this cumulative effect, he gave them a smooth and even rise until he had delivered the word, or words, which contained the comedy idea; he gave these the strongest vocal force in the speech. Their effect corresponded to that of the swell, or diapason, in an organ.

Some actors know this principle, but are not expert enough to approach their cumulation gradually and evenly. Instead, they strike the comedy word abruptly and with a suddenly increased tone, which renders their effort to secure the effect obvious and fails of the purpose. Another fault is to employ the opposite of cumulation and to decrease the tone as the comedy idea is approached. The effect then trails off into ineffectiveness. A wedge enters a piece of wood at its smallest part and splits it at the largest; the actor may well remember this in relation to the principle. This will be discussed later in relation to climax.

We have said that comedy requires a brisk and lively pace. Actors should remember this in respect to the delivery of individual lines. Every one is familiar with the effect of a song when it is dragged and the pace is slow. The actor must deliver his comedy lines with briskness and vivacity. There are many lines which, if delivered at a low-keyed pace, enable the audience to guess what is coming. The actor should keep his tempo ahead of their thought.

In many cases he must even hurry his pace in order to reach the end before the laughter overtakes him. In the melodrama, *Within the Law*, a female criminal had such a line. The inspector had promised her clemency if she would "squeal" on her pals. After making his proposition the inspector asked, "What do you say?" She leaned over his desk, while the audience was tensely waiting for her reply, and answered, "I say you're a great big stiff!" This line received a big laugh for its inelegance, and for its melodramatic effect a burst of applause. She could deliver the "I say" with a slow measure, as it was only an introduction to the main idea. She had to hurry at the end, however, to forestall the anticipation of the audience. In terms of the wedge simile, she became the large end of the wedge as she concluded the line.

When an actor has a line which is good for both laughter and applause and finds it failing to receive its logical reward, the failure may be due to various reasons. In order to gain the best effect, he may need not only to increase his speed, but also to speak the line more forcefully, and to be careful to sustain his tone to the end. The training of vaudeville is probably the best in all the branches of the drama for the principle of briskness and quick tempo.

An actor sometimes drops his voice on the end of his line, or the word which contains the comedy idea. The failure of the line to "get across" is then due to the fact that the audience has been unable to hear the most important word. An old actor once said to a beginner that the first things he should begin to practice were "to be seen, to be heard, to be understood." In comedy, above all, the actor, in the words of Polonius, should "character these precepts" in his memory.

EXERCISES

1. What is a valuable asset for comedy?
2. What is "holding the picture," and why, in comedy?
3. What is "working up a laugh?" Give an example.
4. What is "feeding" a laugh? Devise some comedy line which should be fed by another character.
5. What are the main principles of vaudeville?
6. What is "going stale"? What is "hitting tones too hard"?
7. What do you understand by reserve force?
8. What is The Illusion of the First Time?

9. What physical effects does a performance produce in an audience?
10. What technique is often used after a speech which calls for applause? Why is this done?
11. What technique should be used on the line, "The man who committed the crime stands there"?
12. What is the "tag" of a play?
13. Why is a "break" sometimes placed in a comedy line? Where is it placed?
14. What is cumulation in comedy?
15. Mention several ways by which to "coax" or encourage a laugh.

CHAPTER IX

THE PAUSE

In the previous chapter it was necessary to speak of the pause in connection with certain comedy principles, and elsewhere in the book where it applied to the points discussed. It is very important as a concrete principle and should be given separate space.

A dramatic entertainment is made up of words and actions, with accompanying spaces between the words, between the words and the actions, and between the actions. These spaces may be termed the breathing spells, just as in writing where punctuation marks occur. The punctuation marks denote spaces in the thought where in speech the individual might take a breath, and this fact requires a pause for that purpose.

A performance in drama must be spaced with judicious pauses, always with regard to the logic of their use, to express the varied moods of the play and in order that the performance may not suffer from an unvaried monotony. Despite the splendid training of vaudeville in certain principles, many other principles are neglected, and the pause is one of those most commonly overlooked. When "legitimate" actors first enter this field they are often forced to neglect the principle. This confuses them, for the use of the pause is a natural phase of their work to which they have always been accustomed. Vaudeville races along with unslackened speed, and in its dramatic acts frequent pauses tend to "let down" this fast pace.

On the other hand, when vaudeville actors who are accustomed to this method enter the "legitimate" field, their training can sometimes be detected through their quick tempo unrelieved by spacing or pauses. Their delivery tends to proceed with a regular beat and measure. This quality may not be noticeable in an act of twenty minutes, but might grow monotonous in an entertainment of two hours' length.

The contrast between "legitimate" and vaudeville drama can be likened to the contrast between classical and dance music. Classical and ordinary lyric music, we know, is phrased and spaced, while dance music is measured on a regular beat and rhythm. That form of music which changes its measure to express variety of emotion and feeling is of a higher quality in the art of music. The same is true of drama.

The pause is eloquent. The higher the form of drama, the more it is brought into play to punctuate the wide variety of emotions which high-class drama employs.

Several generations ago there was a celebrated English tragedian named William Charles Macready. He was noted for the eloquence of his pauses and the length to which he could prolong them and still hold the attention of the audience, during which time they could read various emotions upon his face. In his pauses, no matter how prolonged, Macready did not drop the tension or interest of a scene. Through Macready's fame in this principle the expression "Macready pause" has been familiar in the theatre almost up to the present time.

The element of the pause pertains mostly to the feelings; in many instances it presents an emotion which the actor seems to feel rather than outwardly expresses.

THE PAUSE

In motion pictures the pause is constantly used, during which time the story of the picture is carried on in the expressions of the actors' faces. In this work the pause is far more frequent and necessary because words are lacking.

The principle which was mentioned in a previous chapter, that in a play something must be going on all the time, refers emphatically to pauses. When a pause is made it must be filled with an idea toward which the attention of the audience is directed. The student should grasp the sense in which the word "filled" is to be understood. A pause often holds the audience in a tension, an anticipation, or a state of expectancy. The actor should not prolong the pause until the tension of the audience begins to flag. When it does, it is proof that the actor has lost the force of his emotional feeling which produced the tension, and the pause has become a wait. A space or "hole" then occurs in the dramatic texture.

Macready's power to hold his audiences throughout long pauses by the strength of his feeling was an unusual one, and every actor has not this ability. At the same time that he is feeling the emotion which produces the pause, the actor must also sense the audience and gauge the length to which he can prolong his pause and still hold their attention. Experience in the theatre gives the actor this sense; but the innate power of the pause is born with the actor.

In motion pictures the pause often gives the actor more credit for artistry than he deserves. Motion picture art is at many points merely the act of having one's picture taken. A picture star had a scene in which she knelt at her mother's feet and looked up into her face. With the star's beautiful profile shown to the audience and her long dark eyelashes slightly flickering, she seemed to be expressing deep inner feeling, and the effect was most alluring. As a matter of fact she was doing no acting at all, but was merely having her picture taken.

Thus far we have spoken of the pause only in relation to feeling. The actor perhaps reflects this in his face, but does not express it in outward emotion. Pauses, however, have an infinite variety of causes and occasions. Some are often necessary which are not related to the tension of feeling we have described. They may be made in a purely material connection and be related in some manner to the craftsmanship of the direction. Such instances might take place during a courtroom scene when the direction required conformity to the technique of legal procedure. In such a scene, pauses between the lines might occur while the lawyers were preparing their papers before the opening of court, between questions to the witnesses, or during conferences with the client.

Two kinds of lapses in dialogue can be called pauses. They contain either action or thought and are therefore either material or mental. Some students of the theatre may not consider the lapse of dialogue which is filled in with the business of the play to be a pause at all. They may assert that only complete cessation of action as well as speech can be called a pause. Such a pause is mental and is the more difficult to treat. A lapse in the dialogue which contains business, or which results from some requirement of stage direction, is more or less mechanical, does not call so much for the expression of emotion and feeling, and therefore does not require the same delicate sense as the pause which registers thought or feeling only.

For the present purpose we will discard the lapse or pause which is filled in with some action of the play. There are various occasions for it, and as a general rule the actor merely does the mechanical things required by the direction of the play. The other form, or the pause which registers thought or feeling, is worthy of analysis.

What occasions, then, arise for the use of the pause? It cannot be bound by any hard or fast rule since it discards for the most part the use of technique. The actor ceases to speak and to act and merely feels and waits. Since the pause must be filled, its content must be of feeling, and if the actor cannot feel his pause it is mechanical, and therefore without effect.

A pause may telegraph to the audience that something important and dramatic is about to take place. Examples of this kind of pause occurred in *Kick In*. The police inspector sat at his desk awaiting the arrival of two supposed criminals, a man and a woman, whom he was about to question. When they were announced and had entered he did not look up, but continued with his writing. After a long pause he looked up and pretended to see them for the first time. He motioned them to be seated and went on with his writing. Another long pause ensued, during which they fidgeted upon their chairs. Both these pauses showed expert craftsmanship in the direction. In this situation, however, the feeling of the pause was conveyed by the other two and not by the inspector. His pause was a mechanical one filled in with his business of writing. These pauses increased the tension and expectancy in the audience for what was to come.

The inspector, with slow deliberation, finally laid down his pen, placed his cigar on the ash tray, turned slowly in his swivel chair, and faced the other two characters. During these pauses, the criminals had excellent opportunity to employ the principle of reaction, which they showed in their nervous tension while the inspector sat writing and ignored their presence. In a succeeding scene with another criminal, he plied her with one question after another, to which she gave no replies, and the inspector meanwhile waited impatiently for her answers. In this instance, the inspector's pauses between questions brought out forcibly the idea of thwarted purpose. The pause which registers thought or feeling only is usually expressed without physical action. Thought is independent of matter; and physical action in a pause of this nature tends to destroy the effect of the thought or feeling contained in it by distracting the attention of the audience.

However, this rule should not be accepted as invariable. For example, if an actor stops to think, he may place his hand upon his chin and look thoughtfully downward, or may even place his hands in his pockets and stroll thoughtfully to one side before delivering his next speech. In this case he seeks for his reply. From this example it is seen that there is a difference between the pauses of thought and feeling. Scientists believe that thought originates in the mind and feeling in the heart, or emotions. We should not try to analyze too closely, but admit that the pause of thought may often be accompanied with some physical action, while that of feeling only is more often effective when all physical action is eliminated. Whether or not action accompanies either of them, they can both be admitted as pauses.

THE PAUSE

The following example will illustrate a pause, or lapse, in the dialogue which gave one actor an opportunity to dominate a scene. He was seated at a fireplace reading. Another actor stood at a door on the opposite side directing taunting and ugly remarks at him. Finally the latter threw down his book and advanced threateningly on the other. He did not speak until he reached him. This lapse in the dialogue, filled with an ominous action, produced tension and expectancy in the audience. It would not have been as forceful had he spoken while walking.

Certain pauses give added emphasis and weight to the speeches that follow. Here is an example: A family have been seeking a long lost son. One night, without warning, he enters suddenly upon them. As he stands in the doorway the family are naturally startled at sight of him. There is a tense pause in which all the characters remain for a moment motionless. The mother then cries out the name of her son and rushes to him. The members of the family group greet him in turn. They bring him down stage and the mother, through her tears, asks him to explain his long absence. She says, "My boy, why did you never write? We thought you were dead. Where have you been?" The answer which he will make is a startling one; he would not speak it casually and without preparation. The actor must simulate that preparation by means of a pause which shall give the audience the tension and expectancy required. After this pause, in which all the characters eagerly await his answer, he says, "In prison." A person in a like situation would not deliver such an answer with the readiness of casual speech. After this answer another tense pause is quite logical, in which the characters feel the shock of this disclosure. In *The Famous Mrs. Fair*, a long and eloquent pause is made by the parents of a runaway daughter before they proceed to read the note she has left for them. In this case the audience knows what the letter contains; their tension, therefore, is caused by a desire to learn what reaction the letter will produce on the parents.

A slightly different kind of pause was made in a scene between two characters in *Peace on Earth*. They were prisoners in adjoining cells; and through the monotony of their confinement their conversation flagged. Their pauses contained no element of tension, but suggested merely tardy thought before they introduced new topics or gave replies. We know that in real life pauses in conversation usually occur while people think of new things to say.

A character often makes a pause when he sees something which seems to belie his sight. He cannot proceed to action until he has become quite sure of what he has seen. In the large production of the religious pantomime, *The Miracle*, in New York, a statue of the Virgin, which occupies a position before one of the pillars in the cathedral, comes to life, and goes forth on a mission of mercy. The mother superior enters and sees the vacant place. Her mind cannot grasp the fact of the Virgin's disappearance instantly, for to her sense it is a miracle. She stands still for a moment and tries to formulate a thought which will explain this marvel. She thinks she must be mistaken in the location or that the dim light in the church is to blame. During these confusing thoughts she pauses motionless. She then passes her hand across her eyes to see if the fault is not with her sight, and looks again. Finally, when she is certain of the truth, she screams and rushes off to summon the nuns.

The following example is a case in which the mind requires a little time to frame the answer to a serious question. The heroine in *Three Live Ghosts* learns that her lover, who has just returned from the world war, is living under an assumed name and in his youth had been guilty of a crime. She tells him this and asks for an explanation. Up to this time he had thought her ignorant of his past. Before answering he needs a moment to prepare his thought, and he makes a pause before he gives her his explanation.

A person often makes a pause, also, when he needs time to realize the full import of another's words. This kind of pause is quite frequent in real life; when the actor feels and executes it correctly it is effective.

One of the commonest uses of the pause is in enumerating any list of articles, or in speaking words or phrases containing separate ideas. A little boy says to his mother, "Mama, will Santa Claus bring me a lot of things for Christmas?" "What would you like?" she asks. The son pauses for a moment and thinks. Then he says, "A train with lots of cars." Another pause, and then, "A ball, a rocking-horse, a wagon." Again a pause, and then, "and oh, lots of other things." A character is asked to describe some person whom he has seen escaping from the scene of a crime. He says, "From the glimpse I got of him he was tall, dark, had bushy eyebrows and an aquiline nose, had a small moustache, wore a brown overcoat, and carried a cane." Both of the actors, the man and the child, have learned their lines so that both can speak them without hesitancy, but the illusion of truth to life demands that they space the lines with pauses where in real life they would have to stop and think.

A daughter asks her father to make a guess as to which one of her suitors she has asked to dinner. She has a great many, and he mentions one after another. He says, "Well, let's see. Lewis Flanders?" "No," from the daughter. A slight pause, during which the father reflects. Then, "Harold Chambers?" "No." He repeats the same business while he thinks again. "Brice Evans?" "No." This continues through a long list of names. The father varies the manner of his pause and reflection with business, sometimes looking down at the floor, sometimes upward, or sometimes with his hand on his chin, but always pausing to give the right illusion.

A pause is necessary, also, to mark the transition between two different moods in the same speech. For example, if a character has a line in which his temper flares up in anger, and the line immediately following must be expressed calmly, he cannot make the transition from the one to the other without a space, or pause, to serve as a bridge between the two. Extreme moods never change so rapidly as not to render a pause in such a case necessary. The father in *Common Clay* has a dispute about the woman whom the son loves. Anger arises between them and the son exclaims, "You must not speak of her as 'that woman.'" The father: "And you must not address me in such a tone." Both of these lines are spoken with great anger. The father then says, "You were glad to have me stand by you nine years ago when your trouble arose with her." The interpretation of the actor requires that he speak this last line calmly, for it contains cold and quiet reasoning. As it follows just after the one which was spoken in anger, there must be a pause between them during which the father composes his mood.

The pause is also necessary when a character must give the impression of seeking the right word to express his meaning. Here the pause may be used largely as a trick in the reading of comedy lines. Still, when correctly done, tricks can better be called technique, and are allowable when the actor has properly concealed their purpose and method. Stubbins, in *Mrs. Wiggs of the Cabbage Patch*, is played with a drawl. He is about to be married and comes on in his wedding clothes. He has the line, "Well, here I am all dressed for the———sacrifice." A little later he says, "These clothes have been through the ———ordeal before." In both cases his mind seems to work slowly, and he pauses to think of a fitting word in which to express himself. The actor registered his comedy effect more surely because of the pause. We have treated this principle differently in the chapter on Comedy.

Pauses are necessary in telephone conversations. In reality there is no one speaking from the other end, but in the actor's pauses he must give the semblance of listening to another person. To gain the right effect, the actor does well to imagine lines that might be spoken to him, as suggested by his responses, and say them to himself between his vocal lines.

As a general rule, shocks of any kind, such as bad news, and news of all sorts which disturb the mind, are followed by pauses, during which the character feels whatever emotion the news produces. John Barrymore, as Peter Ibbetson, invested the rôle with a generally sombre atmosphere. The pauses with which he emphasized the many sombre emotions of the part were striking in their effect.

Pauses are a very popular medium of expression in the modern play. They have largely taken the place of the older method of making a start upon shocks of various kinds. The older method of acting was more obvious than the new; and instead of showing their thought or feeling by means of the pause, actors generally gave this same feeling an outward physical expression. Sarah Bernhardt, being more or less of the old school, used the start frequently, but with wonderful effect. While the mother superior, mentioned in a previous example, stood without motion and registered a long pause when she noted the Virgin's disappearance, an actress of the old school, and in the same situation, would probably have made a physical start.

Starts are, of course, made in the modern theatre, such as on physical shocks, noise, certain expressions of fear, and so on. The pause, however, is more popular in registering disturbances purely of the mind. It is more suited to the "repressed" method of acting of the present, and might not have been so effective in the "expressed" method of the old school.

The theatre naturally changes as life changes. The acting of a former day was more emotional and flamboyant than today because life was more so. Our present mechanical age is more cold, logical, and matter of fact, and our acting partakes more of a quality of collected thoughts than of unrestrained emotion. Even the art of oratory, as known in a former era, has become greatly subdued, and men with a platform message tend more to deliver calm and straightforward ideas than to be demagogues trying to make an emotional appeal. So the theatre becomes more and more an expression of thoughts and ideas, and somewhat less an expression of broad or violent emotion.

In modern drama, actors and directors often carry the frequent use of the pause to extremes. A performance was criticized for being so filled with pauses, and not always for apparent reasons, that in consequence the play dragged and proceeded on a low-keyed pace. On the other hand an actor made his performance quite effective by using the pause as a general principle. He did this before many of his speeches. The method may have been suggested by the nature of the rôle, or been due to the method of the actor. At any rate, before most of his lines he seemed to think of what he was to say and in so doing created a pause; this heightened the effect of his lines.

If we have no hesitancy in any answer we are to make, a pause before it is not logical. We answer immediately, like the girl in the preceding chapter who called the inspector a "great big stiff." She knew what she was going to answer before he had half stated his proposition. Some statements or questions require an answer immediately upon the other speech, while others require some thought, and these demand a pause while the thought is being formed or the feeling expressed.

The following example involves a comedy line: An English detective shadows a woman who is a society criminal, and meets her in Paris. He appears in the disguise of a French waiter and pretends to speak no English. In the last act, after her capture, they meet again in England, and she hears him speak in his native tongue. She is astonished and exclaims, "Achille! The man who didn't speak English!" The author wanted a comedy line to follow this speech, and the actor had to seem to think of one. His back was turned toward the woman as she spoke the line. He turned to her, made a slight pause, and answered, "Only on Fridays, Madam." Everyone generally thinks for a moment before uttering a "bon mot," and this little pause on the actor's part was not only quite natural, but, through the expectancy for his answer which it aroused in the audience, had great value in creating the laugh.

Many pauses become waits when they occur in places where they do not belong. Among these are pauses caused by inexpert acting, poorly rehearsed performances, the forgetting of lines, and by many other conditions resulting from inartistic acting. Inexpert acting may lack discrimination in the use of pauses and employ them in the wrong places; in poorly rehearsed performances, unnatural spacing may creep in as the result of an uneven rhythm and tempo. In respect to the forgetting of lines, a pause is not an incident in the play but a calamity to the actor.

Such a case was the following: Three actors were having a scene together. Suddenly the dialogue ceased and they stood staring at one another. The stage manager, holding the book in the first entrance, "threw" them the line. It was, "It's a beautiful evening"; but the actors stood speechless as before. Again the stage manager whispered, "It's a beautiful evening"; but still the actors were mute, for none of them uttered a word. One of the actors was standing near the fireplace at the back. The stage manager rushed around to the fireplace opening and hissed, "It's a be-eautiful e-evening." The actor whispered back, "Yes, but who says it?"

This question was a result of stupidity. The line was entirely impersonal; therefore any of the three actors might have said it. The important need was to carry on the dialogue of the play to avoid unnatural lapses in the flow of the story. In one play there was a scene made up almost entirely of impersonal speeches such as that above. Through this very impersonal quality, also, the scene was "tricky," and the actors had to keep their minds on their work to avoid missing a line here and there. However, after several months' run of the play they sometimes became lax and forgot to speak on a cue. In such a case someone else, being familiar with the other actors' lines as well as his own, supplied the line. This was better than trying to prompt the actor who was lax, or had perhaps forgotten, by whispering the line to him, for the uninterrupted flow of the story was preserved thereby.

Those directing non-professional groups of actors should be careful in the matter of spacing and pauses. Oftentimes through inexperience, and sometimes through a lack of that soul-sense which is born in the actor and not made, non-professional actors need mechanical control for certain cases. One director of an amateur group went so far as to beat out a certain number of counts for the important pauses. Even the most undeveloped amateur actor should have some inspirational sense if he conscientiously tries to act, and methods of rehearsal that are too mechanical should be avoided whenever possible. Otherwise, a performance becomes stilted and uninspired.

As a final word regarding pauses, they should have a purpose and a reason. The actor should make their meaning and significance plain; and that class of pause which we have made the main subject of this discussion should transmit its sense and feeling as clearly as if the actor had expressed them in words.

EXERCISES

1. How does vaudeville differ from legitimate drama in respect to pauses?
2. What is the principal cause of the pause?
3. What two broad classes of pauses can you mention?
4. Mention three uses for the pause.
5. When are pauses wrong?

CHAPTER X

READING

Many an actor has been complimented on being "a good reader." In the present day we do not lay so much stress on the virtue of good reading and the added value it may give to acting. In the old school it was considered an asset because of the romantic and Shakespearean drama then more in vogue. These plays were often written in blank verse poetry and, through the romantic style required to act them, graceful and poetical reading was an advantage and rendered the lines attractive, as well as the meanings clear. Correct interpretation in reading was more difficult in this romantic drama because it was filled with long and, as we might consider today, rhetorical and verbose speeches. The degree of the actor's expertness in reading was relatively noticeable.

The modern play, as we know, is more or less of everyday life. We do not live in what may be called a romantic age. We are intensely practical and our speech is terse and to the point. Our plays endeavor to show conditions as we see them about us, and authors make every effort, not only in the action of their plays but in the lines as well, to keep within the commonplace actualities of our everyday life. The blue pencil is freely used upon all lines which even hint at a departure from the matter-of-factness of our present time.

Reading, then, as a special talent, is not so valued as it was in the past, because it is not so necessary in everyday English, and a natural talent for it is not so apparent nor called into such great use. The director has previously worked out the sense which the lines convey, and gives this to the actor at rehearsal if he has missed it in his study. Formerly, the actor was left more to his own devices in all phases of his work.

Nevertheless, good reading is essential in the modern plays as well as in the romantic and classical, for reading is part of the actor's artistic equipment in whatever form of drama he may be engaged.

Man is a trinity of the physical, mental, and spiritual. As an actor, he translates his own person into that of his character, and his expression naturally becomes physical and mental, and, through the spiritual side of his nature, emotional. The physical relates to all of his action and expression through the physical body; the mental to his intellectual interpretation through the mind; and the emotional to the expression of his inspiration and feeling.

The actor uses the art of reading entirely in the intellectual interpretation of his rôle. He does not learn to read his lines through any physical action, nor through inspirational feeling. He decides upon his reading as a purely mental process during his study of the character.

How shall we then define reading? We will say it is that interpretation of the author's lines which shall first bring out the true meaning which the author intended. Then the reading must conform to the characterization which the actor is giving to the part; and, finally, if the nature of the part permits, it must be pleasing to the sense.

The actor may rehearse all of this process in his thought as he studies his rôle. He mentally hears himself giving his lines the requisite emphasis, inflections, phrasing, pauses, and the numerous other shadings which he thinks they require. If the author or director does not agree with the interpretation it is corrected at the rehearsals.

The voice is a physical medium in the actor's list of assets, so a pleasing voice assists him to render his reading attractive. Some actors are guilty of trying to lend an added quality to their reading by assuming a voice not natural to themselves, but which they think their part requires. A leading man, long popular in stock companies, was engaged for a New York production to play the part of a Kentucky mountaineer. He felt that a deep voice best suited this character, though his natural voice would have been quite adequate. The producer said, "Just speak in your natural voice, Mr. Blank." Mr. Blank assented, but the next day he was again corrected, and with no better result. The third day he was dismissed. His trouble no doubt was that he had the habit of listening to his own voice. An actor should never do this. He should merely give heed to his emphasis, inflection, and emotion, and not try to assume a voice which is unnatural; otherwise reading becomes ineffective.

Let us consider for a moment the principle of bringing out the meanings in the lines. In this the actor should give thought to where he shall place his emphasis. As in the delivery of comedy points, he must place the emphasis where the central idea is contained, and these, if properly delivered, must have correct reading also, or the central ideas may be lost.

There is usually only one way to read comedy lines since, individually, they contain only one central idea, and the actor must give that central idea the principal emphasis.

In respect to the serious lines in drama, and this is especially true of Shakespearean plays, there are various and changeable ways in which the same speeches or lines can be rendered and which are equally reasonable. For example, Hamlet's soliloquy on death allows infinite scope for variety of rendition. This is a speech for reading almost entirely, and the varied thoughts tumble so closely upon one another, expressed in Shakespeare's lofty rhetoric, that it is almost impossible to settle upon any crystallized method of reading it. One tragedian said he had studied the speech for twenty years. "The Seven Ages of Man," in *As You Like It*, is another example in which reading is an important feature, besides the portrayal of character that it permits.

The voice has a middle register which is used in even, unemotional tones in ordinary conversation. It rises above this middle position or falls below it. When a rising inflection is used, the voice tends to rise above this middle register, and with a falling inflection it tends to drop below. However, the "middle register" is not the same in all actors. Some voices are pitched high and others low, and the register therefore varies with different people. Tragic and all other forms of serious emotions belong in the highest range of drama and require, more than any other forms, a voice whose register is balanced exactly in the middle of the vocal scale.

It is fortunate for the actor if he has a voice well pitched in the middle register. He has then a vocal margin above and below it. Some actors' voices are pitched too low, either by nature or through bad practice. They have, then, not sufficient scope in vocal range. When high tones are required, the voice has too far to go, and being fixed in the low register, has not flexibility enough for the range.

The voice, then, has three general registers in ordinary use. They are the middle, upper, and lower. The pure technique of reading is largely concerned with rising and falling inflections. Punctuation marks are placed in writing to assist reading and thus clarify the sense. Where we pause at a comma we employ a rising inflection in general instances; where semicolons, colons, and periods occur, we use the falling inflection. The falling inflection is not necessarily a tone on a low register. It can be uttered in a high-pitched key well above the common middle. Always, however, it expresses finality. This is a familiar term in the theatre and a good one, for it describes the purpose of the semicolon, colon, and period which are placed at the ends of finished thoughts.

Tone and inflection are two different things. Tone refers to the position of the voice on, above, or below the middle register, while inflection means the gradation of tone on a rising scale when the thought is sustained and there is more to follow in connection with it, or on a lowering scale to express a finished thought. Thus, a person who is drowning may cry out in a very high key, "Help! Help! Save me!" This employs a falling inflection, nevertheless. On the other hand, Hamlet delivers his Soliloquy on Death in a low tone, though many rising inflections naturally occur in it. For example, he says, "To die, (rising) to sleep, (rising) no more" (falling inflection and finality).

The rising inflection proceeds from the register established as the medium to a tone above this register. It can be illustrated by the following diagram: ⟋. The falling inflection requires a reverse treatment. The tone proceeds from the established register to a tone below it and can be illustrated by the arrow turned downward thus: ↘.

Some actors are unfortunate in not always being able to distinguish between the rising and falling inflections when it is necessary to do so. Many a young actor has repeatedly used a rising inflection on a line which expresses an absolutely definite and finished thought, despite the director's instruction that he shall give it the falling inflection of finality. If the student is doubtful as to how to differentiate between the two, he should consider that the rising inflection corresponds to a comma and the falling to a period.

The reading of a phrase or sentence in parenthesis is usually governed by the reading of the matter that precedes it. The parenthetical statement is a separate thought injected between the links of the main ideas. The attention must be held to these main ideas. Therefore the actor should sustain the tone in the parenthesis by reading it with the same inflection as he used in the lines just preceding it. For example, in the sentence, "When he finally left the Orient (he had been detained there for a year) he was eager to get home," the reading requires a rising inflection after the word "Orient." This rising inflection is repeated after the parenthetical statement in order to sustain the attention for what is to follow. In this sentence the parenthetical statement must have a rising inflection at the end even though it is a complete statement. Said outside of parentheses it would require the falling inflection.

An exception to this rule must be made when the parenthetical matter is a question. Parenthetical marks do not change its reading. Here is an example: "I went to his house alone (Do you blame me?) and told him the whole truth." Here the question needs a rising inflection just as if it stood alone. The statement preceding it also has a rising inflection, but of a different kind; the one inflection does not govern the other.

False reading, like mistakes in punctuation, may alter the whole sense of the lines. One of the earliest known English plays is a comedy called, *Ralph Roister Doister*. In this amusing play, written early in the sixteenth century, a lover wishes to send a love letter to the lady of his choice. He is not able to write, so he employs a public scribe and dictates a letter filled with praises of the lady's charms. After sending the letter, he calls next day at her house for his answer, but to his amazement is met with feminine wrath. It happens that the letter has been badly punctuated, though the words are unchanged, and what he had meant as the ardent praise of a lover has been interpreted by her as criticism and insult. The punctuation governed the lady's reading, and thus perverted the sense.

If the line occurs, "Did you see that, Mr. Francis?", we know from the comma that the question is addressed *to* Mr. Francis. A rising inflection is necessary after the comma and at the end. Written without the comma, thus: "Did you see that Mr. Francis?", we know the question is asked of someone else *concerning* Mr. Francis. The tone should be sustained until the end, when the rising inflection is used.

A little boy's mother told him to go across the street and ask regarding the condition of an elderly sick woman. She had said, "Go and see how old Mrs. *Johnson* is," with the emphasis on the word "Johnson." The little boy thought she said, "Go and see how *old* Mrs. Johnson is," with the emphasis on the word "old." The old lady sent back word, "Tell her it is none of her business." In the first reading the tone and inflection must be sustained until the end, excepting on the last word, and in the second reading the limit of sustension is reached at the word "old."

Sustention of tone is one of the most difficult accomplishments in the whole art of reading. The long and voluminous speeches in the classic plays render this, at times, especially difficult. Tone sustention is also important in the reading of comedy lines. It has the psychological effect of also sustaining and controlling the interest of the audience until the entire idea has been delivered and the speech reaches its conclusion, with a falling inflection, when their response in laughter may be permitted. For example, when a comedy speech contains several phrases or clauses, all developing one comedy point, the tone must be sustained and the rising inflection employed where, in writing, the commas would occur. These rising inflections indicate to the audience that the thought is not yet completed, and the actor thereby controls their interest until he is able to bring his speech to its logical finality and the period.

The following comedy speech completely illustrates this: In *Adam and Eva* an old bachelor discusses matrimony and the advisability of his advertising for a wife. He says, "What about me? A penniless but warm-hearted bachelor, with a bad digestion and insomnia, would like to correspond with a rich widow, object matrimony. I'll get a hell of a lot of answers to that!" Let us analyze this speech and the treatment necessary for it. As written here, it is found to contain a question mark, three commas, one period, and an exclamation point. Through the nature of the scene in which this speech occurs, the "What about me?" is good for a laugh. The actor then waits for that to subside. Where the commas are found in the speech, all punctuating the compound idea, the actor uses a rising inflection in order to sustain the attention of the audience. If he uses a falling inflection at one of these the reading is wrong, and the audience may feel that the signal to laugh has come and may interrupt him before he has completed his task. After the words, "object matrimony," a period is found, and this requires the falling inflection of finality. This falling inflection is a signal to the audience for laughter; but still the idea is not entirely completed, for there is another sentence to follow. The actor must then be careful or the audience will forestall him with their laughter. If he waits too long the laughter will overtake him before he has finished the speech. He therefore continues immediately with the next sentence and without taking a new breath. The principle of breath in relation to reading will be explained in the next chapter.

Here is an example of tone sustention without relation to the rising inflection: In A. A. Milne's *The Dover Road*, a man compliments his butler on the excellence of the fish served at dinner. The butler answers, "Thank you, sir. I will inform the cook." The word "cook" has the falling inflection of finality, as indicated by its period. At the same time its register must be sustained. On analysis we find that the tone of the word "cook" should be on the same register as the word "inform." This may seem to be too minute an analysis, but by a strange psychology in reading, if this speech is not treated with respect to tone, as described, its logical laugh is weakened, if not entirely killed.

Some actors have "a true ear," and therefore do not have difficulty with rising and falling inflections. At the same time, they do not always place their tones correctly, and at the ends of many speeches fail to sustain the tone. This allows the end of a speech to fall below the register which has been established as its medium. As a general rule, the tone must be sustained on the same register at the ends of speeches as in other parts, and in some speeches it must be higher still at the end.

Questions usually require the rising inflection, except in certain instances where finality and definiteness of interrogation are involved, as in, "What are you going to do about it?" We are all familiar with the common interrogations, "How do you do?", "How is the weather?", "Where are you going?", all of which employ falling inflections.

If a butler announces "Dinner is served" with a rising inflection, he is asking it and not telling it, for the wrong inflection has changed a statement into a question. Many speeches have the same arrangement of words for both question and statement, and the correct sense is conveyed in the reading.

Let us take a simple sentence and analyze the varied meanings which can be extracted from it by different readings. The plain question, "What are you doing?" has only four words, yet a different sense is obtained, and sometimes more than one, by placing emphasis on each different word. "*What* are you doing?" may mean, "You have told me you are doing *something,* but *what?*" "What *are* you doing?" may mean, "I didn't ask you what you *were* doing yesterday but what you *are* doing now." "What are *you* doing?" may imply, "The others have told me what *they* are doing, but what of *you?*" And "What are you *doing?*" may mean, "We have heard you talk of your good intention, but what are you really *doing?*" Emphasis on more than one word, or on all of them, serves to stress the entire question. "*What are you doing?*" gives importunity to the words.

The proper emphasis is therefore necessary to translate the meaning correctly, and misinterpretations of the author's idea may result if the proper emphasis is not given. In order to solve any difficulty in emphasis which may arise, the actor will find it of value to reduce his treatment during study to the process of reasoning suggested above.

In many lines it is difficult to determine the exact emphasis that should be used to clarify the sense, especially if the rhetoric is involved. This is largely true of Hamlet's soliloquy. It may have been one of the reasons the tragedian mentioned above had studied the speech for twenty years. In the endeavor to give a speech the correct interpretation, the actor should first know what the speech means and then seek out the predominant ideas. By placing his emphasis on these salient points, he can, in all probability, arrive at the correct reading.

Sometimes an idea that needs to be stressed lies in no one word, but requires a whole clause to express it. An actress had a line of this nature, in which she made comments on a risqué dance which had just been executed by a man and a woman. She was doubtful as to how to read the line; and, in fact, it tested the wits of the director himself. Immediately after the dance steps were finished and while different characters were commenting on them, the lady, referring to the man, said, "It's not the way he does the step, it's the close-up." When the actress tried to find the right reading for this tricky line she rendered it variously with emphasis on three different words. At one time she put the emphasis on "way"; at another, on "does"; and at a third, on "step." She did not know which was right. She had sought for the right emphasis where it was not to be found, for none of them was right. The sentence is compound, and the idea in one clause is contrasted with the idea in the other. The line meant that the impropriety of the dance lay not in the manner in which the step was executed, but in the closeness of the dancers. In this speech the whole of each clause was needed to complete the idea, and she needed to sustain her tone to the end of each. Therefore, she should have placed emphasis on the entire clause in each case and on no particular word. Her trouble resulted because she was not first sure of what the line implied.

Some actors are so inspirational that they give full play to their emotions without analytical criticism of the thought in their lines. They neglect mere intellectual study for the inspirational work of emotional expression. They sometimes fail to realize that reading is purely a scientific part of acting and is an integral part of the work.

In character parts, of course, the actor should modify his reading somewhat to conform to the characteristics of the person portrayed. A Frenchman, for example, will require a tendency toward a cumulative rising inflection. The rising inflection of the common Irish brogue is familiar, as well as a like tendency in the Scotch dialect. These inflections are better described as intonations.

The use of any distinguishing characteristic in speech does not modify the rules in respect to bringing out the sense. At all times the actor must be careful that his characterization shall not predominate to such an extent that it conceals the exact thought which the author wishes to express. Finally, when all the principles have been observed in respect to the author's sense, and the character rounded out with the proper delineation, the actor is free to embellish his reading in any way he can to make it eloquent and attractive.

EXERCISES

1. Into what three parts can the art of acting be divided?
2. What is reading, and to which of these three parts of acting does it belong?
3. In general, where is emphasis placed in reading?
4. What three general registers has the human voice?
5. Name the inflections which accord with the comma; the period; the semicolon; the colon.
6. What is the difference between tone and inflection?
7. What do you understand by sustention of tone? With what inflection is it accomplished?
8. What inflection is usually employed on a question? Give an example of a question in which the falling inflection is used.
9. Give the meanings of the question, "What are you doing?" when emphasis is placed on each different word.

CHAPTER XI

BREATHING

The work of the theatre is completely artificial. Many critics assert that the best performance given by a company in any play is likely to be the first. The actors may have rehearsed for several weeks, and as a result, their general performance has become a process largely mechanical. When the actor appears before a first-night audience, a new condition is brought about under which he works for the first time. His first contact with the audience imparts to him a spontaneity which he has never felt during his rehearsals. During these, he does not feel the same tension that he works under when he is first confronted with a black sea of faces beyond a row of glaring lights. On the first night, therefore, his nerves are strung to a high pitch. He does not feel this so much, if at all, in subsequent performances. This nerve tension is due to his first performance of an untried part. Certain dramatic and comedy values which he has never tested are hidden in his part, and he does not know where these values lie. There may be a laugh in one line and a good emotional effect or a round of applause in another. No one, whether he be author, director, or actor, can be entirely sure of the way the play as a whole, or the individual lines, will be received. The actor, then, goes to his performance completely ignorant of how the play will be received, treats all of his part with the same even fairness, and expends upon each portion the same endeavor.

For this reason, he may be far more spontaneous and natural in his first performance than in any subsequent one. Many an actor, however, whose work inclines to depend more on inspiration than on technique, and who is never made stale through self-consciousness, improves his performance from week to week in tempo, feeling, and embellishment. This is a fortunate quality in any actor. He may be a "bad first-nighter," but may improve as he goes along.

At the first performance of a play the actor learns where to find response from the audience, what scenes and lines "register," and what portions of his part are merely the distances between his points or effects. From then on he knows just how his part should go. Audiences respond in much the same way at each performance; and the actor knows each night beforehand where he may expect his responses. He develops a crystallized method out of the inspiration of his first performance; his acting of the part then may become more mechanical than at the first performance when he has tested his inspirations for the first time.

If an actor has the "art which conceals art," this crystallized method is not apparent. It is said of Marie Tempest that her "illusion of the first time" is so perfect that never in the longest run of a play does she give the impression of any mechanical staleness, but of an illusion entirely fresh and new. This is true of many other actors, also, in greater or less degree. It was said of the famous Joseph Jefferson that in his many years as "Rip Van Winkle" he preserved his freshness by constantly varying his performance so as to give almost a new interpretation whenever he wished a change from the old.

This crystallized method, resulting as it does from many repetitions and the knowledge of where his responses are to be expected, is another cause of self-consciousness in an actor. It may cause tension, as mentioned in another chapter, and have a strong relation to breathing.

When we speak in real life, our breathing is instinctive and natural, for we do not give attention to the involuntary physical operations of our bodies. The mind and body are so coördinated that they act together in harmony without any conscious regulation of this coördination. In the theatre, however, the actor plays artificially and does not speak his lines actually on the impulse of the moment. He must merely *seem* to do so. Therefore, when he suffers from self-consciousness and is thus overanxious for his effects, proper coördination of mind and body have been disturbed. The mind operates properly, excepting in the element of his anxiety; but the body, through solar plexus tension, hampers his breathing and impairs the true delivery of his lines.

At the same time, no matter in what degree the actor may suffer from self-consciousness, a line will produce the right effect if it is properly read, and if the actor has breathed properly before and during its delivery. The fault of improper breathing, when it is caused by self-consciousness, lies in the fact that the actor, as he approaches a line over which he is anxious, has an uncertain feeling in the region of the solar plexus and fails to take the requisite breath for its delivery. The line than lacks vocal impetus because there is not sufficient force behind some of the words. They may then be inarticulate, and the effect is not true to life. When speaking the same line in real life, the person would take the proper breath naturally and without thought. If self-consciousness tends to spoil the actor's effects, he will often find that it can be remedied by premeditated thought for his breathing. A good test is to read his line to himself in private and note the places where he has taken a breath. Away from the audience, this will be natural and spontaneous. Before the footlights, he can reproduce this method artificially and with a natural effect.

The same law applies to singing. When a singer has learned a song in every feature of its requirements, he has fixed upon certain places to breathe and seldom varies them. This is scientific breathing in respect to his expression of the song, and makes his delivery easy and natural.

In the farce, *Nothing but the Truth*, an actor playing the elderly bishop had the comedy line, "He said I should get my money back if I yelled loud enough." This was good for a very big laugh. It contained quite a number of words; and as only one idea was contained in them all, they had to be said in one breath. At the same time, the line had to be spoken with much force and emphasis. A breath to an idea is a good generality. Breaths may be divided among ideas, but single ideas may not be split up with separate breaths. The actor had to have a full breath to "land" this line with the required effect. When the effect of this line began to weaken, due to staleness from a several months' run of the play, the actor found that just as the "psychological moment" for speaking was upon him, a good full breath gained for the line its logical response.

Some actors never suffer from self-consciousness, and therefore do not have to use artificial means to guard against it, nor, indeed, have any thought for their breathing at all. For those who suffer from this fault, scientific analysis of the causes, and knowing the remedy through breathing, will be of use. One actor was conscious of the way he breathed and mechanically regulated all his delivery with premeditated breath arrangement.

Practically the same principle which applies to reading in its relation to punctuation applies to breathing as well. The three are correlated. Just as we make a slight pause in reading where some punctuation mark occurs, so in such places a breath may often be necessary. The pause, marked by the punctuation, gives us time for the breath. It may be said, then, that we space our thoughts with breaths. Reading which is correctly spaced and rendered is the proper expression of these thoughts.

A breath may be necessary where some punctuation marks occur, but it cannot possibly be necessary on all. As a governing principle, as stated previously, a breath is generally necessary when a new thought is to be expressed, and the breath must be sustained until that thought is completed. One or more punctuation marks may occur during the same thought, serving only to mark off its related parts. In such cases, delivery which is broken by breathing destroys the sense. This would be like a freight train disjoined by a broken coupling, when all the cars should follow without a break. Any humorous story requires correct breathing, as well as the proper reading, to secure its effect.

The cowboy's curtain speech in Chapter VIII, when he said, "Stick 'em up, Sheriff. I ain't trustin' *you* any tonight," is a case in point. Here is a speech containing two distinct sentences; but the thoughts are so closely correlated that the only way it may be delivered is in one breath. If the actor had been governed by the period at the end of the first sentence and had taken a breath after it, the thoughts would have been separated and the second would not have been connected, as it should be, with the first. Moreover, the breath would have required a pause, and since this was a curtain speech at the end of a very dramatic scene, the pace of the scene would have been slackened in its most vital spot and the effect greatly injured.

In general, the actor with a moderate dramatic sense will not make this mistake. He can rely upon his inspiration and the "feel" of the scene in the excitement of the moment. In such a case his dramatic sense is a surer guide than intellectual analysis.

When the actor relies on his inspirations he does not always require an understanding of underlying theory. Nevertheless, it can be safely asserted that far too many actors rely entirely on inspirational feeling without consideration for the laws of acting technique. If it were not so, a treatise on acting method would be of little or no use. All fine artists, however, add intellectual analysis to their inspirational feeling in greater or less degree.

There are many times when the actor's technical practice is wrong. At such times, a knowledge of the theory is of value. An actor had a speech in which he gave gratuitous advice to a mother on the raising of her children. He then concluded his speech with the line, "I'm a bachelor and I ought to know." He broke the train of thought in this line with a slight pause in which he took a breath. In this line, also, there was but one comedy idea; the completion of the idea required *both* parts of this compound sentence. At rehearsal the director said, "Say that all in one breath." The actor did so. The two statements which it contained were then correlated, and the actor produced the proper effect.

A similar instance occurred in another play. A detective visits the apartment of a young woman who is supposed to have committed a crime, and questions her about her daily habits. He says, "I see you keep abreast of the times," and then he asks if she reads a certain yellow journal. This satire gets a laugh. The actor had to say the two sentences in one breath. The question was correlated with the statement, and, following closely upon it, made the satire apparent.

In both examples just cited, if the actor had taken a breath between the two parts of his speech, the laugh which the idea contained would not have come. In both cases the whole speech was necessary to complete the idea, and to have separated the speeches into two parts with a breath would have made them into distinct thoughts having no relation to each other. Omitting the breath naturally kept the train of thought unbroken.

Even when an audience hears perfectly what has been said and understands its full meaning, they will not respond unless the actor has delivered the speech with truth to life. We are all familiar with the dreariness of the funniest story when it is badly told. The comedian mentioned in Chapter VII was right in saying, "It's not what you say, but how you say it that counts." The psychology of listening demands verisimilitude, and this must be not only a true likeness in matter but also in the means employed.

The older plays, on account of a somewhat more complex rhetoric, require greater volume in breathing than the tersely expressed plays of the present day. In a modern play, most of the speeches are very short. The long speeches of the old romantic plays require greater exercise for the diaphragm in breathing. As a result of this, constant work in Shakespearean drama tends to make actors deep chested. Grand opera, also, is heavier work for the diaphragm than lighter forms of music. In Shakespeare's plays, especially, more breath is needed to sustain a tone to the end of a thought. Many actors of his plays have not learned to breathe properly, and take breaths in the wrong places or after uncompleted thoughts. Their reading then has a sing-song effect. Shakespeare is like grand opera in that the tones must be sustained with greater volume and length.

EXERCISES

1. What is meant by "crystallization"?
2. How can self-consciousness be remedied?
3. In respect to breathing, how can a comedy line be "landed"?
4. What is the theory of breath in relation to punctuation?
5. Devise some speech and tell how many breaths it requires.
6. When is it sometimes necessary to say two sentences in one breath?
7. Practice telling a funny story in respect to breathing, and reading as well, to secure the right effect.

CHAPTER XII

SUITING THE ACTION TO THE WORD

Shakespeare no doubt first mentioned the principle of suiting the action to the word when, in his Advice to the Players, he said, "Suit the action to the word, the word to the action." In all likelihood, the expression as we use it is a direct quotation from Shakespeare himself. Had we invented a term to describe the principle we probably would have said, *Time* the action with the word, or make the action *simultaneous* with the word. These expressions would not impart so complete a meaning as the words of the poet when he used the word, "suit," to express that relationship which words should bear to action. Throughout his plays we have many another evidence of his genius and understanding in the needs of the theatre.

When Shakespeare used this word, he made a generalization which should cover all possible cases. Action and words are usually related. Words sometimes, but not always, suggest and give impulse to action, and action then becomes the physical accompaniment and the illustration of words. Action is always the result of an impulse; we may not always express this impulse in words, for it may be at times only the silent expression of the thought.

When the action is suited to the word, it conforms with whatever requirements the various principles of technique demand. At times the action must be simultaneous with the words which it is meant to illustrate, as when a person says, "I'm going." He starts to go as he speaks the words. At other times action may precede the words, and at still other times it may follow. Therefore, "suiting" the action to the word includes all of these three methods of treatment.

When he uses the principle of suiting the action to the word, the actor must consider truth to life, as in all other principles. Whether action shall precede, shall follow, or shall be simultaneous with the words to which it belongs, depends upon the nature of the impulse which creates it. That impulse is defined by the words themselves.

First, let us consider several examples in which the action is simultaneous with the words. One such has already been mentioned. If the person is sitting on a sofa he immediately rises as he speaks the words, "I'm going," and starts for the door. The speech is short, and he makes the action practically simultaneous with both the words. If this speech were elaborated, and the idea it contains were lengthened into a longer speech, such as, "I am going to leave your house this very minute," the character would still suit his action to his words, but would very likely divide his action. He would rise from the sofa as he began the speech, and would start for the door at the end of it; the latter action would be simultaneous with the last word.

Many a professional actor, if requested by some director to do the action belonging to the speech with the exact technique we have described, might consider the direction too minute. In fact, many a director might not wish to go into such detail. The actor is supposed to know instinctively how to act on such a speech. He might rise on the first part of the speech and move across the stage as he continued. This would be technically permissible, according to his feeling and inspiration, especially if he delivered the line in a comedy mood. However, in a serious or very dramatic mood, when the intention was to be especially pointed, a better effect could be secured by dividing the action as we have described. In either case, whether for comedy or drama, this would express a surer technique.

In many cases, action that is simultaneous with words comes at the end of a speech. Cumulative, or climactic, effect is important in acting, and the tendency is to sustain action to the ends of completed thoughts. There is a parallel here with sustained tone in reading. A person bows to another, and throwing the hands downward with a gesture of obeisance, says, "I am your humble servant." He completes the bow and the gesture only as he finishes the speech; his action ends then on the word, "servant." If the gesture is omitted, he completes the bow on the final word. We may add here that the head should be bowed with the body. As with the index gesture, the impulse ends at the extremity, which, in this case, is the head. Therefore, the bow from the hips should not be made stiffly, with the torso, neck, and head in a stiff, straight line. As the torso bends forward the head also should bend forward at the neck.

A character may say, "I command you to leave this house." In this case he may swing the arm and index finger outward in a gesture of command, but invariably the gesture is finished only when the speech has been completed, and with the arm at its full length. To complete the gesture on the word "command," the word "leave," or any other word in the speech, would be distinctly wrong. The gesture may be started, however, at any place in the speech.

A good example of divided action can be found in the simple case we have used several times from Chapter II. By this time the student must have realized that all the principles of acting technique are interdependent. The same principles must be treated in their aspect to all the subjects discussed. So the young actress in Chapter II, who turned to the sofa and said, "I'm so tired I must sit down and rest," comes under this principle for further analysis in respect to suiting her action to her words.

In this case, again, she should start her action as she commences her line, and should finish it simultaneously with the last word. The actress would be wrong in sitting at any time before or after finishing the line. She would need to gauge her distance. If she arrived at the sofa sooner than she needed to, she should halt her action so as not to sit too soon. If the sofa were so far away that the line would not carry her the full distance, she should then space her words so as to reach the sofa in time to sit as she spoke the last word.

A person says, "The man who committed the crime stands there." He naturally accompanies this with a gesture, and points at the other on the word, "there."

These few examples, in which speeches and action are finished simultaneously, may be sufficient. There are many other cases in which a gesture or an action does not wait until the completion of the speech. In such cases, the action is made simultaneously with some important *idea* in the speech. Action then occurs on some word in it.

In the speech, "Is that the man?" the word "that" is the important one, and if an index gesture is made, it must be completed on this word. On the other hand, if a person were walking in the fog and could scarcely be seen, and another pointed and said, "Is that a man?", he would complete his gesture on the word "man."

A person, with a sweep of his hand toward a door, says, "This is your room for the night," and makes the gesture on the word "This." A character appeals to Heaven in the words, "Heaven be merciful to me," and raises his eyes upward on the most important word, which is "Heaven."

In most speeches, certain words have special emphasis. Gestures or actions on these words accentuate them in the proper way. When a speech contains such an emphasized word, action or gesture made simultaneous with some other word weakens the force of the speech.

Perhaps the commonest form of suiting the action to the word is when there is no important word in a speech to be emphasized, or when no climactic effect need be made. In such a case, the action proceeds during the progress of the speech, but must at least *begin* with the speech. A person says, "I'll find the name in the telephone book." As he begins his speech he starts across the stage, and continues the speech as he is walking. In this case, he suits his action to the entire speech. Again, a wife says to her husband, who is leaving the house, "Oh, don't leave me alone tonight, dear," and advances to him while she speaks the line. Such cases as these are simple, and should hardly require mention. The natural impulse of any actor is to accompany the speech with the required action, and in the right way. In all the cases thus far defined, there must be simultaneous action, either with the first word, or on the important word in the speech.

Let us now consider action which precedes speech. A person may say, "Won't you sit down," and according to the technique already described, may indicate a chair on the word "down." On the other hand, he may precede the entire speech with a gesture and indicate the chair before speaking. This was done in a certain dramatic scene in Cleves Kinkead's melodrama, *Common Clay*. The subject was impressive, and the actor, by making his gesture first, was better able to suggest anticipation to the audience, and also seem to impress it upon the character addressed. Making the gesture simultaneous with the speech would have been proper at a more casual moment.

It is a rule, then, that to precede a speech with the gesture which illustrates it tends to give that speech a more impressive force. Those playing Indian characters will find that preceding speech with gesture often gives it a significance better suited to their characterizations. An Indian might raise both arms upward and then say, "Great White Spirit, come!" In this case, preceding the speech with the gesture gives it a more romantic treatment. To do so also points out the objective with more impressiveness.

Still again, a character comes into a room and finds it in great disorder after a visit from thieves. He gives a start of surprise, which he accompanies with an appropriate gesture, elevating both hands perhaps, and thus registers the emotion better before he exclaims, "Good Heavens, what has happened?" He also speaks the line while he still has his arms raised. Such a gesture was made in a dramatic scene, when a character entered, and another raising his arms in this way exclaimed, "Thank God, you're here at last."

The following example is given in respect to another kind of action preceding speech. In the comedy, *The Old Soak*, by Don Marquis, the old man says to his son Clemmie, "Don't you talk that way to your Ma, you might —— get you ear twisted." Where the dash occurs, he precedes his final words with the pantomime of twisting Clemmie's ear. Whatever comedy effect lies in the line might be increased by using the technique described. The actor might also make the action simultaneous with the words, according to his discretion.

In *East Is West* there is a scene between an old Chinaman and another man, in which the old man receives an insult from the other. He starts, lays down the pipe he has been smoking, rises from his chair, and advances to the other. He does all this before he speaks. When he gets face to face with the other man he says intensely, "You may be fifty-fifty, but you no call me lie." He has then performed three pieces of business before delivering his line. In this example, action simultaneous with the speech would not have been as effective as separating the one from the other, as shown. The reason is that some action is so important in itself, and contains such dramatic value, that it must be given distinct place and be made to register independently of the words. To perform it simultaneously with speech would weaken its effect.

Rip Van Winkle is driven from his home by his shrewish wife, and goes into the mountains with his gun and his dog, Snyder. He comes on, and looking back, he apparently sees his dog running down the mountain. The dog has been scared by one of the gnomes, who is about to enter. Rip moves his head and body from side to side as if peering through the trees, and then says, "Vot's de matter mit dot dog? Dere he goes down de hill heels over head." He first registers the effect of peering through the trees before he speaks his line. Later, he hears a weird voice calling to him from the mountains, "Rip Van Winkle!" He advances a few steps toward the side wings, cups his mouth in his hands and shouts, "Who is dot trying to frighten me, somebody?" Again he makes his actions precede the words.

A person sees a queer looking object in a room and asks, "What is this strange thing?" It may be an object of some importance in the story, and the stage direction requires that the actor go toward it. In this case, since the question has some dramatic significance, the actor would not make his action follow the question nor be simultaneous with it. He would go to it first and examine it closely before he spoke. Making the action precede the question causes an expectancy in the audience.

Action simultaneous with words or speeches, and action preceding them, are comparatively common; but action following words or speeches is somewhat rare. Still, there are times when this is necessary. A person stands on a cliff and wishes to cast some object which has had an unhappy connection with his life into the sea—a locket, for example. This may be done in all three ways. Referring to some woman whose picture is in the locket, he may say, "Now I shall forget you forever." He may cast the locket away before speaking, may make the action simultaneous, or may hold the locket before him, speak the line, and afterwards cast it from him. The actor's discretion and feeling will be a better guide in such a case.

A mother bids good-bye to her son, who is going off to war. She says, "Go now, my son, and be always brave and true." She then kisses him, puts him gently through the open door, and holds out her arms as he disappears from sight. Again, a character says to another, "This is my last word, for I am leaving you forever." He remains in his position until he has finished his speech before performing the action of going which belongs to it. The principle here involves also that of "keeping the eye on the ball," as described in Chapter V. The action of going belongs logically to the speech, but must not be performed until the line has been completely delivered.

Here is an example of the principle used for a comedy effect: In *Three Live Ghosts*, a grown-up son commands his old mother to sit down. She says, "I won't sit down," and remains standing. He commands her again and she says with more vehemence, "I won't sit down"; but she immediately does so, and registers a comedy effect thereby. In this case, the action must be done immediately following the speech but not sumiltaneous with it, and only after the last word. Here, again, she "keeps her eye on the ball" until she has finished her speech, and then performs the action. As a general rule, the actor makes his action follow the words when the speech is so important as to require special stress or needs to be made impressive, just as in the cases mentioned above where action precedes speech.

The exact technique of distinguishing between action which should be simultaneous with the words, and that which should precede or follow, is difficult for some actors.

One actor repeatedly sat down *while* speaking a line, when the director time and again told him to sit only *after* speaking it. The line needed special emphasis, and its effect could not be marred by a simultaneous action.

Another case of the wrong method follows: In George Cohan's *The Meanest Man in the World*, a young lady was seated at a desk. A young man stood at the telephone. His next line was to show that a question had been asked from the other end concerning the young lady. The actor said into the telephone, "Oh, she's very pretty." He then looked at the girl to show to the audience that she was the girl in question. This treatment was wrong, for he should have looked at her first. He had made his action *follow* his line when it should have *preceded*. Had he preceded the line with the action, it would have telegraphed to the audience that something about the young lady had been asked through the telephone. It would also have produced a slight expectancy in their minds, which would have enhanced the value of the line to follow. Therefore, when he said, "Oh, she's very pretty," the line would have gained the right comedy effect. Making the action follow spoiled it.

Besides the three different classifications already described, action may be divided broadly in another way, namely, action which is, and action which is not, related to words. These two classifications are defined in Chapter II in another way as Definite and Indefinite action, but the principles are allied. Action that is related to words in the manner we have described in this chapter is usually very definite; it is a part of stage business through actual direction, or is made definite through the interpretation and technique of the actor. On the other hand, a reëxamination of the indefinite business described in Chapter II will show that this business is not related to the words in any sense.

In respect to indefinite business, the student is asked to recall two scenes outlined in Chapter II. In one, a young man enters with his tennis racquet, and partakes of afternoon tea with his family. It will be recalled that during the dialogue he strolls about more or less aimlessly. If he had had lines during this action, it would have made no difference at just what point in his action he spoke these lines. The direction would merely require that he be in certain fixed places for certain definite speeches when the time for these arrived.

Indefinite action, or action not related to the words which accompany it, need pay little or no regard to the principle of suiting the action to the word. Let us take an example. In the scene between Dr. David and Dr. Harrison in Chapter II, it will be remembered that Dr. Harrison speaks of the prospective marriage of another young doctor with his daughter. He says, "I'm for it, you know," and strolls to a table and smells of the flowers on it. The business has no connection whatever with his speech, but is merely an elaboration in his action to make him appear at ease; it does not need to be timed in any way to the words; but he finishes it in convenient time to turn back into the conversation. A little later, when he strolls to the back of Dr. David's desk and lights a cigarette, he does this business at any point in his speech that is convenient. He must merely be careful to finish lighting his cigarette to be ready for any definite business that may follow. A generalization on this principle is that the actor may spread indefinite unrelated action out over lines in any way convenient to himself to make him appear natural and at ease, taking care merely to arrive at fixed places in time for definite lines and business.

Suiting the action to the word sometimes involves also finding the objective. A person who says, "I'm going," and starts for the door, needs only to suit his action to his words. He need not first locate his objective, for he knows where the door is, and goes to it instinctively without locating it. Finding the objective, however, is often necessary, in order to employ gesture. The line given above, "I command you to leave this house," can often be spoken without finding the objective, or indeed making a gesture at all; whether it is so treated will depend on the technical instinct of the actor. A more effective technique might be for the actor at some place in the speech to give a swift glance at the door to which he was to point. If he accompanied his gesture with a glance, it would indicate the direction for the person's departure even more pointedly than the gesture alone. Again, on the speech, "This is your room for the night," the actor may effectively give the door a glance of the eye as he speaks and points to it. As a general rule, we must first find an object with our eye before we can point it out to another, unless it be, perhaps, the entire landscape and not some focal point. It may seem too minute to point out the exact words in either of these speeches on which the objective should be located. This can better be left to the general method of the actor. Still, for the sake of the beginner, if we analyze closely, we find that in the first speech the look can be given on the word, "leave," and in the second on the word, "this."

In many cases, finding the objective must be timed

exactly. Take, for example, the young lady in Chapter IV who ran in to show her mother a necklace which her uncle had given her. After speaking her entrance line she was to look about the room, and finding her mother absent, was then to say, "Why, where is she?" Had she first looked about the room, as she should have done, to locate her mother and then discovered that she was gone, she would have found her objective. It would have been an objective of idea, and not of place or thing. Then on the line, "Why, where is she?", she should have turned to the other person, and would thus have suited her action to her words.

We will conclude this chapter with one more illustration. In the last act of *Othello* the Moor says, "I have another weapon in this chamber; It is a sword of Spain, the ice-brook's temper." He then looks about for it and locates it upon the side wall. Thus he has found his objective. He says, "O, here it is," and he suits his action to his words by going to the sword as he speaks them.

In respect to this whole principle, the student should learn to distinguish between action with, and action without, words, but he should do only one thing at a time when direction or technique so requires.

EXERCISES

1. In what three ways should action be suited to words?
2. How would you suit your action to your words on the speech, "I am going to leave your house this very minute"?
3. On what word would you complete your gesture in the line, "I command you to leave this house"?
4. If you walked to a sofa on the line, "I'm so tired I must sit down and rest," what technique of action would you employ?

5. On what word would you point in the speech, "Is that the man?"?
6. What is one purpose attained by making a gesture precede a speech, such as, "Won't you sit down?"?
7. Why should some action be made distinct from words?
8. Give examples of action simultaneous with, preceding, and following words.
9. What kind of action is not related to words?

CHAPTER XIII

CLIMAX

Every musician knows the significance of the signs given above. They appear above the notes of a musical composition to indicate the treatment of the expression in playing or singing the music. The figure at the left indicates that the music is to be swelled out into a broader, fuller tone; and the figure at the right, that this tone is then to be moderated, and reduced to the normal tone which governs the general expression of the music. The figure at the left corresponds to climax, and that at the right to anti-climax. Climax resembles climbing to the top of a hill, and anti-climax descending the hill on the other side.

The principle of climax enters constantly into all the expressions of life. In every kind of endeavor it can be found in operation, in some phase at least, and it prevents monotony of expression, just as the two figures at the head of this chapter enter into the expression of a musical composition to denote an emotional phrasing, and to overcome a monotonous evenness which would occur without them.

Climax has many different forms. It may be expressed in words, or in ideas alone. We often hear people say,

CLIMAX

"As a climax to this he told about such and such a thing." The person has reserved his biggest subject or piece of news until the last, in order to lead his hearers thereby to the highest point of interest.

The orator begins his address in a quiet, even key, and as he proceeds, he presents one topic after another with the intention of so arranging his subject as to give it an impressive force of climax. A minister pursues the same plan; and as he proceeds, he gives his delivery a more climactic stress. In any well-written sermon, the most forceful ideas and the most impressive expressions are placed at or near the end. This is done to obey the law of climax.

Climax also operates in the arrangement of public programs. Even in our school days, when we appeared on the program of the speaking exhibitions, we were anxious lest the speaker who preceded us should have better success than we. If he did, then anti-climax was the result of our own effort. A singer, when making out the program for a recital of her pupils, is careful to arrange the sequence of names so that cleverness may not appear too far up on the program, while mediocrity appears at the end.

In vaudeville performances, a person may wonder why the acts are sometimes played in a different sequence from that which appears on the program. After the first performance, the manager has found that the relative merit of certain acts is not as represented or expected, and he has shifted them about. The quality of a vaudeville bill should improve as it advances. Therefore, when certain acts far along on the program are found inferior to those ahead, their positions are changed. There is a place on a vaudeville bill called "the best spot." This is about two-thirds of the way along; and in this "spot" the "feature" act is placed. If we are to observe the principle of climax the question might be asked, Why not at the end? Of the two figures at the head of this chapter, one indicates a swelling of the tone, or climax, while the other indicates a diminishing, or anti-climax. The music must get back to its normal level of tone. So in vaudeville, after the big feature of the program, the quality of the bill must get back to the normal level from which its progression of climax started. After the feature act, therefore, the entertainment diminishes somewhat in merit. This may be likened to the right-hand figure above.

The same principle is observed in the construction of plays. The simple marks at the head of this chapter illustrate a universal law. If we climb a hill we must also descend it, and if we rise to any other height, either of anger, joy, grief, or other emotion, we must also descend to our normal level of expression. The theatre endeavors to be merely a transcription of life, and we "hold the mirror up to nature" as we find it. So in the writing of plays, the skillful author places his biggest emotions and scenes not at the end, but somewhere before that end is reached.

In some of his plays Shakespeare places his dramatic climaxes very far along, especially in *Hamlet* and *Othello*. But even in these plays he does not dismiss his audience until the mind, which has been stirred by these tremendous climaxes, is brought to rest with some colloquial and comparatively unemotional lines. In some modern plays, in which the authors have placed their big dramatic situation, or dénouement, at the very end, there has been too abrupt an effect produced thereby. An audience cannot be sent out of the theatre with their emotions stirred to a high pitch. The thought must be composed when they leave the theatre, as when they entered it; in well-constructed plays this is done in closing scenes or acts.

There is perhaps too great a tendency in our modern theatre to cut out of manuscripts at the original rehearsals of plays lines and scenes that may be considered superfluous. As a result of this many plays are too short for an "honest" evening's entertainment; for the dialogue has been "cut to the bone." Such cutting occurs too often at the end. A police melodrama was produced which had its highest climax not only in the last act, but at the very end of the act. This climax contained the dénouement; and the curtain fell immediately upon it. The effect was such as to produce a shock to the mind, which had no time to compose itself before the play was over. This play, by the way, was a failure.

A four-act play generally has its big dramatic climax at the end of the third act. *The Merchant of Venice*, a five-act play, has its big scene in the fourth act, in which Shylock is punished for his trickery. The fifth and last is then devoted to comedy, in which the mood of the audience is lightened, and the threads of the sub-plot, containing the love interest, are knitted together.

Strong climaxes in plays may be placed at the ends of acts. The curtain then descends upon the stress of some high emotion. The rule prevails, nevertheless, that the climax must not be placed too near the end of the last act, for the reason we have mentioned.

Climax, then, is the highest point reached in any section

of a dramatic performance, in any part of a scene, or in any part of a speech. Since climax is one of the three important principles used in vaudeville, as mentioned elsewhere, the vaudevillean endeavors to make the end of his act contain its highest climax—the juggler with his best feat, the magician with his best trick, the singer with her best song, and so on.

Many an old melodrama had a murder committed in the first act. The rest of the play was then devoted to unraveling the mystery and apprehending the villain. Here is an example: The hero came on just after the villain had committed the murder, found the body of the murdered man, and as he bent over it, the other characters entered, the villain among them, and the hero was accused of the crime. With a start, the hero dropped the smoking revolver which the villain had placed beside the body, and in melodramatic tones, with one hand raised, exclaimed, "Before God I swear that I am innocent." Then the curtain fell. This was climax, and the melodramatic actor of that day was a master in its production. Today we would call this the bombastic method of "machine-made drama." Still, the actor of that day had training in the principles of this broad type of climax which is largely denied the actor of the present in our colloquial, matter-of-fact drama. In modern plays, this type of climax has become almost a lost art. It can still be practiced to its fullest extent only in the classic drama.

A notable scene in Shakespeare, which illustrates this, is that between Macduff and Malcolm in Act IV, Scene III, of *Macbeth*. Shakespeare seems to have followed the rule of never placing his climax at the very end even of a scene; but the modern producer knows that the fall

of the curtain simultaneous with a dramatic climax helps
to obtain a greater amount of applause. In this scene
Macduff learns of the slaughter of his family by Macbeth,
the highest climax coming when, after receiving the ter-
rible news, he kneels upon the stage, raises his sword
toward heaven, and exclaims:

> But gentle heaven,
> Cut short all intermission; front to front
> Bring thou this fiend of Scotland and myself;
> Within my sword's length set him; if he scape,
> Heaven forgive him too!

There are a few lines more which follow before the scene
closes. Modern producers usually eliminate these in
order to get a "hand" as the scene closes on the lines just
quoted. Shakespeare showed his masterful art in dram-
aturgy even in this, namely, bringing his audience back
to the normal level of thought with his following lines.

In the old melodramas, when an actor reached one of
these dramatic climaxes at the end of an act, he held his
position while the curtain fell. He remained in this position during the second picture, while the curtain was
rising and falling again. This converted dramatic action
into tableau, and we can see that it was not true to life.
In our modern plays, in order to present exact realism,
such fixed tableaus on second curtains are abandoned.

Since climax is "the top of a hill," then having had an
ascent it must also have a descent. Many climaxes occur
in every play, and the emotional stress must always be
reduced to the normal level in order that it may rise again
to another height. The big climax is sometimes reached
through a succession of smaller climaxes. The succession

of climaxes of any nature in a performance can be likened to the figure below:

The climactic heights vary in distance, from minute climaxes that occur in individual lines, to the highest climax of all, which may occur at the end of an act. The above figure is only an incomplete suggestion, and the student is asked to imagine each one of these straight lines broken into many smaller lines to represent even the smallest of inflections.

Let us consider climax in respect to the actual delivery of lines. The author, rather than the actor, naturally attends to the climax of idea in the writing of his play. The actor's technique is concerned with the delivery of the lines the author has written. The essence of the principle lies in this: to climb a hill we must start at the bottom; to produce a climax, the tone and force at the beginning must be held in reserve and under control until they are swelled out into their greater note at the end.

A performance was spoiled in one act because the actors reached the climax in voice and feeling long before the lines called for it, with the result that both the actors and the audience were tired out before the actual climax arrived.

Climax in the reading of lines operates in comedy, as well as in serious drama. The character of the mood does not change the principle. Mrs. Fiske was an adept in the reading of comedy lines with climactic effect. In the vocal force which she employed, her reading of many comedy lines had the wedge shape of the left-hand figure heading this chapter. This may be termed aptly a "rising inflection of phrasing." Laughter is only an excitation of the risible faculties, and this method literally forced the responsive laughter from her audience. Since climax is one of the three main principles in vaudeville art, and its use is largely for the purpose of laughter, the vaudevillean often works for years before he masters the principle. When he does so, he becomes the best sheer "laugh-getter" in the theatre. Many actors never master this principle at all; and we must impress upon the student that this principle is one of the most important features of dramatic art.

Many actors have little sense of the principle and start at the top of their climax instead of at the bottom. When they reach the logical point for their climactic effect they are then no higher than when they started, or else have expended themselves in an excess of effort, and really end at the bottom of tone instead of at the top.

In the melodramatic speech, "Before God I swear that I am innocent!" the actor had to strike a higher note than any before reached, either by himself or any of the other characters. This whole speech had to be given a higher note than any preceding it, and the highest note in the speech itself had to be on the word "innocent." In the production of this climax, or "curtain," as it may be called, since the curtain fell on these words, more than one character was naturally concerned. Suppose that on some speech preceding this "curtain speech" another character had pitched his tone at the very top note. When several actors are concerned in such a dramatic climax, the one who produces the final climax, in an expression of the theatre, must "top" all the others. In this case the actor who starts the climax must not begin too high. If he does so, the actor who must finish the climax has not the full vocal force necessary to produce the "topping," or climactic, effect. The result is then anti-climax. Sometimes all the actors engaged in such a task of climax production shout at the top pitch, with the result that they make only noise and do not gain the right effect.

Here is a case, in *The Breaking Point*, in which three actors were involved in such a climax: Three men and a woman were on the stage. The scene was dramatic. One man rushed to the drawer of a desk and secured a revolver from it.

A SHERIFF: Drop that gun, Jud.
A WOMAN: Jud, for God's sake!
A DOCTOR: Dick!

The man is an amnesia victim, and when the doctor exclaims, "Dick," which is his real name, it recalls him to himself. The word "Dick" reaches the highest point in the climax. No matter how high the others may have spoken, the doctor must "top" their tones with a higher tone and a greater force. After the doctor's exclamation, the tones then drop to the normal level, and a quiet scene ensues.

The following is another example of a collection of speeches which formed a climax in the progress of a scene: In *Common Clay*, a young man brings the woman he loves to his home. His father, who opposes their marriage, objects to this. He summons this son and says, "Why did you bring that woman here?" The son, with some heat, answers, "You must not refer to her as 'that woman.'" The father angrily retorts, "And you must not address me in such a tone." Here the moods of the two characters flare up in anger, which the father "tops" in a climax on his speech. These three speeches must proceed in a rising mood, so that the force of the father's last speech contains a climactic tone over the other two. The speech following these is also the father's, but it is in a quiet tone. As he reduces this speech to the normal level of tone he must take a little time for the descent to that level. He makes a slight pause, as one generally does when he composes himself after an outburst of anger, and then says, "You were glad to have me stand by you nine years ago when your trouble arose with her. I am still standing by you, my son." The scene then proceeds quietly.

Rip Van Winkle, after his twenty years' sleep, finds himself a stranger in his native village. He is not recognized by his wife, nor by his future son-in-law now grown to manhood. At last he appeals to his little daughter, Meenie, who is now a woman. She recognizes him, and taking her in his arms, he exclaims, "Tank Gott! Tank Gott! Somebody knows me now, somebody knows me now!" The response to such a speech in this old style of drama was generally a round of applause. However, the actor needed to observe the principle of climax to make the speech register that applause. To do this, he had to be careful not to start the speech with too great an amount of force, in order to have a reserve of power to swell it out into the proper climax at the end. Here, again, he had to start at the bottom of his hill.

We shall consider an example or two of climax in relation to comedy lines. A character may have the line,

"The man's an idiot!" If this is spoken in a comedy sense, the humorous effect can be secured by swelling the tone at the end so that the greatest force is expended on the word "idiot." A mood of anger or irritation also gives an impulse for climactic effect with which to conclude the speech.

This mood of irritation is employed as the impulse in the following example: In *Adam and Eva*, a life insurance agent tries to insure another man's life and pulls from his pocket some policy blanks. After a few lines the other says, "You don't mean to say you're a life insurance agent?" The other replies, "What the deuce did you think I was, an elephant trainer?" A sure laugh rewards this line if the actor is careful of his diapason, or swell, at the end, when he gives his greatest force to the words, "an elephant trainer." Again, a character, in response to the question, "What will you do if war breaks out?" answered, "If war breaks out I'll head for the Canadian wilds." This was good for a laugh; but the actor weakened his effect by placing "I'll head for the Canadian wilds" on a descending scale of anti-climax instead of an ascending scale of climax, as he should have done.

After much practice in this principle, the actor will discover that a good pair of vocal "bellows," assisted by good breathing and action of the diaphragm, will assist materially in producing the proper effect. But at all times he must seek to appear natural through the "art which conceals art."

The student is asked to recall what was said in the chapter on Reading about register and tone. He will find there is a strong analogy between reading and climax. In all cases, if climax is to be produced properly, the register and tone must be sustained. Therefore, when climax is so produced, the reading is correctly rendered as well. In fact, correct climax is practically impossible without correct reading. Correct reading, however, can be rendered without any climax at all. Reading, in its abstract sense, is purely a process of the intellect; but climax, on the other hand, always involves the emotions. A person may say, "The man is dead," and when he speaks this in a cold, unemotional tone, he may have sustained his reading and tone in the proper way, but may attain no climactic effect. On the other hand, if he delivers this with a stress of emotion, he has then injected feeling into the speech; and while he may not change his reading, the line attains a climactic effect because he has laid his greatest stress on the word "dead" at the end.

When the student has thoroughly studied the contents of this chapter and has absorbed its theory, he cannot at once convert that theory into practice. The correct expression of the various phases of climax is not to be acquired in a day. The principle needs constant practice, but with close attention to its laws, an actor can completely master it in time.

EXERCISES

1. What two kinds of climax are there in drama?
2. Mention one or two examples of climax.
3. How is climax used in the construction of plays?
4. Why should a play not end abruptly with a big climax?
5. In the old melodramas, what was the treatment in respect to action at the end of an act?
6. What is the main point in the principle of climax?

[191]

7. Practice saying, "Before God, I swear that I am innocent," with a climactic effect. What should you do?
8. When several persons are concerned in a dramatic climax, what must be done?
9. Devise a speech to be delivered with climactic effect.
10. Why is there an analogy between reading and climax?

CHAPTER XIV

TEMPO AND RHYTHM

The principles of tempo and rhythm, which we combine as the subjects of this chapter, may be considered to represent two distinct principles. As a matter of fact the principles are so interdependent as to be almost one and the same.

Science has discovered that everything on our planet and in connection with it, both in the enveloping atmosphere and the pervading ether, is in constant motion through an action which we call vibration. This vibration governs the most refined material substance, and even the ether itself, whereby atoms and even electrons and æons are in a constant state of motion. In the figure above, an attempt has been made to illustrate in some degree how vibration operates. A point running along this line of successive curves would naturally travel from side to side. If we suppose this drawing to be perfectly symmetrical, and the speed of the point constant and even, then it would take precisely the same time to reach the apex of one curve as another. It would also travel with an evenly sustained tempo. The length of all the curves being exactly the same, the even tempo of the point as it went around each successive curve would give an example of rhythm.

Vibration, then, involves the principles of tempo and rhythm acting together in such a way that the one cannot be dissociated from the other. If the rhythm were jarred from its even flow, such as would occur if one curve were shorter than another, the tempo would be uneven as well. Were the tempo of the point's transit in the vibration uneven, it would require curves of unequal length for its progression, and thus interrupt the even flow of the rhythm.

What has this purely physical aspect of tempo and rhythm to do with acting? In physics we learn that sound is produced through vibration in the ether; and acting, of course, has a vital relation to sound. Any single sound wave, whether propelled from the mouth in the form of speech, or produced in any other way, has in itself perfect rhythm and tempo through a natural action of physical law; but when the intellect of the individual is concerned in the delivery of successions of words, his tempo and rhythm may not be exact, and their flow is thus uneven. Tempo and rhythm, then, are important principles in the art of acting.

Havelock Ellis, in his book, *The Dance of Life*, declares that all life is rhythmic. In any normal and orderly action there is perfect vibration, which involves correct rhythm and tempo; but in distorted conditions of human life, such as deranged conditions of the human body, rhythmic action has been disturbed.

We require and employ a rhythmic action in many things we do. When we walk we do so at a certain more or less constant tempo, and this tempo establishes a fixed rhythm to accompany it. If we quicken or retard our steps the tempo is changed, and the rhythm of our steps accords with the newly established time. The blows of a hammer on a nail are made as a rule with an even spacing in respect to tempo, and this tempo establishes a perfect rhythm of action.

Certain courses in physical culture are found to be not only more effective, but more enjoyable as well, if accompanied with music. The music is rhythmic, and its swing prompts the person to time his physical action with this even swing of the sound, and thus to establish a perfect rhythm in his action. These exercises are meant for health, and rhythm being an element of health through vibratory action, the necessary relationship between the normal physical and mental vibrations is thus established.

Of late years music has also been employed to accompany the work of typewriting students when they practice their action on the keyboard. It is found that speed and perfection of movement cannot be accomplished so quickly by the mental process alone. The rhythmic swing of the music affords a vibratory element apart from the intellectual, assists the student to find the keys more quickly without thought, and increases his speed by giving him the habit of unbroken tempo and rhythm.

Rhythm is essentially a quality of the senses. It is something one feels, rather than a thing one calculates and fixes by intellectual analysis. The rhythm of the dance is perhaps the commonest example of this element of sense and feeling, and the dancers get its swing through the measured strains of the music. The swing caters principally to the senses, and tempo and rhythm are two important principles upon which it is based.

Tempo can be controlled by intellectual calculation in acting more easily than rhythm. A person can regulate tempo at will. It can be quickened or retarded as the individual desires, and is easily defined as fast or slow. No examples can be given to illustrate how perfect rhythm can be produced. It is part of the soul of acting rather than the technique, and falls within the category of those inspirations which are "born and not made" in an actor.

In the same way that some actors are "tone deaf" in the reading of lines, others do not possess a perfect sense of rhythm. The finest artists, however, are likely to possess it. On the other hand, the actor under direction can express tempo in any desired measure.

Poetry, we know, has a rhythmic flow. In classical plays, when these are written in metrical verse, a sense of rhythm does much to render the delivery attractive. Modern actors, who are accustomed to the matter-of-fact lines of present day plays, often have difficulty with blank verse drama because they are not schooled in the rhythmic sense necessary for these plays. Their delivery of the lines is broken, staccato, and halting. There is an analogy to the dance in blank verse drama in that it should "go with a swing."

Bulwer Lytton's *The Lady of Lyons* was included in the repertoires of two stars who played at a theatre in Chicago within a few weeks of each other. This play is written in romantic blank verse. The first actor played the piece in the manner of our everyday speech. His delivery was broken, matter-of-fact, and greatly lacking in the rhythmic flow which the lines required. The second actor, who followed a few weeks later, had been trained in the legitimate drama, and was essentially a "blank verse actor." His rhythmic delivery of the romantic verse presented a contrast which was striking to any observer who witnessed both performances. In modern plays, the rhythm of delivery is broken largely by the pauses which the performances contain. Shakespearean lines proceed with fewer of these staccato pauses, and the rhythm is therefore more constant.

Varying degrees of tempo are necessary in all plays, in different scenes, sections of scenes, or speeches. Rhythm is not necessary only in poetic drama. It is necessary as a pervading element in any performance. The better a play is rehearsed and performed, the more evenly its tempo and rhythm will be expressed. For this reason, plays presented in stock companies, when only a week is given for preparation, are found to be somewhat lacking in these principles. Hesitancy in the lines, unsureness in the business, and a general uncertainty on the part of the actors, all tend to interrupt the rhythmic flow of the performance, and in many places halt its tempo.

Some critics of the theatre go so far as to assert that a sense of rhythm is the underlying secret of acting. This is merely a theory, but may be as tenable as any other on this point. Though rhythm cannot be bound under technical laws, yet a perfect rhythmic sense does much to develop a true technique through practice.

A critic and a prominent actor met in the foyer of a theatre during an entr'acte of a play given by John Drew. The critic said to the actor, "Did you notice how the scene lagged before Mr. Drew entered, how dull it seemed, and how it brightened up as soon as he came on? It seemed to take on a new lease of life. How do you account for that?" The actor replied, "Rhythm." "What do you mean?" said the critic. "Mr. Drew," said the actor, "has a perfect sense of rhythm. The scene lagged before he entered, not through any special lack of interest in the lines, but because the actors did not have the perfect rhythmic sense. When he entered he spoke his lines with a true tempo and rhythm. He not only produced the right effects in his own lines but inspired the others with his manner as well, and the whole scene was carried along in the right spirit."

Good directors have a correct sense of rhythm and keep it constantly in mind while directing their productions. Through this sense they are able to produce a performance which moves with brightness and vigor.

Correct tempo and rhythm command and maintain attention. An actor delivered Mark Antony's oration from *Julius Cæsar* and gave it with a rapid tempo and a rhythm unbroken by many pauses. The steady uninterrupted flow of the lines held the audience in a tension; their attention was never allowed to flag, and, in the vernacular of the theatre, they "sat upon the edges of their seats."

The psychological moment for picking up a cue, as discussed in Chapter II, has a strong relation to tempo and rhythm; for in the passage from one speech to another in separate mouths tempo and rhythm can be maintained, or, through the halting progression of the scene, they can be disturbed. One actor can preserve these principles in his own speech, but when the "bridge" is crossed between his speech and the next, the rhythm of a scene can be broken by an unrhythmic sense in the next actor to speak. Such a break in rhythm occurs when he does not pick up his cue at the psychological moment. Actors get the "feel" of a scene, and through its flow an intuitive sense of just when they are to speak each line. They get ready to speak as much through the sense of rhythm as through the auditory sense when they hear their cues pronounced.

An actress playing a leading part in a production was known among her colleagues as being "hard to play with." The principal reason was that she had no rhythmic sense. An actor played a scene with this actress. When he opened his mouth to speak and had taken a breath to do so, he received a slight shock in the solar plexus, because she had not delivered the cue when it was expected. Her performance was always uneven through a lack of the very important principle we are discussing.

There is only one logical author of a play. That is the person who has written it. Actors often have a desire to turn author for their own amusement. They interpolate lines and act for their own benefit rather than for the benefit of the audience or their colleagues. These lines are usually unexpected; the surprise they occasion throws the rhythmic sense of the other actors off balance for the moment, and their minds must be led back into the rhythmic path. The same thing often happens when actors momentarily forget their lines. This is especially true if a play has been running for some time. The break in the dialogue may cause confusion; and the other actors are quite likely, either to forget their lines for the moment or else to stumble in them.

The late Augustin Daly was one of the greatest dramatic producers in America, and his company was the representative head of the drama in this country. Mr. Daly remembered every tone and inflection in any of his performances. Every response from the audience was fixed in his mind, and at any time he knew, from the character and volume of the laughter or applause, what lines were being spoken. The performances flowed rhythmically on a fixed time, and did not vary. At one time there was in the company a young woman who years afterwards became a leading actress. In a play she was cast as a maid. One night Mr. Daly was in the front of the house and heard a very big laugh from the audience. From the progression of the performance he knew that no laugh belonged in that place. He hurried angrily back to the stage, sought out the stage manager and asked hotly, "Who got that laugh?" The stage manager informed him, and also told him that the actress had put in a certain funny line. Mr. Daly immediately wrote her notice of dismissal.

Performances that are carefully rehearsed and performed by the best artists have a rhythm and tempo so exact that the time of playing may not vary more than a minute or two throughout successive performances. In professional productions, the "playing time" of each act is noted and recorded. If this time varies, it may be due to either a quickening or lessening of tempo. By noting this change in playing time, a tempo that is too slow or too fast can be rectified.

A man not an actor, whose business brought him many times back of the scenes during the run of a play in which a fine company were appearing, was surprised to discover that every tone and inflection throughout the play was always the same. An actor played the same part for several months, and was noticed never to vary his performance from one night to the next in so much as the smallest gesture.

This may be termed "crystallization." When the actor has developed his performance to the limit of his ability, he should endeavor to crystallize his method so that not only his readings, inflections, emphases, and other necessary points in his playing, will become fixed, but that his tempo and rhythm will remain unchanged. The last is quite as necessary as any other feature.

Let us examine a few examples of tempo and see how this principle can be violated. We have said that comedy, and especially farce, must proceed with a more rapid pace than emotional drama. The reason is founded purely on science. Low notes on any musical instrument vibrate at a slower rate than high ones. Sombre emotions correspond to these low notes, and are expressed in the lower tones of the voice. The vocal sounds vibrate at a slower rate and the readings are slower as well. Comedy is found to employ the higher tones of the voice, and the vibrations are therefore higher. The readings of separate lines are also delivered at a higher rate of speed. Speed is, however, necessary in many sections of serious drama, as mentioned some pages back, where Antony's oration was delivered at a rapid pace. The difference between the tempo used in comedy and that in serious emotion is a generalization to apply to the *average* pace of an entire performance. All plays, whether drama or farce, must observe the laws of expression, whereby they are given color and are not rendered monotonous by an unvarying tempo. This point will be further discussed in the following chapter.

The response in laughter received by comedy must be controlled by the acquired art of the actor, as well as by his natural inspiration. Of the many laws which bear upon this control, tempo is one of the most important. Before the curtain rises on a farce the director will often say, "Now make it bright, and keep it going." He knows that a slow pace in such a play will do much to destroy the comedy effects. In tempo, especially, farce in vaudeville falls short of the true principle of holding the mirror up to nature, for other principles are often sacrificed for unvarying speed. The performance then lacks variety, phrasing, expression, and true characterization, and becomes merely a medium for getting laughs.

In very recent years a new term has crept into the theatre. This is "speed." Modern life has been keyed, by accelerated motion in automobiles, aeroplanes, and other high-powered machines, to a high and stimulated vibration. Our lives hurry more than they once did. Since the theatre seeks to transcribe real life, hurry seems to be transported to the stage and expresses itself in the principle of speed. Two plays called, respectively, *Broadway* and *The Front Page* were designedly acted with the greatest "speed" it was possible to attain. Since these plays portrayed certain vulgarities of contemporary life and contained many crude elements of comedy and farce, a very rapid tempo throughout was no doubt permissible in them. Another play was characterized by the critics as proceeding at a "jazz tempo." This play was of a very serious nature; so here speed, when unrestrictedly applied, was out of place.

A director, who seemed to be a modern disciple of "speed," directed some actors in the opening scene of a play to quicken their pace to a very high tempo. His idea was that since the opening lines could not be greatly concerned with the development of the story, but merely introduced the plot, they should be got over as quickly as possible. A day or two later the manager of the company dropped in and declared with some indignation that he couldn't tell "what it was all about." Whereupon, the actors were directed to slow down to a normal, conversational tempo. During this mad race of words one of the actors had asserted that it had been impossible for him to enunciate distinctly all of his syllables. This method of acting, especially in the opening scenes of a play, would have shocked a director of a past generation. Many a director in that day was heard to say in an opening scene, or on some long speech, "This is plot; be sure they hear it."

Two things should be borne in mind from these examples. One is that "speed" should not be applied to an entire play without regard to the separate moods and qualities of the scenes. Some scenes or sections of scenes, may need to go with a very rapid tempo, while others must proceed much more slowly. When one director said, as his very first comment before starting rehearsals, "This play must go with speed," one might have asked, "Shouldn't that depend on what we are saying?" In all cases tempo should be governed completely by what it might be in real life in a similar circumstance. The other thing to bear in mind is that at no time should an actor speak so fast that clear enunciation is rendered impossible.

Correct tempo is almost invariably necessary for the production of true climax. The physical action of ascending a hill tends to retard the pace; but, on the contrary, the ascension of the hill of climax requires a more or less increased tempo. This operates in all phases of emotional drama as well as in comedy. The application of the principle refers here to the climax of words, and not to the climax of ideas. In the melodramatic scene mentioned in the preceding chapter and ending with the line, "Before

God I swear that I am innocent!" the actor could not speak the words with a leisurely tempo. From the beginning of the climax, which was several speeches before the end, its tempo increased, not only in the individual speeches of the actors, but in an acceleration of the whole, and that acceleration needed to be maintained until the curtain fell.

On the other hand, there is a danger in this acceleration. When climax must be produced on a certain rapid and dramatic tempo, it requires more volume of breath than colloquial speech. Some actors, if attempting to give the right effect by the technical rules we are explaining, might become self-conscious and hurry their effort. This anxiety and hurry would deprive them of much of the necessary volume of breath, and the effect would be thin and weak. We can walk fast without hurrying, and the same principle must be observed in rapid tempo when it is associated with climax. Taking sufficient breath, then, enables the actor to produce the proper volume in climax, and at the same time the requisite speed in tempo.

The student knows that he should give a brisk tempo to farce. He should also learn that tempo is most necessary in individual comedy lines, but that he must avoid the practice of hurrying them. Laughter sometimes overtakes the actor before he has completely delivered his line. If this laughter is thoroughly rounded, and thus indicates a full understanding by the audience of the point involved, it does not matter. In *Common Clay*, an actor had the speech, "You deal in downfalls by the thousands, while I'm only a poor little retailer who has to give his personal attention to each job." This speech received a laugh and a round of applause. At the same time, the audience grasped the idea before it was finished, and really never heard the last words, for they anticipated the actor with their response. Nevertheless, he had delivered the speech correctly, and the final words were hardly necessary. One reason why lines sometimes do not ring true to life, and therefore do not gain the correct response even when the audience fully grasps the ideas which they contain, is that the actor has not given his tempo the proper acceleration.

In *Within the Law*, the girl will be remembered who said to the police inspector, "I say you're a great big stiff!" An audience would get the idea contained in this speech if it were delivered in any way whatever. The speech received its logical applause, however, through the increase of tempo at the end, added to the proper volume of climax.

The speech of the bachelor mentioned in Chapter X, who, to secure a means of subsistence, contemplated matrimony, shows another example of the principle. After describing the subject matter of his advertisement for a wife it will be remembered that he concluded with, "I'll get a hell of a lot of answers to that." As explained in that chapter, he had to begin the final sentence without taking a breath in order that the laughter might not overtake him. If he had allowed it to do so, the effect would have been much weaker than if the audience had received the complete idea. Besides using the principle explained regarding breath in his delivery, he had also to accelerate his tempo in order to reach the post, as it were, before the audience. We find, then, that many comedy lines involve a race between the actor's tempo and the audience's thought. An observer can often see an audience with their mouths open ready to laugh, and impatient for the opportunity to do so. To use a common expression of the street, the actor is able to "beat them to it" through the proper use and control of tempo.

EXERCISES

1. Give some examples of rhythmic action in everyday life.
2. Define the difference between tempo and rhythm.
3. Mention two ways in which rhythm may be disturbed in dialogue.
4. What do you understand by "crystallization"?
5. How does the general tempo of farce differ from that of serious drama?
6. Say something about breath in relation to tempo and climax when they are projected together.
7. What is meant in this chapter by "beating the audience to it"?

CHAPTER XV

LIGHT AND SHADE

The expression light and shade is used both literally and figuratively in all art, excepting, perhaps, music and literature. It is used literally in the drama in respect to physical effects. The significance of the expression in its figurative sense is gained from the physical effects of nature. The difference between light and shade lies in the degree of light, or contrast, imparted. The same principle in acting can be completely defined by the one word, contrast, used above.

Contrast operates in all conditions of nature and in relative degrees. It can be seen in the various hues of vegetation, both in the colors themselves and when their shades are lightened or darkened by different degrees of light from the sun's rays. It can be noted in different volumes of sound, which change from high to low, from loud to soft, and vibrate in many degrees of tone. It is seen in all physical action, which may be fast or slow, violent or subdued. It operates even in thought, which may be calm and quiet, or emotional and excited.

The principle of light and shade is an important element in all branches of art. The varying expression of music is familiar, by which it becomes loud or soft, swells into fuller tones, or is reduced to pianissimo effects. Pauses which occur to assist phrasing, rapid tempo which for the moment quickens the movement, and frequent increases of volume, all contribute to that contrast in music which we define as light and shade. The principle must be largely ignored in dance music, for this has a special purpose which light and shade would defeat.

Any visitor to the picture galleries of the Metropolitan Museum in New York may stop before the celebrated painting of Washington Crossing the Delaware. If he examines this picture closely and is a good judge of art, he may be struck with a singular idea. The painting is famous, and since it has a place in the distinguished collection, apparently is of great merit. Its fame, however, is due merely to its historical commemoration of the well-known event which it illustrates. The painter's name is not even remembered and an attendant will tell us that the painting finds a place there only through its historical significance. In what lies its deficiency? The figures seem true to drawing, and the grouping is artistic. There may be several reasons for its mediocrity, but not the least of these is that the painting is flat, lacks color, and has not that vividness which makes pictorial art immortal.

When one leaves this picture, he may pause in another room of the Museum before what connoisseurs consider the greatest picture there. The same artist painted what is frequently spoken of as the greatest picture in the world—the Sistine Madonna in the gallery at Dresden. It was Raphael, and the painting in the Metropolitan Museum is The Madonna Enthroned with Saints, already mentioned in the chapter on The Law of Attention. Besides possessing the centralization of interest described in that chapter, this painting has a depth and richness of color, and a contrast in light and shade, which are lacking in that of Washington. The painter of the Renaissance had many secrets of mixing colors which are lost to modern times, and the rich colors of this painting seem as fresh as when first applied. The deep contrasts in the colors cause the figures to stand out as if vibrant with life.

In dramatic plays, light and shade is shown in many different ways. There are all kinds of people in the world —differing in nationality, character, and years; and the world is peopled with infancy, childhood, youth, maturity, and old age. In a play, the contrast in characters must therefore be the same as in life. Youth may be likened to light, and age to shade. In the world of the theatre, the correct transcription of life demands that there be a contrast of youth and age when human sympathies, conflicts, and interests are interrelated. We must find here the light and the shade of character and age; few successful plays are without these elements. Some playwrights attempt to discard the element of old age in their plays, feeling that, in the present fashion of the theatre, only youth and love are attractive. They fail to see that since age presents a strong contrast to youth, light and shade in character drawing are secured through the contrasting ideas of age and youth. Plays without this contrast of mature thought and that of adolescence lack color, and the "pictures" are flat, like a painting without light and shade in its coloring. Such plays often fail.

A different quality in contrast is secured through another medium. This is through contrasted conditions of society. *The Two Orphans* is said to be the greatest melodrama ever written. It possesses this contrast of youth and age in abundance and presents a powerful contrast also between the lavish display of the highest society and the sordid squalor of the lowest. When the two worlds meet and conflict, the contrast in the social elements is striking.

Still another feature of light and shade is found in different types of characters who meet on the same social scale, or in the same environment. The very differences in costume which these characters sometimes present offer a contrast in color which appeals to the eye. If a Hindoo, for example, is introduced into a modern drawing room, as happened in *The Eyes of Youth*, he does not fail to show a contrast in color which relieves the monotony of seeing all the characters looking, acting, talking, and being, very much the same.

Still another quality of broad contrast in play construction should be mentioned. It is that which lies between the serious and the comic elements. In the comedy drama of two generations ago, the comic element was given separate place, and was played in separate scenes by the comedians. The serious scenes were devoted to the story and were usually devoid of humorous lines. These scenes followed each other turn and turn about, as it were, the comedians holding the stage for a while, to be followed by the lovers, perhaps, who carried on the serious thread of the story. Comedy was introduced in these dramas in separate scenes to furnish what was called "comedy relief." Today the comedy relief in drama is worked into the entire fabric of the play and may be expressed by any, or all, of the characters. It springs usually out of the situations of the plot.

Comedy can be termed the light, and tragedy, or serious emotion, the shade, in plays. Shakespeare's *The Merchant of Venice* has the light and shade in the form of a main plot containing Shylock and his story, and the sub-plot of Portia's romance with Bassanio. The two distinct stories are carried on by different sets of characters, the main point of contact between them occurring in the courtroom scene in Act IV.

Contrast in light and shade can be narrowed down still further, and we find comedy relief created by occasional lines of comedy interspersed throughout serious scenes as a play proceeds. It can be narrowed down further still to include all the differences in moods and expression, and even the slightest inflections and emphases in the reading of lines. The principle is then not only contrast between comedy and serious emotion, but a contrast, as well, in the methods of expression of any mood, whether of comedy or emotion.

This principle embraces many others which were described in preceding chapters. It is impossible here to review all the principles previously discussed which must be included in this one. Some of the important ones should be mentioned. Light and shade can be termed variety in the art of acting; and since variety springs out of contrast, the student will readily perceive how comprehensive light and shade must be.

Lines spoken on an even tone without emotional expression of any kind, having no emphasis, no rising or falling inflections, and unaccompanied with physical action, could be likened to a note monotonously repeated on a musical instrument. The slightest departure from this formula in reading and action would introduce in some degree the principle of light and shade. Gesture in its proper place contributes to the principle through the illustration which it gives to speech. All the various readings of comedy lines play an important part. The pause is a strong element which imparts variety to a performance, while the actor has limitless opportunities in reading, along this line, to bring out the correct sense. Suiting the action to the word with the correct technique again contributes to the principle, and climax adds one of the strongest features in which light and shade are expressed. Varying tempo, with its accompanying rhythm, lends color as well. It can be seen, then, that light and shade in acting is a compendium, as it were, in which the majority of the technical principles are found.

The dramatic acts of vaudeville should be mentioned once more in this connection. Though they are acted with good tempo and climax, both of which contribute to light and shade, these principles are not used in vaudeville with the variety in which they must be employed in legitimate drama. The tempo of a dramatic vaudeville act is, as a general rule, fixed and unvaried, while any climax the act may contain is placed at the end. Throughout, any variety through changing tempo is lacking, pauses are largely eliminated, and the entertainment thereby lacks the color of variety, and has a monotony of tone and delivery which is not true to the highest standards.

Very careful rehearsals of plays are necessary if all possible variations in light and shade are to be obtained. The actor should thoroughly weigh and consider each line, with the supervision of the director, in order that he may give its full value in expression. When he has subjected all his lines to careful analysis, alone and with the help of the director, he then puts together the whole product in a rhythmic flow, with the correct tempos at various parts, the proper climaxes interspersed, and the correct action. A performance, after all, is a mosaic of minute particles, each one specially considered and placed, to produce finally a perfect whole. The director of a stock company complained that in a certain scene all the actors were taking one another's tones, all speaking in the same key, and that as a result the scene lacked variety and the actors were not giving independent characterizations of their rôles. Through their limited time for preparation they were thinking of lines and failing to give thought to performance. As a result of this the scene was devoid of light and shade.

Let us point out a few specific examples in which the principle of light and shade should be observed in separate speeches. In *Nothing but the Truth*, dishonest speculators inveigle the elderly bishop into investing his money in worthless stock. A friend informs him of the deception and tells him that he will get his money back if he shouts his demand so loud that the whole house can hear. He meets the brokers and demands the return of his money. They refuse it. A comedy scene ensues in which he proceeds to follow the advice given him. He rushes to the several doors and bawls his demand to the household in general. He has the line, "I'll tell everyone, everyone. I want my seven hundred dollars." He should speak the first part of his speech, which is "I'll tell everyone," in an average key. The second part, "everyone" he should deliver a little louder; and on the third part, "I want my seven hundred dollars," he should rush to a door and shout at the top of his lungs. He repeats the line in the same tone as he rushes to another door. A little later, after he has received the money, he concludes that he should have interest for its use. He hurriedly figures out the amount and says, "I want thirty-five dollars."

He speaks this in an ordinary tone. "What for?" says one of the men. "My interest," replies the bishop. "Not on your life," says the other, or words to that effect. Again the bishop uses his effective method. He says quietly, "I want my interest." Then a little louder, "I'll tell everyone." Louder still, "everyone." And finally at the top of his voice and repeating it at several doors, he shouts, "I want my interest! I want my interest." Still later, when he finds he has the cheats in his power, and thinking that turn about is fair play, he decides that this is a good time to secure a donation for charity which they had promised him. He taps one of them on the shoulder and says quietly, "You promised me a donation." Considering the present mood of this character, a refusal is natural and is not slow in coming. Whereupon the bishop petulantly says, "Oh dear, you promised," and turning to the other he says, still quietly, "He promised me a donation." Then he uses his effective method and increases his tone as he says, "I'll tell everyone, everyone. I want a donation! I want a donation!"

These speeches give an example of light and shade in relation to climax. The line that is shouted receives climactic force, and the tones are afterwards reduced to the normal level in order that they may receive impetus to rise again. The light and shade are obtained in the difference between the normal and the loud tone.

An actor who played this bishop did not vary his tones and volume with the technique we have described. He spoke in such loud tones throughout the scene that when the times came for him to shout there was not enough difference in his vocal effects. His whole scene was therefore noisy and greatly lacked variety of expression. Though these lines are discussed here as showing an example of light and shade, they could easily have been included in Chapter VIII as affording an excellent example of climax.

Many rôles in which laughter is mingled with tears afford excellent examples of light and shade. The old play *Rip Van Winkle* is a good example of this. In this play humor and pathos are in such close relationship that the actor must be careful to produce the proper variety of expression in each line. In the last scene, Rip accuses the villain of having attempted to steal his property. He says, "Vere den iss dot paper you wrote for Rip Van Winkle to sign ven he vas drunk, but ven he vas too sober enough not to do dot, eh? Don't you know dot Rip Van Winkle like a goot feller he put him in de game bag?" He then reaches into his tattered game bag, where the mortgage deed has lain during his twenty years' sleep, and shows the paper. It is yellow with age, and in comic amazement he exclaims, "Mein Gott in Himmel, is dot de same paper?" The scene is dramatic, and the comic expression in the midst of it gets a laugh. The actor must be careful to make a quick change in his expression from melodrama to comedy, however, in order to produce the laugh.

The following example occurs in Hamlet's second soliloquy, Act II, Scene II. It employs light and shade in great variety, and embraces many different phases of this principle in relation to the principles of technique as a whole. Variety in mood, gesture, action, tempo, climax, and tone, are all found in it. The scene is given as one actor's conception might interpret it. The players have just arrived at the castle, and Hamlet has asked them to give the court a "taste" of their "quality." The first player has spoken his dramatic speech concerning the sack of Troy by the Greeks. At the end of this scene, Hamlet has directed the player to insert the "some dozen or fifteen lines" which he "shall set down" for the play to be presented before the murderous uncle, and has dismissed the players. He is now alone. He sits upon the throne steps at the left and says,—

O what a rogue and peasant slave am I!
Is it not monstrous that this player here,
  (*with a gesture toward the spot where the player has stood*)
But in a fiction, in a dream of passion,
Could force his soul so to his own conceit
That from her working all his visage wann'd,
Tears in his eyes, dejection in's aspect,
A broken voice, and his whole function suiting
With forms to his conceit! And all for nothing!
For Hecuba!
  (*He expresses melancholy contempt on "Hecuba"; then with a rising tone of contempt:*)
What's Hecuba to him or he to Hecuba,
That he should weep for her?
  (*He then rises and advances to centre, and with tones of awe on a low register:*)
                              What would he do
Had he the motive and the cue for passion
That I have?
  (*He expresses a little more force in the next lines.*)
      He would drown the stage with tears
And cleave the general ear with horrid speech,
Make mad the guilty and appal the free,
Confound the ignorant, and amaze indeed
The very faculties of eyes and ears.

(His voice now reaches a low tone of melancholy.)
Yet I,
A dull and muddy mettled rascal, peak,
Like John-a-dreams, unpregnant of my cause,
And can say nothing;
>*(He expresses the "nothing" bitterly. His tone then begins to rise into a stress of anger on:)*
>>No, not for a king,
Upon whose property and most dear life
A damn'd defeat was made.
>*(This reaches a slight climax, and he shakes his fist at the empty throne where the king has sat. He now reduces his tones to the normal level and they take on a note of question.)*
>>>Am I a coward?
Who calls me villain, breaks my pate across,
>*(The next line about his beard is cut, but was used in Shakespeare's time because Richard Burbage, the original Hamlet, probably wore one.)*

Tweaks me by the nose, gives me the lie i' the throat
As deep as to the lungs, who does me this?
>*(He gives a slight increase of volume and a small climax at the end. His voice then sinks into deepest melancholy as he says:)*

Why I should take it; for it cannot be
>*(The word "Why" is changed from the obsolete and theatrical "Swounds.")*

But I am pigeon-livered and lack gall
To make oppression bitter, or ere this
I should have fatted all the region kites
>*(now flying into a torrent of rage and hurling the manuscript of the play which he has in his hand at the empty throne chair)*

With this slave's offal!

(He now rushes up to the throne and expresses the pantomime of throttling the king.)

Bloody, bawdy villain!

Remorseless, treacherous, lecherous, kindless villain!

(This frenzy reaches the highest climax and stress in the scene. Its force exhausts him for the moment, and he staggers against the chair to get his breath and recover his control. A pause ensues. The "O, vengeance" is usually cut. His mood again changes to one of deep melancholy, and he uses very low tones.)

Why, what an ass am I! This is most brave,

That I, the son of a dear father murdered,

(He comes off the throne to centre.)

Prompted to my revenge by heaven and hell

(again a slight rise of emphasis and tone on the last)

Must, like a (bawd), unpack my heart with words,

And fall a cursing, like a very drab,

A scullion!

(Now with self-reproof and some disgust:)

Fie upon't! Foh!

(He gently beats his forehead with his clenched fist.)

About, my brain!

(This takes him to a chair at the right, where he sits. His emotion now changes to cold calculation in a moderate tone.)

I have heard

That guilty creatures sitting at a play

Have by the very cunning of the scene

Been struck so to the soul that presently

They have proclaimed their malefactions;

For murder, though it have no tongue, will speak

With most miraculous organ.

(He now leans a little forward and expresses intense purpose.)

> I'll have these players
Play something like the murder of my father
Before mine uncle;

> *(intensely, and almost hissing it)*
>> I'll observe his looks;

> *(with a rising tone)*
I'll tent him to the quick;

> *(then intensely)*
>> If he but blench,

> *(with much stress)*
I know my course.

> *(On the last he rises with triumph in his tone. He then goes up to the left upper entrance and expresses in this action strong purpose. A thought halts him and changes his tone. He pauses, turns, and almost whispers in awestruck tones:)*
>> The spirit that I have seen

> *(in a whisper)*
May be the devil; and the devil hath power
To assume a pleasing shape; yea, perhaps
Out of my weakness and my melancholy,
As is he very potent with such spirits,
Abuses me

> *(Here he again employs the awestruck tones on:)*
>> to damn me.

> *(The manuscript is again in his hand. He looks down at it and is reminded of his original intention. With dramatic force he says:)*
>> I'll have grounds
More relative than this;

> *(pointing to the manuscript in his hand, and giving strong emphasis and a note of triumph to the word "play")*
>> The play's the thing

(*and with intense stress, almost between his teeth*)
Wherein I'll catch the conscience of the king.
   (*At the end he shakes his fist toward where the king
   went off and raises the end of the speech to a climax.
   He makes his exit as the curtain falls.*)

EXERCISES

1. What is light and shade in acting?
2. What is the main difference between dance music and other forms?
3. In what ways are light and shade expressed by authors in their plays?
4. Mention a way in which it can be expressed by the actors in their performance.
5. Why is drama in vaudeville often lacking in light and shade?
6. Rehearse the scene about the bishop who had been cheated by the speculators, expressing the proper degrees of light and shade.
7. Study Hamlet's soliloquy in Act II to become familiar with its light and shade.

CHAPTER XVI

POINTS IN ACTION

Many principles in acting are more or less heterogeneous in respect to classification, and therefore cannot be discussed under any special principle. These principles are nevertheless important and it is the intention in this chapter to gather them together in a section of their own. They cannot be placed under any comprehensive law and will be mentioned in turn without respect to any relationship one to another. The only common nature they possess is that they all relate to action.

FADING INTO MOTION

A young actor who had spent his few years upon the stage in the cheaper class of dramatic companies was selected for a part in a first-class production. The intensive rehearsals which took place in order to gain the utmost from the actors were contrary to his experience. The actor was therefore very nervous, and a spasmodic method in his action which had never been corrected became more pronounced. When actors have plenty of time to develop their delineations they can perform the business of their action with ease and sureness of method. They become relaxed, and are free from the stiffness and tension which are apparent in many quickly prepared performances, in which the actor must think primarily of his lines. This young actor carried his inexperienced methods into the new field. When he was told to move to certain places at stated times, he did so with a soldier-like precision. This fault has been mentioned in a previous chapter. The director noticed his mistake and said to him, "In your movements fade into motion, and do not go so abruptly."

Fading into motion does not, of course, apply as a principle to all action. When this direction was given the actor it related to some business in which abrupt action was not natural, and in which relaxation of movement was the prime requisite. The principle of Indefinite Action is directly related to that of Fading into Motion.

No indefinite action should be spasmodic or abrupt; but rather the movement fades into the action gradually and easily, as having no definite purpose. Sometimes, in cases of definite action also, the actor should "fade into" his motion. For example, he may be going with a definite purpose to sit at a table. Though the intention is definite, at the same time the action need not be hurried.

The young tennis player in Chapter II, who came home for afternoon tea and strolled about with a teacup in his hand, had no definite purpose in his action, and naturally faded into his motion from one place to another.

Suppose a person is hunting about in a room for some lost object. As he moves from one place to another, he fades into motion here and there in the uncertain way of persons so occupied. When he finally sees the lost object his action becomes definite, and he then moves toward it abruptly. All abrupt movement falls within the category of definite action. In practically all cases, however, when movement is very spasmodic it is not artistic nor even natural in either definite or indefinite action. To use a homely simile, moving on the stage at any time as if "shot out of a gun" does not contribute to grace and ease of action.

WALKING BACKWARDS

In Chapter II something was said about the need, at times, of backing away from a character in order to make room for someone else who enters the scene, and that to turn and walk deliberately to the new position is not good technique. An example or two should be given to include other phases of the principle. Suppose a person knocks at a door from the outside. A character on the stage goes to the door and opens it for the other's entrance. The person opening the door may need to remain there until the other has passed by him into the room. When he opens the door he is naturally squarely in the way of the person who is to enter, and he must then get several feet away from the door in order to allow the proper room. To turn and walk deliberately to the several feet of distance would be wrong, so he merely backs off to the requisite distance. When the character has passed, it may be his duty to close the door after him.

The reason for his backing away instead of walking away relates also to the law of attention. At all times the actor must stay in the play, and he must observe the law of attention in order to do so. In such a simple situation as this one, if the actor turns away from the new centre of interest which is about to enter in the form of another character, he removes his interest for the moment and gets "out of the play." There are some situations, of course, required by the direction of the play, in which a character opening a door for another might walk deliberately away to another spot. This might be to centre.

He might say, "Come in, please," and his deliberate movement from the door after opening it would indicate to the other that he should freely enter the room. The direction might require that the person opening the door should be on the right for the scene to follow. If the other needed to be on the right, then the person opening the door would allow him to pass and would use the technique described. In the melodrama, *Cornered*, a butler precedes a policeman into a room, when the policeman has demanded permission to search the house. The butler walks deliberately to centre ahead of the policeman and says, "Certainly you may look, but you won't find anything."

The student should discriminate in the business of turning away from other characters and do it only when he has a definite reason; he must guard against taking himself out of the play.

POISE

This principle relates also to the section in Chapter II, "What Shall I Do with My Hands?" A very simple expedient will assure a correct and comfortable pose when the hands are at the sides. First, the actor should stand squarely on both feet and keep them fairly close together. Some military training has advocated for soldiers a parallel position for the feet, with the toes pointing straight forward; but this seems far too rigid. The toes should point outward slightly, but not too much. Then the actor may sway his whole body forward until the heels are lifted nearly off the floor and the whole weight of the body falls on the balls of the feet. This posture will automatically tend to throw the chest out and draw in the chin. The actor will then be able, not only to appear comfortable to the observer but to feel comfortable as well, while his hands hang loosely at his sides. Many a professional actor actually *looks* strained and uncomfortable while his hands hang down; and he generally feels so because he has not properly distributed his weight along a vertical axis. In moving to some other point the body may be thrown still further forward. This will automatically create an impulse for one foot to move forward as well, and the other will naturally follow. Walking, as well as all other physical movements, is born of an impulse originating in the brain. This impulse impels the torso constantly forward and the legs merely follow; they do not lead. Therefore, the proper movement for the legs is by a swing from the hips; the bend at the knees is secondary and is produced only as a *result* of the movement at the hips.

In sitting, the torso should be fairly erect, not slumped, with its axis, represented by the spinal column, kept from too much deviation laterally—that is, to the right or left.

It seems that women do not look as natural and comfortable as men do with their hands hanging loosely at the sides. This may be due to the female form, which has in general hips wider than shoulders. A woman's hands seem more graceful and natural at or above her waist than below it. The young actress may be advised, therefore, not to allow both hands to hang at her sides for long at a time. The leading woman of the French production of *Topaze* in Paris was observed very often with one hand hanging by her side while the other was held at her waist in front. In this posture she looked well poised and natural.

SURPRISE

A playwright has declared that the three most important elements in drama can be defined as the three S's.
They are surprise, suspense, and sympathy. We are not
concerned here with the last two, and with the first only
in its relation to action. The element of surprise may
underlie some of the biggest situations in drama, but is
also most important in the minute technique of action.

The technique of this principle is the opposite of that
which the actor uses to telegraph certain ideas to the
audience, because an opposite effect is desired. It is of
prime importance in the execution of many comedy
points. Action can raise a laugh as well as words. When
the actor keeps his words ahead of the thought of the
audience, and, to do so, speaks with the correct tempo
for that purpose, he produces the necessary surprise; this
is an element integral to the psychology of laughter.
Tempo must be employed in action, as well, in order that
the audience may not anticipate the action.

Every child is familiar with the tricks of circus clowns,
who strike one another with inflated bladders and slap-
sticks, though these tricks are almost obsolete now even
in such a physical form of entertainment as a circus. We
remember the speed with which the clowns struck one
another with these implements, and the surprise with
which the business was done. The same sort of business
was also done with a broom or a ladder, when one clown
whirled about and knocked down another, who "received
the slap" by clapping his own hands. The comedy effects
were produced purely through the element of surprise,
for the clowns did not allow the audience to anticipate

the business. In these cases, anticipation by the audience would have spoiled the effects.

In *Mrs. Wiggs of the Cabbage Patch*, Stubbins enters a room, and after closing the door, turns and knocks upon it. This gets a laugh. The man might turn and slowly raise his hand to knock; but if he performed the business in this way the idea would be first telegraphed to the audience and the comedy effect spoiled. Their anticipation is forestalled only when the actor does the business quickly, though he must not seem to hurry it, and the surprise thus produced raises the laugh.

Again, in *Charley's Aunt*, Fancourt Babberly, dressed as the "Aunt," takes the opportunity afforded by his feminine attire to hug and kiss his chums' sweethearts, and they kick and punch him when the girls are not looking. In this business the hilarious comedy effects are secured by the unexpectancy of the actions, as well as by the actions themselves. The actor must use discretion to determine when action may be done with a deliberateness that allows the thought of an audience to proceed at a pace with it, and when it must be done so quickly as to cause surprise.

DRUNKEN SCENES

The effect of alcohol on the system is to paralyze temporarily the mental faculties. Since these are the motor force for physical action, the movements of the body become uncertain and retarded, and lack vital force. The person under the influence of alcohol is unsteady on his legs; and his movements, instead of being normally active, are lethargic and heavy. When he plays a drunken scene the actor often forgets this, remembers only that the movements of the legs must be unsteady, gives them too much briskness, and moves quickly from side to side in a manner which defeats the illusion. A drunken man is heavy and ponderous, and he is rather inactive than active. He moves as little as need be, and his action, whatever it may be, is retarded rather than quick and spasmodic. He is not inclined to move his feet unless to move to another place, and only tends to sway his body slightly while in a standing position. When he walks it is with a slow and cumbersome movement. The young actor who attempts a drunken scene should avoid all quickness of motion. There should be no precision or grace in gesture; he should thicken his speech and slur the consonant sounds, since alcohol paralyzes the vocal muscles. He should also speak with a slower tempo.

RISING

It is not good practice for an actor to rise from a chair or sofa by obviously grasping the arm of it, though this is natural for elderly people. Also, while sitting, as well as while standing, fairly erect postures are the more commendable. When a person is sitting and is about to rise he may prepare himself just before doing so by retiring one foot under the central weight of his body. When he rises, the weight of the body falls on the foot under him and he need not throw his body ungracefully forward, nor grasp the arm of the chair or sofa. A graceful position while one is sitting may be acquired with one foot extended and the other partly under the body. The foot to be extended should be the one *down* stage. This will depend on the direction in which the actor is facing.

In no case should an actor rise by lifting both feet a

few inches from the floor and banging them down again to give him impetus. This is often done by incompetent actors and is extremely awkward. In general, also, an actor should not lean upon the furniture when he happens to be standing near it. Doing so disturbs the dignity of erectness mentioned above, unless some business requires it, as when he leans over the back of a chair or sofa to talk to someone sitting on it. An amateur actor, to whom the furniture seemed a refuge for his awkwardness, was observed clinging to the back of a chair on one side. As he crossed the stage he reached toward a chair on the other side. This gave the impression that he was helpless without furniture to lean on, which was no doubt true.

Arrested Action

Suppose a burglar breaks into a house, finds the safe where the family valuables are stored, and while he is fumbling with the combination the butler enters, levels a pistol at the burglar, and says, "Come away from that safe!" The burglar may do two things. He may give a physical start and turn quickly. On the other hand, while he is bent over the combination, the command from behind may startle him into a motionless position. The latter would be an example of arrested action on his part. If he were to attempt to escape, the first method would be the logical one; but if he were to consider himself caught, the second would be the more effective.

A person often employs arrested action when, during some physical action, he is startled in the midst of it by sudden surprise or some unforeseen interruption. An actor uses such arrested action to register more effectively the dramatic stress of a situation. The action being arrested, and a slight picture, or tableau, being thus produced, there is a better dramatic effect presented to the minds of the audience. An effective instance was noticed in a performance by the Washington Square Players in New York. A character sitting on a couch reached behind him without looking, for a possession which he had always kept in that place, but which had been stolen a few moments before. The character paused, with his hand still raised to the vacant place, before finally turning around. This arrested action projected the seriousness of his loss.

Such treatment is of value also in comedy scenes. In *The Goldfish*, a "professor of deportment" gives a lesson in manners to a wealthy but illiterate woman and instructs her in the correct etiquette for a visit to the opera. He sits beside her in an imaginary box and shows her the manner in which she should applaud. While both of them have their hands raised in the act of applauding, a third character enters and speaks. His voice arrests the pair in their action, but they do not lower their hands. They merely turn their heads toward him with their hands still in the air, and hold the picture. The arrested action prolongs a laugh, which follows as a result of the interrupted situation.

STRUGGLES

Acting is not play, but work, despite the misleading term, "play," which is applied to a dramatic entertainment. The most important medium through which to relieve the strain of acting is reserve force. Without this, acting is often exhausting. The late Sarah Bernhardt, who was an adept in the technique of her art, was completely false in the way that acting *should* be false in order to justify its name. This means to seem, but not to be. She made the claim that if she ever allowed herself really to feel her parts she would soon "tear herself to pieces." In her perfect simulation without real feeling she proved herself a superlative genius.

As a general principle, the actor should never lose himself completely in his part. This would be giving too much play to the inspirational side of his work, and too much subordination to the intellectual. Thus he might rant, or give vent to "inexplicable dumb shows," and commit many other extravagant mistakes which would indicate lack of control both of mind and body. He must "keep his wits about him." Some great artists have made a practice of speaking to no one off stage during a performance in order that they might completely submerge themselves in the spirit of their rôles. This does not refute the principle, however. Other fine artists, on the other hand, can be completely out of the mood of their parts up to the moment of entering upon a scene, and then pick it up instantly. This exemplifies the principle completely, for the actor must act first with his body, next with his mind, and last, but not least, with his spirit.

The work of acting is concerned largely with the physical actions of a performance. In the old melodramas and classic tragedies, this physical action was sometimes very strenuous. The actors had, then, to spare themselves as much as possible; and in order to do this, they learned to simulate the fights and struggles which so often occurred. In these encounters, they rehearsed the movements laid out for the struggles, and, with practice, made them seem real without really expending so much force as they would in real life. This, after all, is the truer art. A struggle on the stage as it might be done in real life would not be as effective as when the action contained reserve force, without which all dramatic art is deficient. In sword fights or struggles, therefore, motions which are correct but which allow the actors to preserve the proper amount of reserve force, present by far the better illusion. On the other hand, if the actors carry this simulation to extremes, they may present a burlesque of the action. The burlesque struggle, so often seen in comic motion pictures, in which the actors join hands and swing them from side to side, is familiar. In all physical encounters the actor must not expend himself in physical action, but at the same time must seek the illusion of truth to life.

ELIMINATING ACTION

Matter and mind can be given as a simple classification of all existing substance. A man expresses physical action through matter, which is his body, and thought through his spirit, or mind. At many times, action must accompany the expression of thought, as already explained in Suiting the Action to the Word. At many other times, the proper expression of thought requires the elimination of physical action in order that the thought may have a better effect. In such cases, the actor often makes the mistake of allowing what we have described elsewhere as foreign physical action to creep in and disturb the proper projection of the thought. This foreign action grows out of a lack of repose, and tends to distract the attention of the audience from the thought expressed. There are many times, of course, when characteristic action having no relation to technique may accompany words, but these are excepted here.

Comedy at times requires the elimination of action, and the actor must discriminate as to when it is necessary. In *Rip Van Winkle*, Rip meets the gnomes in the mountains and has a humorous scene with them. The grandfather informs him that all his boys are dumb, and that there are no girls in the family. Rip has the line, "Dumb girls. Vot goot vifes dey vould make!" A comedy point is contained in this line. Its proper effect requires that all action during the line shall be eliminated. Rip therefore stands perfectly still with face front, since this is an "aside" speech, and delivers the line without physical action of any kind.

Again, in *Common Clay*, a young reprobate stands at a door, and before he makes his exit, delivers the line, "I'll be a gentleman if I have to go to the penitentiary to do so." After he goes off, a character on the stage turns front, and, without motion, says, "Going to the penitentiary to be a gentleman!" He remains motionless until the laugh which this line causes has subsided before he turns to another on the stage and says, "Sam, he doesn't know what a gentleman is." In many instances, serious emotions as well require this technique, especially if they are quietly expressed.

CLEAR-CUT ACTION

This principle has been touched upon in connection with previous principles, but deserves a special section to illustrate and emphasize it more fully. The difference between action when it is connected and performed with the words of a play in a definite and clear-cut manner, and when it is blurred in execution, or does not suit the words, is like the difference in an effect seen through a microscope when an object is placed in or out of focus. To make his action distinct and clear-cut, the actor must first determine just what he is going to do. If he is to divide his action into several parts, he must decide which part is to come first and which to follow. In such a circumstance he must then try to do only one thing at a time.

Let us cite an example or two: A character is absorbed in a newspaper. Another approaches him with a box of candy and invites him to have some. In this case, the actor might divide his action into four parts, and he should completely finish each part before he proceeds to the next. First, he might look up at the person speaking; second, down at the candy; third, back again to the other, when he might say, "No, thanks"; and fourth, back at his newspaper.

A capable director often instructs an actor to divide his action in such a way, and even tells him the number of parts it should contain. The business given above need not always be performed in the manner described. The point is that when it is done with this technique it must not be blurred. According to his technical method in such a situation, the actor might decline the candy without even glancing away from his paper.

In *Adam and Eva*, the elderly bachelor mentioned before goes to a door and says to a person on the stage, "I shall leave your house forever." Many parts have business just before the actor's exit which, in a term of the theatre, is called a "trick exit." This term means that when the actor is given certain business at an exit, if he does the business neatly and with clear-cut precision, it may be "good" for a round of applause. After completely finishing his line, the old man (1) turns to the door; (2) draws himself up proudly; (3) puts his hands behind him; (4) stalks off. If the actor divides this action in a clear-cut manner, but at the same time does not make it mechanical and stilted, it receives the right response.

In still another example, in the melodrama, *Cornered*, a criminal masquerading as a gentleman makes his escape under the eyes of a police inspector. He goes jauntily to the door, turns, says, "Good day. Pleased to have met you," hooks his cane over his left arm, places his silk hat breezily upon his head, taps the top of it with his hand, turns to the door, and exits. He divides his action where the commas are placed in these lines. This "trick exit," also, when neatly done, brings a "hand."

There is another kind of "trick exit" which does not gain its effect in the way just described. For example, if a person makes an exit in a fit of laughter, hysterics, or some such violent emotion, which requires much vocal force added to climax, a round of applause will often follow. It is necessary that the actor prolong his effect until he is well off the stage. In A. A. Milne's *Mr. Pim Passes By*, there is an excellent example of such an exit, when Olivia Marsden leaves the room hysterically shouting, "A fish bone! Morality depends upon such a little thing." She may elaborate the effect of her exit by repeating, "A fish bone! A fish bone!" as she goes off. Applause thus produced is not in itself a proof of good acting throughout the entire rôle of the actor, for that may be mediocre in general. On the other hand, when applause follows an exit that is made quietly and with no such effect as described above, the actor knows it is a genuine tribute to his work.

Mrs. Midget's final exit in *Outward Bound*, by Sutton Vane, is a splendid exit quietly done, that never fails to bring a hand. The little charwoman finds her son, and together they start on their way to work out their salvation. The son does not realize that she is his mother. She knows and follows him out saying, "He wants me! He wants me! I'm coming." Though this exit is quiet, it contains an impressive idea, and it is this that gets the "hand." Examples of the entirely unpretentious exit occurred with the late Henry Irving, who usually received applause after all his exits, of whatever nature.

AD LIBITUM

This Latin phrase, which means "at liberty," applies to lines which the actor may invent himself in certain situations, or action which he may perform in any way that suits him. The expression is shortened to "ad lib"; it is used as a verb or adjective, and the whole practice is called "ad lib-ing."

Ad lib-ing may be done by one person or several at a time. An actor may have an exit in which he calls after a person who has left the room. He may say, "Here, come back, come back, I say, I want to talk to you," and so forth. As he leaves the stage, he may ad lib his lines at his own discretion until his voice dies away in the distance. When several actors at a time ad lib together, they say anything that carries out the idea. A person comes into a room and joins a party of merrymakers. They all say such lines as, "Oh, here he is now," "Well, here's Bobby," "What kept you so long?", "Oh, here you are, we've been waiting for you," and so on. In the mob scenes of *Julius Cæsar* the citizens ad lib in the shouts.

Actors can commit two faults when they ad lib in a group. One is for them all to say the same thing. This fault is observed in the choruses of musical comedies, when the girls all shout "Yes," "No," or "Certainly we will," in exact unison, and all use the same words. This is wrong, for in real life they would not all think of the same words to express their thought. This fault in musical choruses is of course due to the direction. The second fault is that the ad lib lines sometimes do not start on the exact cue, and are sometimes prolonged beyond a reasonable time. In one play much ad lib-ing was done by a mob; but it got so out of control that it drowned many of the speeches of the actors, which should have been heard. Sometimes, among a group, definite speeches are given to the several actors so that they may not all speak the same line. The actors speak the different lines at the same time and thus give the effect of a babel of voices.

Miscellaneous Points

Under this title we shall mention several principles which are not all connected with technique in acting, but which the student should understand.

Some writers on the theatre define as one of the principles of acting *The Illusion of Unconsciousness of What Could Not Be Known.* This is a somewhat abstruse principle, and difficult at first to comprehend. In substance it means this: The actor knows in reality everything that transpires in the play before it happens. In the semblance of his character he is supposed to be ignorant of future

events. He would be so in real life. He must not anticipate. In many situations he must present the illusion of
being completely unaware of something which may be
imminent. One example should suffice. Suppose a criminal is hiding in the dark waiting to commit a crime. A
character comes on and the criminal creeps up behind
him. This character is to receive a blow upon the head
and must fall unconscious. The actor playing this part
naturally has full knowledge of the business shortly to be
done. At the same time, he must be free from all tension
in his movement, and must assume an ease which will
give the complete illusion that he is unaware of what is
about to happen.

MANNERISMS

Only a generalization need be made on this subject.
In most cases mannerisms detract from art. They belong
to the individual and not his characterization, and have
no value in his performance unless, by chance, they happen
to suit the manner of his portrayal. Wagging the head
and shifting the feet, described in Chapter II, may be defined as mannerisms. A leading actor had the mannerism
of twitching the fingers of his left hand while it was at his
side, and the director jokingly told him to tie his fingers
down. When the actor can rid himself of all mannerism
he can then begin to write his art of acting "upon a clean
slate."

LAUGHING

Some people do not laugh audibly, or when they make
any sound at all in laughing it is breathy and does not have
the resonant quality of natural laughter. If the young

actor cannot laugh naturally he should try to learn to do so, for laughing is very often required by his parts.

Laughing is produced by a contraction, accompanied with a slight tension, of the diaphragm, while the breath is expelled from the lungs in short, quick gasps. The vocal chords contract at the same time to give resonance, as in speech, to the sound produced by the breath as it passes out.

To practice laughing let the student say "Ha, ha, ha," as if he were merely saying the three little words. In doing this there is very little tension of the diaphragm, but merely a gentle contraction. Let the student say the words again with a conscious tightening and contraction of the diaphragm, and at the same time forcing the breath outward in quick staccato sounds. He must be careful to make the sounds resonant, as in speech. The proper tension of the diaphragm and the effort to "pump" the air out in short jerky sounds, will accomplish this with practice. A beautiful laugh is as rare as a beautiful speaking voice, and is an accomplishment well worth while.

BREATHLESSNESS

Sometimes a character must give the illusion of being out of breath. Let us say he is supposed to have been running from a distance, and he comes into the scene breathlessly describing some startling event. In real life breathlessness halts the speech and renders the delivery staccato and jerky. In order to imitate nature the actor should expel his breath as he talks in short quick gasps. This will also cause some movement of the head and body, as of a person in agitation of mind.

Hokum

This word was formerly a part of American slang, but is now found in unabridged dictionaries as an accepted word in our language. No one knows its origin, except that it arose out of the theatre and belongs essentially to it. Some years ago the lexicographers sought a definition for it and asked some prominent actors for its true meaning. One explanation of the word gave it as derived from "hocus-pocus," the expression of the magician in performing his illusions, and which means something that cheats or tricks. Hokum, however, as we now understand it, does not cheat or trick, for it is quite obvious.

The finally accepted definition was, Any line or piece of business that raises a "sure fire" laugh. This definition may be strictly true, for hokum always has such an effect. At the same time, many a brilliant line in high-class comedy raises a sure fire laugh which is not hokum at all. Hokum, however, is confined within that class of comedy which is easily reducible to burlesque or the grotesque; and any comedy point that cannot be so reduced is not hokum.

Some farces are criticized as having too much hokum in them; yet hokum is often quite true to life, and the comedies of Shakespeare abound in it. The mock duel in *Twelfth Night* is a good example. If a person slips on a banana peel and goes sprawling, this is true to life and we laugh, for we are always amused at the comical mishaps of others. This business on the stage would be pure hokum. The danger of employing hokum on the stage lies in the fact that it can so easily be reduced to burlesque; and for this reason it is often condemned. The actor should be careful, therefore, that when he has hokum to perform he shall do it with the moderation of truth to life, without which it degenerates into "horseplay."

When plays become very old, but are still performed, like *Charley's Aunt* and *The Old Homestead*, actors have a tendency to overdraw the legitimate hokum in them, and introduce still more which has not a natural, but a burlesque, quality. This is sometimes done even in Shakespeare, for the authors are not present to protect their property. A law regarding hokum should be, If a character would not act in such a manner in real life, then the performer should not act thus on the stage.

Different Kinds of Drama

Tragedy: The drama of tragedy is defined as a play in which doom is foreshadowed by forces of destiny not set in motion by, and beyond the control of, the person upon whom the doom falls. *Hamlet*, in which the Prince meets his doom through no cause set in motion by himself, is a perfect example.

Melodrama: Melodrama is a play setting forth a conflict of good and evil forces, with good ultimately triumphant. In such a play, evil is punished through the operation of forces set in motion by itself, and the play has a happy ending. *The Two Orphans* is a true melodrama. A melodrama was originally a play of this type with music. Shakespeare's *Macbeth*, though generally styled a tragedy, is, in the opinion of some critics, a melodrama. They hold this view because Macbeth brings his doom upon himself. The play was at one time done with a musical setting.

Romantic Drama: This type of drama is a play in which the time is generally set back to those periods in history which we call the days of romance. It has a happy ending. The romantic drama has incidents which are more or less fanciful and unreal. *Richelieu*, by Bulwer Lytton, is a good example.

Comedy-Drama: Comedy-drama is a play which mingles serious with comic elements, the latter furnishing comedy relief. It has a happy ending. *The Merchant of Venice* is a classic example.

Domestic Drama: This is a drama of any nature dealing with conditions of the home.

Society Drama: A serious play in which the story concerns the lives of society people. Society comedy also concerns society people, but has a lighter and more humorous nature.

Comedy: This class of drama is one of light and amusing nature, in which there are no serious incidents, and with invariably a happy ending. It often presents a harmless satire on human society. Sheridan's *The School for Scandal* is a classic example.

Light Comedy: Light comedy is a play of a lighter and more airy style than a comedy.

Farce: Farce may be defined as a play containing extravagance of situation and character, in which the situations are merely possible, but not always probable. Its accumulation of absurdities is meant solely for purposes of laughter.

Social Drama: This takes up problems of social and economic life, takes one form of argument or another in an attempt to present a special point of view, and contains strong elements of propaganda in order to sway public opinion. The new "class struggle" drama, which has recently made its appearance, is a definite form.

Grand Opera: This corresponds more or less to tragedy in drama. All of its dialogue is sung, and it has a chorus.

Comic Opera: Comic opera corresponds largely to comedy in drama, but possesses a somewhat more fanciful and romantic quality. Some of its dialogue is sung and some of it spoken. It also has a chorus.

Musical Comedy: Musical comedy is a growth out of the comic opera. It is of a lighter nature, the music not being so heavy and having more the form of interpolated specialties. It generally has a modern theme.

Revue: The revue is an entertainment on a lavish scale with dialogue, lyrics, and a chorus. It contains various specialties, songs, and especially skits satirizing topics of the day. It is a modern growth out of the old-time extravaganza, which was also produced on a lavish scale, with ballets and various spectacles, and which dealt often with fairy tales or other fanciful subjects. The Ziegfeld Follies is an example of the revue.

Burlesque: This is an entertainment of words and music, containing a chorus, and in which every aspect of life is travestied *ad absurdum.*

Vaudeville: In the old days, vaudeville was called "Variety." It is defined today as a collection of various units called "acts" of any nature whatever and having no relation to one another, made into a unified entertainment.

DIFFERENT KINDS OF PARTS

Star Part: The star part is any part in a play for a man or a woman, of sufficient importance to merit portrayal by a star.

Leading Part: This is a part for a man or a woman which

carries the principal love, or romantic, interest of the play.

Heavy Part: In the old melodramas the heavy part was that of the "villain" of the play. In modern plays, it is called the "second" part, and is the second in importance. The part is played by the "second" man or woman.

Juvenile Part: This is any "straight" part for a young man or woman.

Character Part: A character part is any part for a man or a woman for which some special characterization is necessary or in which maturity is portrayed.

Comedy Part: A comedy part is any male or female part requiring the unction of comedy.

Character Comedy Part: This part is one requiring characterization along comic lines.

Light Comedy Part: This is a straight comedy part, generally for a young person, either man or woman.

General Business, or *General Utility Part:* This part is one of any nature, of subordinate importance. In former days such a part was called a "walking gentleman." Rosencrantz and Guildenstern in *Hamlet* are good examples.

Ingenue Part: The ingenue part is that of a young girl supposedly ingenuous in her nature. It may be either serious or comic.

EXERCISES

1. Explain "fading into motion." Give an example.
2. Describe some situation which would require an actor to take a few steps backward.
3. What are the three S's in drama?
4. What do you understand by "the element of surprise"?

POINTS IN ACTION

5. Give an example of "arrested action."
6. What is meant by "eliminating action"?
7. Mention a few mannerisms which can creep into one's performance.
8. What is the difference between a tragedy and a melodrama?
9. What is the difference between a comedy and a farce?
10. What is the difference between grand and comic opera?
11. What is "anticipation"?
12. What does "ad lib" mean?
13. What is a "trick exit"?

CHAPTER XVII

THE STUDY OF A CHARACTER

Let us now consider the actor's work in studying his character, and the more important of the two mental processes which he employs. We referred to these in Chapter I where the first process, involving the methods for commiting lines to memory, was explained. The more important process is an intellectual one. It is intellectual despite the accepted understanding that acting involves the inspirational impulse of the emotions. Some people think that an abundance of intellect is a hindrance rather than an aid to art. This depends entirely upon the relative degrees of intellect and inspiration which an actor may apply. Acting is physical, or mechanical; mental, or intellectual; and spiritual, or emotional.

Though the emotional inspirations are of prime importance in acting, at the same time the actor employs these only when he has completed his study and begins really to play his part. The study of the part is an intellectual process, since it has place in his thought and not his emotions. He practices the physical or mechanical elements of his performance at rehearsals, and builds the intellectual and the emotional structure thereon.

Some actors depend more upon intellectual analysis than upon emotional inspiration for their effects. Mrs. Fiske seemed to be one of these.

Eva Le Gallienne, in her book, *At 33*, says that she has found in her companies two kinds of actors. One kind work from the "inside out." That is, they have an inner, intellectual conception of the basic qualities of the person they are to portray, but no concrete idea along technical lines of how to portray that character. They seek by experiment at rehearsal to have the externals grow naturally out of their inner instinct. Such actors should be left at first largely to their own devices and not rehearsed too rigidly. The other kind of actors seek from minute and careful direction at rehearsals, and from the development of the situations about them, to find their characterizations. Such actors work "from the outside in." They can be minutely directed from the beginning of rehearsals.

An interesting incident is told of the great French actor, Talma. Through news of the sudden death of one of his loved ones he was stricken with great grief. In the very midst of one of his outbursts of emotion his mind was suddenly caught with the thought of what his physical action had been at the moment. He thought, "I must remember how I did this." No doubt, in some later performance he translated into conscious technique what he had done as a sheer reflex in his period of real grief.

To be fitted for the work of the theatre the actor must study life and people. He should endeavor to grow in an understanding of human psychology, human motives, human virtues, and failings. There is much necessity in his work for interpretation of human motives and impulses. There are many times when he must inquire of himself, What would the person do in this case? when trying to determine the motives of the character he is studying. He may ask himself, What would *I* do in a similar situation? His solution will be correct only so far as he has approximated a correct understanding of human virtues, failings, and motives.

The actor, then, who endeavors to attain great success must seek to have as wide an understanding of human nature as an ever alert observation will allow. A physician does not cure disease successfully without an expert preliminary diagnosis.

Many people hold the opinion that the actor should know life through actual contact. There is a difference of opinion here as to the relative value of theory and practice. To observe life carefully may be as effective as actual experience in various situations. An actor may be able to imitate intoxication successfully, though he has never been under the influence of liquor; to observe drunkenness has been sufficient. It is said that Edmund Kean once carefully observed a drunken man and wished his "Cassio" might have been present to gain a suggestion from the man's actions. An actor should have a "kodak mind" in order to photograph impressions of human character upon his memory.

Actors who have plenty of leisure for preparation in a rôle often visit foreign countries where the locales of their play are laid, in order to absorb the atmosphere of those places and to gain ideas for their own delineations. By reason of our cosmopolitan mixture of races, America furnishes vast varieties of types and "genre." The East Side in New York has often been very useful to actors, who have visited its neighborhoods for the character suggestions which they required.

In make-up, also, the actor must practice observation, for in this he is able to arrive at a correct visual presentation of his character. The manner in which he shall dress, make up his face, wear his hair or his beard, can be suggested by the "make-ups" he has seen in life.

Acting has been defined by some directors as "projected imagination." This means that in studying his part the actor should form the image of the character in his imagination. In his performance he projects that image into outward form. It is quite possible that a large element of autosuggestion is used in the whole process.

When an actor begins to study his part he should, if possible, read the entire play. Through a unified conception of the play as a whole he gains a conception of his own character's relation to the story. His character is sometimes vividly marked, or its motives clearly defined, through the lines of the other characters. Though his part may be finished in the first act, some lines in the last may be a clear index to the character.

Some directors take exception to this and insist that the actor be given his part only. They think that the direction of a play is like the direction of an orchestra, in that it is no more necessary for the player to be familiar with the entire work in the one case than in the other. Such a method might restrict the actor's understanding of his character for the reasons given above. For example, in Eleanor Robson and Harriet Ford's excellent mystery melodrama, *In the Next Room*, an art collector is mysteriously murdered at the end of the first act and his body is found lying on the stage. In the next act his young niece describes to a detective the position in which the body was found. Should the actor, finishing his work, as he did in the first act, have been ignorant of this description, he might have employed an entirely incorrect posture for his body after the murder.

The careless actor is often regardless of the story of the play. An actor playing in a Shakespearean repertoire company giving *King Lear* got through his part in the second act. He asked a colleague one day, "How does the darned thing end, anyhow?"

If he is not able to read the entire play, because it is in typewritten script fresh from the author's hands, the actor should pay close attention to the rehearsals. New plays are generally first read to the company for this purpose. From this first reading the actor gains a general understanding of his character,—what kind of person he is, what his motives are, his relation to the other characters, and the story itself.

When the actor has clearly grasped these features, he must then decide upon what characterization he shall give his part in order to bring out the qualities of the character with truth to life. The author generally has a clear idea as to how the parts which he has created should be played. Still, the actor can often bring more to a part by sheer creation and embellishment than the author himself was able to think into it. When this is done, the actor is more than successful; he has become not only an interpreter but a creator as well.

Some of the parts in Shakespeare's plays have such tremendous possibilities that no creative conception can be an improvement upon them. The ultimate creation of these great parts was accomplished by the poet himself. Merely to interpret them to the fullness of the poet's wonderful vision is to rise to splendid heights. That actor who seeks to create innovations or novelties for these parts only falls short of the splendid achievement which lies in pure interpretation, and succeeds only in depicting these characters as different people from what they really are.

On the other hand, many parts in modern plays have little given to them by the author, who may not possess much talent in character drawing, and may be little more than a teller of stories. In such cases, the actor is expected to give a characterization and conception through his creative imagination. Managers often engage for such parts high-salaried actors who can invest them with some delineation which the author was not able to write into the lines.

In one such case an actor was highly successful. On first glance he found his part a "bad" one. It was of the sort called "heavy," after the manner of the "heavy villains" in the melodramas. If he played it "straight" and interpreted only what he found in the lines, it would have been cold and ineffective. The actor found there was great latitude for the creative principle; by giving the part a certain peculiar characterization he was able to give it distinction, and a bad part became a good one.

Actors resort to many devices to give prominence to rôles that have been given distinguishing characteristics by the author. Lisping, stuttering, and limping, have all been resorted to. The case of the elder Sothern, whose fame sprang out of the accident of tripping over a lady's train on his first entrance as "Lord Dundreary," a mishap which was hilariously greeted, and which led to an elaboration of his rôle, is a part of dramatic history.

The best parts are naturally those which the author has delineated so clearly that the actor has only to interpret what he finds in them. When he has fixed his interpretation in mind, the actor may then add any embellishment along creative lines of which he is capable. Interpretation need not interfere at all with creation, so long as too much license in creation does not pervert correct interpretation, and thus distort the author's original idea.

When the actor has formed his idea of the correct interpretation of his part, or has gained a creative conception of it, he should then determine the mood, or moods, in which the part should be played in various scenes. The mood of a character may change swiftly from one scene to another. All parts, however, do not have a distinct mood in every scene, and the same mood may be constant throughout a portrayal. The greatest example we have of a pervading mood is found in *Hamlet*, in which the Prince's mood of melancholy is constant from beginning to end. Hamlet has a few light spots, in which his mood seems to be gay—but seems only, for any great actor will show the pervading mood beneath it.

In many parts, as has been said, no special mood is expressed. Since acting is an expression of the emotions, and the emotions are closely related to mood, these parts cannot be the best ones.

A new plan for the development of young actors has recently been gaining vogue. It is called "improvisation," and is practiced in what is called "studio work." The students are given an improvised plot for a scene, and they carry it out in their own words. The purpose of this method is to develop in them natural impulse and inspiration, which, as a habit, they can later impart to the lines of an author. The ultimate aim is to teach them to speak naturally in dialogue and to grow out of a tendency just "to speak lines." "Affective memory" is another principle which studio work seeks to develop. In the expression of any emotion, whether of hate, fear, love, or any other, the student is asked to remember some corresponding feeling which he may have experienced in real life. For example, if the emotion to be expressed is fear, and the student has at some time been frightened at the sight of a snake, then by recalling to memory his experience with the snake his memory of that incident "affects" and directs his emotion of fear to be expressed in the scene. This method of study is practiced in some of the Continental theatres.

When a rôle is distinguished wholly or in part by particular moods, the actor must be careful to make his playing consistent with the mood he carries. In *Hamlet*, the Prince delivers no speech which is not colored with his pervading mood of melancholy, however natural, or even gay, the same words might be in another's mouth. When a scene among several actors is governed by any special mood, they should all tinge their lines with that particular mood.

An actor found that his part was governed throughout by the mood of ill humor. Therefore, he needed only to be consistent in his grouchiness. If he said, "Good Morning," "How do you do?", or "Thank you," which are speeches polite enough in themselves, in this part they had to be spoken in a tone of ill humor; and this consistent ill humor was the keynote of the characterization.

Sometimes an entire play must be performed in a general mood which is shared by many of the characters. The actors must then grasp the pervading mood, for if they do not the effect may be spoiled.

The atmosphere created by the actor is most important. It serves as the background upon which the many colors of the tapestry are woven. For example, there was the spirited mood of youth in *Romeo and Juliet* as played by Jane Cowl's company, and the mood of impending doom in the Actors' Theatre production of *The Wild Duck*.

Milne's comedy, *Mr. Pim Passes By*, is styled a tragi-comedy. Mrs. Marsden receives the false news that her first husband is still alive. The author's treatment makes this a situation for comedy. The Marsdens, then, had to show a mood of despair, but had to give it a comic aspect in order that the effect should have the touch of light comedy required. In a performance of this play, the actors grasped the tragic aspect, but in the playing were unable to offer the tincture of comedy required. They thus played this bubbling comedy with slight suggestion of its real nature, for they were too serious in many scenes.

It is a good practice for the actor, just before he enters upon a scene, to settle upon himself the mood which he shall carry on with him. Failure to do this beforehand, especially if the mood must be a highly emotional one, often leaves him unprepared for several lines of the scene. He gets into the mood later only through the force of the lines themselves. While waiting outside for his cue he can think of what his mood is to be, whether of joy, sadness, or any other emotion, and thus he can be fully pervaded with it when he enters. One old actor used to act snatches of his part in his dressing room while dressing; and it was said that Sarah Bernhardt used to arrive at the theatre a couple of hours before the performance and would speak to no one until the play was over. This was that she might thoroughly saturate herself with the spirit of the part she was to play.

Some parts have no consistent mood in any scene; the

moods change quickly from one speech to another and express varying emotions throughout. The actor then determines the moods and emotions which belong to the separate scenes or lines. There may be joy in one line, sadness in another, or sympathy in a third. The actor must interpret from the line the mood or emotion it should express. He must also, of course, select the right reading in order to bring out the proper sense.

He should thoroughly understand the meaning of what he says, even though it be on a subject of which he has had no previous knowledge. A story is told of William Terriss, leading man with the late Henry Irving. At rehearsal the actor spoke a long emotional speech with apparently good effect. Mr. Irving said, "Very good, William, but do you know what it means?" Mr. Terriss answered, "Lord bless you, Governor, no, I had trouble enough to learn it." After the meaning was explained to Mr. Terriss, he must have spoken the lines with surer effect. He relied too much upon his inspiration without intellectual understanding, although in this case, by chance, he rendered the lines with good effect.

A very essential feature during the study of a part is for the actor to form a correct mental vision of his part from which he can reproduce his actual performance. This vision must include the principles we have already mentioned; with the aid of rehearsals, the actor adds the mechanical business of the part to that vision. It is said that an actor never produces a perfect similitude of the vision he has formed; still, the more fixed the vision in his mind, the closer he can come to its realization in actual performance. It is well to try to visualize some famous actor in the rôle one is studying and to try to act it as *he* would. In all cases it is of value to study the technical methods of the best artists, just as students of painting study the great masters.

Rehearsals of a play have one essential purpose, which is for the actors to obtain and fix in their minds a vision of their relationships one to another. Except for this requirement, rehearsals would not be necessary. A performer who is to deliver a dramatic selection alone may rehearse it by himself. If he chooses only to *think* it to himself, with every word, every emphasis, and every action carefully thought out and visualized, he can deliver it without mistake, even though he has not spoken a word aloud beforehand.

During his study the actor should think out his technique, always forming a mental picture of himself in the act of expressing the emotions and performing the mechanical business of his conception. This vision should contain every aspect of his performance, physical, mental, and emotional. When he goes to rehearsal he may have to make many physical adjustments and changes on account of changes in his relationships to the other characters. Sooner or later the business in the main becomes "set," and the actor rehearses until his performance has the appearance of spontaneity. He should, of course, be thoroughly familiar with his lines. Without this sureness the spontaneity which is so necessary cannot be acquired. Because they lack this sureness, stock companies, who have for the most part only a week for preparing a play, give performances that lack spontaneity, being jerky and uneven.

When an actor has only a short time in which to prepare himself, he must largely subordinate the intellectual process of study to that of committing the lines to memory, since, at all costs, the latter must be done. In such a case, at his first performance he is under a tension for lines, and much of the intellectual structure he may have built for the interpretation of his character, if any at all, is cast aside. On this score, much can be said in favor of the "souffleur" in European theatres, who sits under a prompter's box. This is a small hood at the footlights from which the lines of the play are given to the actor just ahead of his speech. It relieves his tension in thinking for lines and thus allows him greater freedom for the spontaneous expression of his performance.

The actor, then, must be careful that his performance gives the delineation of a character and not merely the reading of lines. Failure to follow this principle is seen in many dramatic acts in vaudeville, though the actors themselves are not so much to blame as the peculiar conditions which render such failure necessary.

The following principle is a very important one and should be given much attention. This may be called "The Elimination of the Non-Essential." It has been hinted at in the chapter on Gesture, but needs further discussion.

The art of the cartoonist suggests rather than gives a correct illustration of life. The painter is more likely, through a wealth of detail, to represent a scene much as it catches the eye; but the cartoonist is satisfied to present only so much as will carry out his idea. For example, if he shows a scene in a room it is sufficient to draw a vertical line or two and a few lateral lines to represent corners and baseboards, with perhaps a picture for suggestive effect. The story told by the cartoon has no relation to the walls;

these are merely suggested for its setting. In this way irrelevant embellishment, which is not essential to bringing out the idea, has been omitted and the idea has greater emphasis. Set over against this principle is that of embellishment. This is a governing principle in the paintings of certain artists, notably Meissonier, Gérôme, and others like them, whose work is distinguished by elaborate detail.

The same principle of eliminating the non-essential should be true in the delineation of a character. In studying his rôle the actor should discriminate between that which is essential to the presentation of his ideas, and that which is redundant and unnecessary. An artist often uses as few strokes as possible to outline a figure, and the actor should use as few "strokes" as need be to outline his. Eliminating all gesture that does not have a meaning and a value we have already mentioned; and in Chapter I, violations of repose, such as useless movements of the head, feet, and hands, were also spoken of. All of these physical actions, since they have no relation to the characterization, are non-essential and should be eliminated.

Eliminating the non-essential refers mostly to pure interpretation of what one finds in the lines. On the other hand, the principle of embellishment is distinctly creative. Both these principles must be observed at the same time. Although the actor seeks to embellish his performance as much as possible with business, gestures, and various other elaborations, he must still be careful that what he does has value and is in keeping with the character. Upon examining his performance, he may find that he should eliminate many non-essentials from the creation he has made.

THE STUDY OF A CHARACTER

After playing a part for a number of months, an actor found that by introducing a piece of new business he secured a substantial laugh. The business was quite in keeping with the character and was therefore a worthwhile embellishment. In an endeavor to embellish their characters as much as possible, actors often use the creative principle too much, and put in business which is out of keeping and which distorts the character from truth. Comedians who do this verge from pure comedy into burlesque. We have a traditional case in that of the gravedigger in *Hamlet* who, to get a laugh, took off seven vests.

An art lover who visits the picture galleries of the Metropolitan Museum in New York may notice especially the paintings of Rembrandt, Van Dyke, Franz Hals, Gainsborough, and others of the more famous coterie. He will be struck with the fact that though the separate collections have a style distinct from one another, the individual paintings in each collection have a uniform personality. This personality enables a connoisseur to distinguish the authorship of a painting even when the painter's name is not upon it, because the painter's own personality shows through his work.

The actor should preserve his own identity in all his parts, and when the demands of a part require an individuality foreign to the actor's own, he should not attempt the part. Actors who follow another in a rôle, and are required to play it with all the manner and method of their predecessor, although these may be totally foreign to their own style, lose their own individuality thereby and also their effectiveness.

Stanislavsky, the director of the Moscow Art Theatre Company, said he never allowed an actor to change his voice for a part. He believed that if the actor did so he was thereby hampered in his effort to be convincing. The actor may, however, change the manner of using his voice. For example, Rip Van Winkle, after twenty years' sleep, uses a thin, weak voice, but the actor should preserve the individuality of his own vocal organ. He should also express whatever characterization he uses through the medium of his own personality, and attempt to assume no other.

Refinement and culture are an asset in all art. The selection of a really uncouth actor for an uncouth part is often a mistake. Such a practice is prevalent today, but has not always been considered necessary. Art is cultural, and a personality of culture shining through a part, no matter of how rough or uncouth an aspect, refines the performance, and the actor gains credit for a greater degree of art.

Finally, in his study of a character, the actor should maintain an ideal of integrity and conscientious purpose, and not descend to cheap methods and tricks, which will appeal only to the unintelligent. Such a practice would also be untrue to life, and would only travesty the ideal which true art requires.

EXERCISES

1. In studying a character, which of the three elements of acting is employed?
2. What would you expect to do first in order to gain a conception of your character?
3. What is the difference between interpretation and creation in the performance of a part?
4. Mention one or two ways in which an insignificant part can be given some effect.

5. What is the pervading mood of Hamlet?
6. How may one be consistent in mood?
7. Why do actors rehearse together?
8. What is The Elimination of the Non-Essential?
9. What is Embellishment?

CHAPTER XVIII

ACTION AND DISTRACTION

In this chapter something will be said of action in the respect in which it may present distraction. In the preceding chapter the principles of Embellishment and Eliminating the Non-Essential were described and contrasted so far as they applied to an actor's individual performance, but were not considered in relation to the play itself. In the present discussion these principles will be contrasted in their relation to the performance as a whole.

A young actor once spent several hours in a private rehearsal, with himself as actor and director, working out an elaborate characterization and practicing many gestures, vocal effects, and various other business, for an eccentric part which he was to play. He went to the rehearsal the next day prepared with his conception and well rehearsed in all the business of his action. The rehearsal demonstrated that man is a social being who does not live alone; he is governed in a large measure by his environment, and must regulate his own actions by his relation to other people. The actor found that much of the business with which he had hoped to embellish his performance had to be eliminated because it would have interfered with the business of the other actors. Had he been allowed to "keep in" all of the action and business he had invented, it would have become distraction from the work of the others. A great deal of it, also, would have been distraction from his own performance. Action introduced into a part to embellish an individual's performance must be so governed that it does not distract the attention from some important emphasis in the actor's own lines, and also that it does not distract attention from the work of the other characters. The director should see that both these principles are observed.

The actor must distinguish, then, between action which may be introduced along the line of embellishment, and that which may hamper his best effects by being perverted into distraction.

Many of our leading actors have an inspirational or temperamental sense which enables them to elaborate their performances with a richness of personal action. This lends color and variety to their work. A poor actor is often criticized as being "a stick." This means that he is stiff and unpliable. If the actor lacks a loose, free, and easy manner in his postures, and does not introduce any of the gestures, movements, and other expressions of action which are natural in real life, this criticism can justly be applied to him.

Mannerisms, such as shifting on the feet and moving the head while speaking, which have been mentioned previously, are personal actions, but cannot be considered embellishments. They succeed only in being serious distractions. In fact, mannerisms of all kinds must be so considered. On the other hand, any action which tends to render the words more effective or the portrayal more colorful, and is true to character, is an embellishment up to that point where it may become a distraction from the actor's own work or that of his fellow actors.

A featured actress in a New York production indulged in these little embellishments in action of which we speak.

In her case, her effort to color her performance with personal action produced distinct mannerism. This assumed two forms. She played her entire part, it seemed, with her handkerchief crumpled into a ball in her hand. Much of the time she would look down at the handkerchief, unfold it, and again crumple it up into a ball. When not thus engaged she was busy with the other mannerism. Her hair seemed to have a habit of getting down into her mouth, and whenever she desired to deliver a satirical line with special effect she picked the hair, real or imaginary, out of the corner of her mouth. These actions were the result of her effort to appear loose and at ease, but were so constant throughout her performance that they greatly detracted from a true effect, and were entirely false.

A person may sit at a table smoking a cigar. As he talks to another across the table he may occasionally fleck the ash from his cigar into an ash tray. This lends color and naturalness to his speech, and not only suggests freedom and ease, but is also quite true to life. On the other hand, if something dramatic or pointed were said by himself or another character, such an action would become distraction by diverting attention from the words. The subject of Eliminating Action, discussed in the previous chapter, applies to this phase of the principle.

Again, a person talking to another may embellish his performance, when the situation permits, by flecking some imaginary dust off the other's coat lapel. A moment later he may pat the other on the shoulder to emphasize his words, or may slap him on the back in a spirit of good humor. A young girl, in attempting to wheedle her father into granting some request, may take hold of his coat lapels, arrange his tie, pat him on the cheek, fumble with his watch chain, or do any other action which will relieve stiffness and present the illusion of an easy familiarity. Still again, a person in a revery may drum with his fingers on the table, or, while speaking, may lean forward in his chair and make imaginary figures on the ground with his cane. A parasol in the hands of a lady is an expressive implement in certain situations of embarrassment with which to draw figures in the sand. All of these colorful actions are of value in the principle of embellishment, if done at times when they do not result in distraction by taking emphasis away from words which may be more important. A common rule in regard to them may be that they can always be done with perfect safety during one's *own* speeches; but when done during the speeches of other characters they are dangerous.

Feet are very noticeable on the stage. When an actor sits on a table, he will often swing his feet while delivering his lines. This action is very apparent, and if it is done in serious dramatic moments, the action ceases to be correct and becomes a distraction.

Shakespearean, and classic drama in general, is direct, more or less declamatory, and recitative. There is much less occasion in this drama for the various colorings in performance which we are discussing. These plays make use of classic and graceful pose to a large extent. Their essential feature is the appeal they make to the eye through grace in gesture and movement, and a more rigid adherence to fixed technique in action and posture. Some of the gesture that is characteristic, and therefore permissible, in modern plays would appear grotesque if the actors were dressed in costume. For instance, it would look out of place if a character, dressed in a dignified Elizabethan court costume, sat upon a table and swung his legs. Even if he leaned forward in a chair with both elbows on his knees, an action so familiar in life today, it would violate the grace which that kind of costume suggests. Even the walk of modern life is not completely suited to these plays. In trousers a man walks largely from the knees, while in tights, or fleshings, as they are called, this modern walk is not appropriate, and the classic actor must learn to walk mostly from the hips. This practice was often carried to extremes by bombastic actors of a former day, and developed into an extravagant stride.

It may be appropriate to mention here that when the actor kneels upon one knee to another—business which is so often done in classic costume plays—he should leave his body open to the view of the audience by kneeling upon the *down stage* knee, if he is facing either to the right or the left.

A star had a scene in the last act of a play, in which he bade good-bye forever to the woman he loved. He escorted her to a door, and after a few words of farewell she made her exit through it. The actor then closed the door and leaned against it with his hand on the knob. He had no line, but showed in his face the grief he was supposed to feel at parting. There was a distraction in this business. The expression of grief on his face was the focal point of interest, and the audience needed to give that their whole attention. While he leaned against the door, the fingers of the hand that held the door knob kept closing and unclosing on it, thus distracting the attention of the audience from the focal point, which should have been the actor's face, and causing attention to centre on this physical action, which played a minor part in expressing the emotion. Here again, eliminating all action after the pose was made would have centred attention upon the emotion expressed in the face.

Let us cite an example or two in which the action of one character may distract attention from another. In a stock company, where the direction was not very exact in respect to the relative positions of the actors and they were permitted within limitations to select certain positions at will, one of the characters sat at the side of the stage and sang a song to the accompaniment of a guitar. As mentioned in Chapter II, the centre of the stage is that focal point toward which the eyes of an audience most readily travel. Now this "specialty" naturally claimed the centre of interest, but while it was going on, another actor took up his position at the stage centre and stood looking out toward the audience. In this position, prominent as it was in comparison with that of the performer at the side, he became a serious distraction from the other, who should have gained the full attention of the audience. A cat walking on to the stage could not have distracted the audience's attention more effectively.

One more example will suffice to illustrate this point. In Mary Roberts Rinehart's *The Breaking Point*, an amnesia victim has just been brought to his proper senses. He sits crouched in a chair beside a desk in a doctor's office. The doctor stands off at one side. A woman stands behind the desk with her back to the audience. This position puts her "out of the picture." All the attention of the audience is centred on the man in the chair, while he tries to recall the past and readjust the events upon which up to that time his memory has been a blank. The scene is dramatic, and the man in the chair should be the only active element in it. The actress who played the woman had a restless temperament and unconsciously made little movements of her body. She raised her hands to her hair or shifted her position; this disturbed a fixed repose which she should have assumed while she was out of the picture, and distracted attention from the man in the chair, who should have been for the time being the focal point.

It is a fixed rule in the theatre that an actor should not walk "on another actor's lines." This expression means, while another character is speaking. Slight exceptions can be made to this rule, as in the case of "moving backgrounds," treated elsewhere in this book. The student should always remember, however, that the principles outlined in this study of acting technique are in general fundamental ones. They should be observed when possible except where exceptions to the rule may be allowed.

All action belongs logically to the person who performs it. Observing the fundamental principle, then, the actor should not perform definite action during the lines of another character. Doing so seriously distracts attention from the lines of the speaker. This is often done in real life, of course, as when a person leaves a room while another is addressing those present. Even in real life this may distract attention. As was said in a previous chapter, the make-believe of the theatre should not always be like real life.

All of the principles defined in this section are for the production of a perfect ensemble effect, with that of the whole, and not of any one part, given first consideration.

ACTION AND DISTRACTION

EXERCISES

1. When may action become distraction.
2. Mention some actions which may become distractions.
3. What is "embellishment"? Mention a few actions in embellishment.
4. Mention some actions not appropriate to classic drama.

CHAPTER XIX

COÖPERATION

The principle of Coöperation, like that of Light and Shade, is one of the important comprehensive principles in the technique of acting which embraces many of the others. Coöperation is just what the term implies; there is no more important element in the whole field of dramatic art.

The recently developed science of Sociology is "an attempt to account for the origin, growth, structure, and activities of society by the operation of physical, vital, and psychical causes working together in a process of evolution." Society is "any group of sentient beings who are more or less alike, who recognize more or less clearly that fact, and who have recognized common interests in their social relationships." These definitions show that man is a social being who enjoys intercommunication with, and assistance from, his neighbors in order to live with his fullest expression. The life of the hermit is not natural, for such a man attempts to individualize his existence. The social life is a coöperative life. The reflection of real life, as seen on the stage, must carry with it the coöperative principle if it is to be true to life at all.

Coöperation in the theatre, as implied in the name, does not relate to individual performances, but to ensemble effects, considering the performance as a whole. In stock companies a term is employed which has much of the sense of coöperation. This term is "teamwork."

COÖPERATION

It is coöperation up to a certain point; but while coöperation is based purely on scientific technique, the "teamwork" of a stock company refers to that familiarity of the actors one with another through constant association, which makes them acquainted with individual mannerisms, and helps them to smooth out the hitches that result from uncertainty in lines and business. The actors assist one another in this way to make the play go smoothly.

In Dumas' romantic drama, *The Three Musketeers*, the well-known line, "One for all and all for one," brings down the curtain on one of the acts. In this speech the musketeers pledge themselves to mutual assistance. This expression has the sense of coöperation perfectly applied. Individualism implies a sense opposite to that of coöperation. It is a matter for regret that there are far too many individualists on the stage. The individualist would have had no place in the fraternity of the three musketeers, or if he had, the motto in his own mind might have read, "All for one and that one for himself."

It may be asked, What is the real purpose of the theatre? The answer, at first thought, is simple, and may be stated, To give an entertainment. But entertainment can be good or bad, so analysis of the question must be made in order to illuminate the answer. Since man does not live and act alone, for life is coöperative, then in the imitation life of the theatre he should coöperate in like manner.

The "star system," so called, is that in which a star player appears in a play surrounded by a "supporting" cast. The system does not always have an injurious effect upon the principle of coöperation, but in many cases the star system does abuse this principle. Many stars are individualists in the strictest sense, and subordinate all the effects of a play to their own prominence and advantage. They adjust the situations to serve their own personal effects at the expense of other effects which might arise out of similar situations in real life. They cut lines and business of subordinate characters, if these are found to offer opportunity to the actors playing them, and may even rearrange the play, usually to its detriment, in order to give themselves relative prominence. Any star who wrote his own play might make the dialogue unbalanced by writing no lines of any great effect for the other characters and by giving all the comedy "points," and all values in situation, to himself. Besides, he might so arrange all positions and general stage business that he always occupied the centre of attention. In this case the "all" would be assisting the "one," and the one would be assisting only himself. In such a play there would be distinct operation of his company by the star, but no coöperation with them. A play so written could never endure as a classic in dramatic literature. The object of coöperation, then, is to produce a finished product in which, as in an Italian mosaic, no one piece stands out alone, but in which each is fitted to another to present a perfect whole.

This principle tends to disparage the star system. It need not be antagonistic to it, however, unless the star system causes one-sided performances such as have been described above. The public goes to the theatre for one purpose—to be entertained. The value of any actor to a company, whether he be the star or one of the supernumeraries, lies in the percentage of efficiency which he brings to the performance as a whole. The star, who is often a recognized artist, brings a high percentage of individual merit. His value, however, lies not so much in that merit alone as in the percentage of efficiency which he can contribute to the complete effect of the play. After all, "the play's the thing," and the public goes to see plays more than players.

"All star casts" often give poor performances of plays, while ordinary actors can give good ones. Stars seem to have the quality of individualism more strongly marked than they do the coöperative principle. Coöperation is active and reactive. To be active is to be positive; to be reactive is to be negative. When a star has the habit of the active-positive in his performance while the other actors are forced to be only reactive and negative, he is not very comfortable in a company in which many others have his own habit. The positive pole of the magnet requires the negative pole in order to express its force. Stars assembled in an all star cast are often a collection of positive poles without any negative pole balance. Each tries to gain individualistic prominence, does not properly coöperate, and the performance, as a result, is poor.

A featured player appeared in a new production. An actor who had rather unusual critical insight sat in the audience on the first night. The next day a friend asked him his opinion of the performance and he said, "It is a good play, but Mr. Blank walked right away from it." The player was an excellent artist but a gross individualist. He had sought his own personal success at any cost. Instead of coöperating with his associates in an effort to make the play successful, he had aimed only at personal success for himself. The newspapers no doubt accorded it to him, but in a few weeks the play was withdrawn, a failure. In another case a comedian was seen to ruin the success of a stock company in a single season by the intensive use of the individualistic method.

Again, a star was playing a summer stock engagement in a western city. There was a comedian in the company who seldom knew his lines, and in one of the plays this comedian had a long and important part. The exact lines of the author did not greatly concern him, for if he could not remember them he substituted his own. In one act he played an important scene with the star. It happened on the first night that any lines he might have learned deserted him, but he continued to talk nevertheless. The star, who received no cues, was taken at a great disadvantage, was unable to speak, and the comedian, in a rapid fire of his own words, which contained, however, some semblance of the idea, finally made his exit and received a generous round of applause. The audience thought the comedian had done some fine acting, but the star's work was completely spoiled, and the scene, as a collective dramatic performance, was ruined.

Another incident may be cited in contrast to this, which operated to conserve the principle. A fine light comedian, whose presence in a cast always helped the play to gain success, played a long run in a New York production. The same critical observer mentioned above saw the play and considered it an excellent one. Later, he saw the piece played by a stock company. This time he was surprised to discover what he thought were serious flaws in its construction. He then realized that these flaws were noticeable only because the leading rôle was played by an actor of only average ability. The actor in New York had been able to gloss over these faults with his excellent technique and to act his part in such a way as to conceal the flaws in the play completely. He had devoted himself to the playing of the whole play in so far as it lay in his power, and had subordinated the individualistic principle of playing himself. The truly coöperative actor not only plays his own part but assists all his fellow actors to play theirs.

In the chapter on Tempo and Rhythm, the actress who did not possess a rhythmic sense, and thus disturbed the even flow of the performance, showed also a violation of the principle of coöperation. Methods in acting may be either constructive or destructive. Individualism tends to produce destructive results, but the coöperative principle is entirely constructive.

Perhaps the finest dramatic company America has ever had was that managed and directed by Augustin Daly. There was no star in this company, and its whole purpose was to present a play with an evenly balanced and coöperative performance, in which each actor contributed to the effect of the whole. Mr. Daly knew that the secret of success in the theatre lay in perfect coöperation. As a result, the fame of his company spread throughout the country, and the members gained enhanced reputations through their association with this fine company.

Let us turn from generalization on this principle to technical analysis. Suppose two persons are sitting together in conversation. While one speaks the other listens. Here we have the principle of attention; it is an integral element of coöperation. The person who speaks is active and positive, while the one who listens is passive and receptive. Thoughts can be conveyed without words and transmitted by means of gesture, facial expression, and various movements of the body. While one character is speaking the other needs to show that he is hearing what is being said. He may do this in various ways. The speaker may say, "You remember when we met Nelson today? Well, you know what I said to him?" and so on. The listener may have no words during this account, but still may reply to the questions. He naturally nods his head in affirmative answer, and the speaker continues. A few moments later the speaker may make some humorous remark, and without words, the listener may smile, or laugh silently. We often see this passage of ideas actively and vocally expressed, and reactively and silently received in real life. Here, again, we have the principle of action and reaction, which is another integral element of co-operation. Acting without adherence to this principle is usually not true to life, yet the individualist in the theatre tends to ignore it altogether! A dramatic critic of the eighteenth century records that Sarah Siddons' reaction as Lady Macbeth to the acting of her brother, John Kemble, as Macbeth, was so wonderful that his gaze was continually fixed upon her face.

Augustus Thomas was once trying out a new play with a stock company in San Francisco. Two men were having a scene together. At a point in the scene one of them delivered a certain line. The playwright said to the other, "Let that line register upon you." The actor answered, "What do you mean, sir?" Mr. Thomas replied, "Well, you know that when you press a key upon a cash register a bell rings and the drawer opens. The machine "registers" the amount of the purchase. In other words, it responds to what has been done. Let us see by some action or expression on your part that the remark has registered upon your mind." The actor then understood the idea.

COÖPERATION

It is sometimes more difficult to react to a speech than to deliver one; much attention therefore should be given to the important matter of reaction.

No better example of coöperative reaction can be found than in the old melodramas. As stated previously, these usually contained a stereotyped villain. The actor who played the villain was therefore generally sure of his requirements. The author often made this character a butt for the witty or caustic remarks of other characters, for he knew this would delight the audience and they would respond with laughter or applause. The comedy Irishwoman called him a "dirty spalpeen"; the heroine told him he would some day be brought to justice; or the hero declared that he was an unmitigated scoundrel. In the face of these remarks in real life no one could be unmoved. The actor-villain who knew his business reacted in the proper manner to the lines. He might give a quick scowl of resentment, do some action which said, "Foiled," louder than words, and in general would react in a manner to show that the remark had told upon him. The audience gave their response to the speaker of the line, but it was the villain who had really created it. This fact was often tested, and it was found that if the villain failed to react there was often no response from the audience.

The monologist in vaudeville is essentially an individualist. He often writes much of his own material, and being the only actor, he is himself the whole entertainment in his act. In this work he has no experience in coöperative reaction, and is sometimes entirely ignorant of the principle. If he afterwards enters the "legitimate" field, where the principle is in operation, he is often found to be difficult to play with, for he has never been bound by the limitations naturally set by collective and coöperative art.

The comedy team in vaudeville must employ coöperative methods. Such a team usually consists of two men who do a talking act. In the English "music halls" such entertainment is called "patter." One of these two, often ridiculously dressed, is the comedian, and the other, generally in normal dress, is the "straight" man. For its motif the act usually has the straight man giving rapid accounts of certain matters, while the comedian interrupts, misunderstands, or interjects comedy lines. The comedian gets most of the laughs, but does so mostly through the straight man's reaction to what he says. The straight man may grow angry or confused at the comedian's jokes, but at all times maintains a rapid tempo, which is necessary in order to carry over the gags of the comedian. For this reason a good straight man is most necessary, and coöperation in this kind of act must be practiced in its fullest sense.

The "straight" man does what is called "feeding." It would be well if more actors, when playing scenes with others, would react in the "feeding" manner. This sort of reaction helps the other actor to get his points over, and contains much compensation in that, since it is true to life, it helps the feeder to play his own part in a better way.

Let us revert to the incident mentioned in Chapter II of the two young men who were playing with a mechanical dancing doll. On the entrance of the minister, the confusion of the young man who was the more involved, the shocked expression of the minister, and the attitude of the friend, all contributed to making the comedy situation go. Where more than one person is concerned in registering any comedy point, the coöperative principle must, of course, be employed.

Proper reaction gives impulse to the person who has set it in motion. Suppose two persons are having a scene together. One is engaged in making some explanation to the other, who at times expresses indignation, tries to interrupt, and is greatly worked up by the person's statements. He indicates his moods without words, for he may have no lines during this account. The person may say, "Don't you see, that was how it happened." Here the other may start to speak, but the character, raising his hand, may say, "Now wait a moment and I will explain. Your wife—" The other again makes a sign of protest and the first says, "Well, I thought it was your wife," and so on. Should the second person remain unmoved during the speech, the speaker would have no impulse with which to deliver his line, "Now wait a moment," and so forth. Again, a lawyer says to a lady, who is bringing suit for breach of promise, "He shall marry you as a punishment." The lady gives an indignant start, which imparts to the lawyer the impulse to say, "No, no, I don't mean that." In this way proper reaction from another character, when that reaction is logically placed, gives stimulus to the next line which is to be spoken.

In a play a country doctor is asked his business and announces proudly, "I am a physician, sir." The other says contemptuously, "Veterinary?" The reaction of the doctor, who gives the other an indignant look on this question, produces a laugh; without this reaction the point would lose most of its effect.

In *Othello*, during the jealousy scene, when Iago pours

into the Moor's ear jealous suspicions of his wife and Cassio, Othello has many opportunities to react without words to Iago's insinuations. After his suspicions are thoroughly aroused, his appetite is whetted to hear Iago's false report, and Iago says,

> Therefore as I am bound,
> Receive it from me.
>> (*Othello makes an eager start, which gives Iago an impulse to say:*)
>> I speak not yet of proof.
> Look to your wife; observe her well with Cassio:
>> (*There is an aspirated exclamation here from Othello.*)
>> (*A few lines later:*)
> She did deceive her father marrying you.
>> (*Othello here looks front in questioning surprise.*)
>> (*A moment later:*)
> She that so young could give out such a seeming
> To seel her father's eyes up close as oak,
> He thought 'twas witchcraft;
>> (*Here Othello feels convinced of his wife's treachery and utters a groan.*)
>> But I'm much to blame;
> I humbly do beseech you of your pardon
> For too much loving you.
>> (*A few lines later:*)
> I hope you will consider what is spoke
> Comes from my love.
>> (*Another groan from Othello.*)
>> But I do see you're moved.
>> (*Still later:*)
>> Cassio's my worthy friend.
>> (*Othello groans, "Ah!"*)
> My lord, I see you're moved.

[280]

COÖPERATION

In this scene, the moods of Othello, as expressed in his interpolated groans or movements, dovetail perfectly with the insinuations of Iago, and in each instance give Iago impulse and greater power of expression for his next lines. In such coöperation one actor can aid another to increase the spirit of his work. When such coöperative treatment is not given, it is common to hear an actor say, "He does not give me anything." The actor misses the impulse which proper reaction would impart to his own lines.

Besides the principles of attention and reaction, coöperation contains another, which can be described as simultaneous action. This means that actors must work together in unity and concord, like a team of horses drawing a load up a hill. Coöperation is necessary in most, if not all, comedy love scenes, as well as in comedy generally. An example follows from the rural comedy, *Mrs. Wiggs of the Cabbage Patch*, in which the three integral elements of coöperation thus far described are found. Mr. Hiram Stubbins is an idle and sottish village character who wishes to obtain a cook and housekeeper, and has advertised in a matrimonial journal for a wife. Miss Hazy, a forlorn and ugly old maid, has answered the advertisement. Mr. Stubbins comes on dressed for the wedding, meets Miss Hazy, and an eccentric love scene takes place. After some dialogue between them Stubbins hears the wedding march being played in another room. Miss Hazy remarks that the family are practicing for the ceremony.

STUBBINS: We might as well practice, too. (*They are sitting side by side, and he places his arm about her waist. She rises in confusion and moves away a step. The force of her action throws Stubbins sideways on to her chair.*

He recovers himself, looks about to see if they are still alone, moves his chair close to where she is now standing, and takes her on his knee. Up to this point, the action is not particularly coöperative, being done largely by Stubbins alone. Miss Hazy, beyond the action of rising, merely stands bashfully with her eyes cast down. As she is drawn on to Stubbins' knee, however, she turns her face to him, and with a grimace he turns his face away. She wears a long wedding veil. He draws it down over her face to conceal her ugliness, and then trots her on his knee to the sound of the music. Again looking about to be sure they are alone he starts to kiss her, and rolls up the long veil to do so. As he sees her face he again turns away in comic disgust, but finally turns and kisses her with his eyes closed. They both then lay their heads together, sigh, and "strike" a picture of comic bliss.)

MISS HAZY (*without moving*): Hiram.

STUBBINS (*in the same position*): Huh?

MISS HAZY (*still not moving*): Am I the only girl you ever kissed?

STUBBINS: Well, not exactly. (*Miss Hazy gives him a quick look.*) But I kin conscientiously say you're the last. (*At that they repeat the business of putting their heads together, the sighs, and the blissful looks. At the end of the scene they make their exit dancing to the time of the music, which is still playing.*)

Perfect coöperation occurs in several places in this scene. As Stubbins places his arm about Miss Hazy's waist, she must rise at just the right time for his comedy effect of falling on her chair. As she is drawn on to his knee, she must immediately turn her face close to his so that he may make his grimace at her ugliness. After the kiss, the business of putting the heads together and the

[282]

sighs must be done simultaneously and in unison. When Hiram is asked if she is the first girl he ever kissed and says, "Well, not exactly," her look at him must be immediate, and is of value in giving him a better impulse to look back at her with his line, "But I kin conscientiously say you're the last." Finally, the dance on the exit must be practiced so as to be in step and in time to the music.

Coöperation should now be discussed along a broader line. Hitherto, we have defined it only in respect to personal contacts in separate scenes. Coöperation also involves a broader set of relationships, which often includes all the persons in a play. A unique and interesting model of a German village was exhibited a few years ago in a metropolitan department store. The streets and shops were shown with the various industries going on. Mannikins were set in motion by means of concealed machinery, which caused them to perform the activities of real life. The baker was seen raking his loaves out of the oven, the butcher chopping his meat, the guests in the tavern drinking their beer. Here was a little drama of life shown with mannikins. The point in this example is that the activities in one house were in no way related to those in another, except through the machinery concealed beneath the whole. Although each integral part was independent in itself, yet the exhibition, as a whole, showed a concrete unity of action. There is an analogy between the workings of this mechanical exhibit and the principle of coöperation in the theatre, as we shall try to show.

The Moscow Art Theatre Company, mentioned in a previous chapter, came to New York in 1923. They were heralded as the greatest dramatic company in the world.

When they opened in New York City their performance in many respects gained great praise from the critics. Among other things, the critics noted the ensemble effects of this company and said they showed marked contrast to those of the native theatre. The critics attempted to find a reason for this; but probably the real one was a perfect coöperation, an outstanding feature in the acting of the Russian players. The company carried a large body of supernumeraries, and it was remarked that each individual among them performed his separate bit as if it were most important and he had been separately rehearsed in it. Bodies of supernumeraries in the average theatre are rehearsed, for the most part, collectively and en masse; but each individual in this "super" body seemed to have been specially placed like a unit in a mosaic.

There seems to be a tendency in American and English theatres toward focalization of interest. For example, a spot light is often trained from the gallery on to different parts of the stage in order to illuminate those parts and concentrate attention there, while the rest of the stage is in darkness. So, in drama, attention is directed to various positions where the central action of the story is being carried on, while it is diverted from other parts of the scene by the characters placing themselves out of the picture.

The Continental theatre employs the ensemble rather than the spotlight method. The ensemble method is in many respects like the three-ring circus. The eye must travel everywhere to take it all in. The spotlight method can be likened to a one-ring circus, in which the attention of the audience is demanded for only one thing at a time.

Let us see how the ensemble method operates. An

example will suffice from a performance by the Yiddish Art Theatre in New York. The play was a Russian piece called in English *The Inspector General.* In one drawing-room scene a dialogue was carried on between two of the important characters at the centre. On the left was a table, at which two old men sat playing cards. At the back on a sofa were a young man and a woman in animated conversation, while at the right stood two other characters engaged, it seemed, in a heated argument in dumb show. In our American theatre the dialogue would have claimed the centre of interest and all other parts of the stage picture would have been subordinated to it. In this transplanted, but nevertheless Continental, theatre, the action at the sides and back might be made as prominent as the actors desired. After all, this was true to life. The student may protest, and rightly, that such action violates some of the principles which have been emphasized in these chapters, such as the law of attention and the need of avoiding distraction. The answer is that each method is perhaps better suited to the audiences of the countries in which it is used. Some persons enjoy a three-ring better than a one-ring circus, though each has its reason for being.

The ensemble method of dramatic art often presents a more colorful and variegated picture than the focalized method of our own theatre. These different methods can be seen, as well, in painting and photography. By a process of focus, the photographer throws his central figure into bold relief, and some painters subordinate their background to the interest of their principal subject. On the other hand, the paintings of Meissonier show an ensemble effect, in which he gives the most unimportant of his figures a wealth of detail. Though the Moscow Art Players followed the method of ensemble effect, they no doubt discriminated as to when the central ideas needed to be projected without distraction.

Anything that might happen in real life, if it were put upon the stage, might not be true art. The coöperative ensemble effect in acting can be carried to extremes. A critic was discussing these Russian players. Speaking of their tendency toward the embellishment of detail, and their development of what may be termed "side line action," he gave the following example; it is an extreme case, but may serve to illustrate the idea: The Russians are perhaps presenting *Hamlet*. While the prince is having his first soliloquy in Act 1, Scene II, in our productions he is alone. But the court has just left the scene. The Russians might consider it quite logical, in order to lend color and background to the scene, to bring back several of the courtiers, who might stroll across at the back, or pause and stand in a group in conversation. In their opinion, this would have an added advantage in that it would accentuate the loneliness of Hamlet, since the courtiers would pay no attention to him as they passed. Suppose, again, that during the Soliloquy on Death, while Hamlet mused at one side, the King entered and went to the throne to recover his sceptre which he had mislaid there, and without noticing Hamlet, made his exit. This, again, would accentuate the loneliness of Hamlet, and from this interpolation of business an embellishment would be accomplished. These features lie more in the province of directorship than in that of dramatic technique, but the two fields of work are closely related.

COÖPERATION

EXERCISES

1. Why do people in organized society coöperate with one another?
2. Why is the life of the hermit an unnatural life?
3. From what play does the line, "One for all and all for one," come? By what author?
4. In what way may the "star system" be a detriment to art?
5. Why do "all star" casts often give poor performances?
6. What is reaction?
7. Mention one way in which two actors can coöperate in a conversation.
8. What do you understand by "impulse" from another person during a dialogue? Give an example.
9. Explain what is meant by the "ensemble method" of production. The "spotlight" method.

CHAPTER XX

HAMLET'S ADVICE TO THE PLAYERS

William Shakespeare wrote this excellent advice over three hundred years ago. It embodies another proof of the greatness of his philosophy. He knew that if a performance in the theatre is to possess the requisite qualities for success, it must be governed by certain fixed laws. To judge from the contents of this advice, those laws were repeatedly transgressed in that day as in this. Actors have been fundamentally the same always, and we find the poet's advice just as necessary today as it was then. When we examine these lines closely, we cannot believe that bombastic methods of acting could have been greatly tolerated by the poet himself, even though much is supposed to have been allowed in his time which would not be accepted now.

Shakespeare must have understood many of the secrets of success in the theatre. Just what the real secrets are may be matter for dispute. Ideas vary, and perhaps no special laws can be laid down as rigid and infallible. Nevertheless, in writing this advice, Shakespeare probably came closer to expressing the secrets of success in many of their principles than other people do who try to explain them along different lines. In this place Shakespeare speaks more intimately to the actor and student than anywhere else in his dramas, and gives him no more valuable advice than in the following lines:

HAMLET'S ADVICE TO THE PLAYERS

HAMLET: Speak the speech, I pray you, as I pronounced it to you, trippingly on the tongue: but if you mouth it, as many of your players do, I had as lief the town crier spoke my lines. Nor do not saw the air too much with your hand, thus, but use all gently: for in the very torrent, tempest, and as I may say, the whirlwind of passion, you must acquire and beget a temperance that may give it smoothness. O, it offends me to the soul to hear a robustious, periwig-pated fellow tear a passion to tatters, to very rags, to split the ears of the groundlings, who for the most part are capable of noth· ing but inexplicable dumb shows and noise: I would have such a fellow whipped for o'erdoing Termagant: it out-herods Herod: pray you, avoid it.

FIRST PLAYER: I warrant your honor.

HAMLET: Be not too tame, neither, but let your own discretion be your tutor: suit the action to the word, the word to the action: with this special observance, that you o'erstep not the modesty of nature: for anything so overdone is from the purpose of playing, whose end, both at the first and now, was and is, to hold, as t'were, the mirror up to nature: to show virtue her own feature, scorn her own image, and the very age and body of the time his form and pressure. Now this overdone, or come tardy off, though it make the unskillful laugh, cannot but make the judicious grieve: the censure of the which one must in your allowance o'erweigh a whole theatre of others. O, there be players that I have seen play, and heard others praise, and that highly, not to speak it profanely, that, neither having the accent of Christians, nor the gait of Christian, pagan, nor man, have so strutted and bellowed that I have thought some of nature's journeymen had made men and not made them well, they imitated humanity so abominably.

FIRST PLAYER: I hope we have reformed that indifferently with us, sir.

HAMLET: O, reform it altogether. And let those that play your clowns speak no more than is set down for them: for there be of them that will themselves laugh, to set on some quantity of barren spectators to laugh too, though in the meantime some necessary portion of the play be then to be considered: That's villainous, and shows a most pitiful ambition in the fool that uses it. Go, make you ready.

This Advice to the Players expresses a fine understanding of the needs of the theatre in its effort to express pure art, and splendidly analyzes the violations of most important principles. Yet for three hundred and more years since it was written, thoughtless and selfish actors have disregarded it. Some of the shortcomings mentioned in this advice are the results of insufficient art, while others are distinctly due to wilful neglect or personal ego.

Let us examine the lines more closely and study their meaning. "Speak the speech, I pray you, as I pronounced it to you," may be taken to mean that Hamlet, having written a short scene which should illustrate the murder of his father by his uncle, wished the scene to be played, and the lines spoken, just as he had given it to the players. An author often finds that the actors are not speaking his lines as he has written them. He has spent much time in phrasing his sentences so as to bring out the finer shades of meaning. When lines are not spoken as written, they may injure the effect of the play; for any variation in rendition may result in a change in the ideas the author wishes to express. An actor had the exit line, "And now the Baronet wins," but said instead, "And now the Baronet's wine." He had read his part carelessly, and since an exit accompanied the line he probably thought the Baronet was going off to get a drink. An actor serves the good of the play by learning his lines exactly.

" . . . trippingly on the tongue: but if you mouth it as many of your players do. . . ." This, no doubt, refers to that virtue in acting which we know as good diction, and to its opposite, bad enunciation and utterance. Clear and distinct speech is a comfort to an audience, while bad elocution is a fault committed far too often on our stage. Distinct speech is not in itself a proof of fine acting, and poor diction is a fault of many excellent artists. Stars have sometimes hurt their own success by not allowing their audiences to hear all of what they say. The audience is entitled to what it pays to hear, and the best effect of a play is hampered when part of its story is impaired, due to vocal sounds being lost while in transit to the ear. Then Hamlet says, "I had as lief the town crier spoke my lines." He had in mind the town crier of his own day who used to go his rounds at all times of the day or night and cry his message or command, the words sometimes so distorted by frequent repetition as to be impossible perhaps to understand. Who can really distinguish the words of our own street hawkers? Heaven forbid that Shakespeare's actors should have so mutilated their speech as to sound like these! The modern actor should realize that as his duty is to be seen, to be heard, to be understood, so the audience's desire is to see, to hear, and to understand.

Then Shakespeare has Hamlet say, "do not saw the air too much with your hand, thus, but use all gently." He knew that many actors were guilty of extravagance in gesture; this was a natural accompaniment to their bombast. Using "all gently," was distinctly a reference to reserve force, which should be observed in action as well as in speech. Shakespeare knew that "in the very torrent, tempest and . . . whirlwind of passion," "smoothness," a necessary element of acting, can come only with the temperate use of action or speech, which holds much stored-up power.

"O, it offends me to the soul to hear a periwig-pated fellow tear a passion to tatters." The association of ideas in Shakespeare's mind between periwigged pates and ranting was quite natural. Any actor who is inartistic and careless in the adjustment of wigs and other make-up will be equally inartistic in his general performance. The poet was no doubt as great an enemy to an ill-fitting wig as the modern manager is. The skillful artist is never seen carelessly dressed for his part.

"Inexplicable dumb shows" are meaningless movements which result from extravagant and purposeless use of the hands and other parts of the body, and "noise" the inartistic declamation which results from allowing tone to get beyond control. When the expression of emotion ceases to withhold a proper amount of reserve force, it breaks the bounds of restraint and becomes mere noise, which lacks correct expression.

Shakespeare knew the actor could be "too tame" also, and thus go to the opposite extreme. This is under-acting and is probably the commonest fault of the beginner. When the actor gains confidence and experience he may overdo his work if he has no great artistic instinct which will impart moderation to it.

Suiting "the action to the word, the word to the action"

needs no further discussion, and "holding the mirror up to nature" is, or should be, the whole purpose of dramatic art. Many followers of the new schools of Impressionism, Expressionism, Futurism, and numerous other conceptions which are creeping into the theatre, will not agree entirely with this last general principle. The discussions in this book are concerned only with what seems true to everyday life.

There were actors in Shakespeare's time no doubt, as there are today, who looked upon his dramatic poetry as something foreign to nature and needing, therefore, to be treated in an unreal way. Hence they ranted, sawed the air with their hands, used a stage manner, and were altogether unnatural. We can imagine hearing Shakespeare say, "It is true that my characters speak in blank verse poetry, which is not the language of the street. In their speech they are poets, but in their actions they are everyday human beings like us all. I beseech you 'to this special observance,' that in playing them you o'erstep not the modesty of nature, but perform them with that naturalness which they deserve."

". . . though it make the unskillful laugh, it cannot but make the judicious grieve." An appeal to the appreciation of an "unskillful" audience is not as praiseworthy as an effort to please the tastes of the more cultured few. The cultured do not enjoy the antics of an uncultured actor in his appeal to "the groundlings," or, as we say now, "the gallery"; a dignified effort to reach the highest intelligence receives its just reward.

"And let those that play your clowns speak no more than is set down for them." In this sentence Shakespeare put his finger on one of the worst practices in the theatre of this or any other time. What it was called in Shakespeare's day we do not know, but today we condemn it under the name of "gagging." This practice has a place, it must be allowed, in certain forms of dramatic entertainment. Burlesque, vaudeville, and musical comedy, are often built up or improved with this practice when done by comedians who have the cleverness and wit to originate funny lines and business. The form of drama we call "legitimate," in contradistinction to those forms just mentioned, is only distorted, and its concrete unity injured, by this practice. Each time some thoughtless actor puts in a gag on the spur of the moment, seeking thereby to elaborate his performance and gain an added credit for himself, the rhythmic continuity which the author has laid down is for the moment interrupted, and at a time, perhaps, when "some necessary portion of the play (is) then to be considered."

An actor had an exit on which the audience usually gave him a round of applause. One night, as he had delivered his final line and was about to make his exit, another actor was struck with an idea for a laugh and spoke some line for that purpose. The audience was checked in their intention and withheld their applause in order to hear what was being said. The line did not get the laugh, and, besides, it "killed the hand."

Authors especially object to their plays being injured in this way. A comedian in a play had been introducing some gags into his part. The author went to the actor and said, "I want you to cut out those very bad gags you have been putting into your part. Some of my friends have seen the play and are blaming me for them."

Gagging usually betrays itself, for the lines, not being

rehearsed beforehand, are generally squeezed into places that are foreign to the continuity of the story. In most cases they break the flow of dialogue, often interrupt some actor in the act of speaking, and are sometimes delivered simultaneously with other speeches. In all cases they are foreign matter introduced into the dramatic substance and are usually recognized as such. When this is seen by the audience, they resent the presumption of the actor in elaborating upon the work of the author. The actor's business in the theatre is to work, and gagging is an effort on his part to play. When actors play in this manner they laugh with themselves and "set on some quantity of barren spectators," who do not recognize the falseness of the effort, "to laugh too." But "the judicious grieve" and their illusion is spoiled. Shakespeare never uttered truer words, than when he said gagging is "villainous and shows a most pitiful ambition in the fool that uses it."

EXERCISES

1. At what time did William Shakespeare live? In the reign of what monarch?
2. Study the Advice to the Players so that you understand the meaning of all its expressions. Consult Furness' Variorum for reference.
3. Name some faults committed by actors in respect to this advice.
4. What do you understand by "periwig-pated"? "inexplicable dumb shows"? "holding the mirror up to nature"?
5. Who were "groundlings" in Shakespeare's time?
6. Why were the comedians in Shakespeare's day often called "clowns"?
7. What is "gagging"? What do you think of it, and why?

CHAPTER XXI

MAKE–UP

It used often to be said that a good make-up was "half the battle." In the present day this statement is not heard so often. The art of make-up, as it was understood in a former generation, is not practiced today in the same degree. The theatre has begun to find the art of less use by reason of various new conditions which have taken the place of the old. In the motion pictures, however, make-up is called into greater use than elsewhere by reason of the far greater variety of situations, scenes, human types, and stories dealing with all conditions of human experience. But even in the pictures the necessity for what we understand as "make-up" is eliminated as much as possible.

This is due to a recent evolution in the theatre. The public expects to see natural types in plays, and the managers comply with public demand. A method of selecting actors is used in the theatre today which is called "the type system."

Many old daguerreotypes and photographs show our grandparents with beards, chin whiskers, side whiskers, moustaches, and in general longer hair than fashion permits today. In former generations, actors naturally wore the same kind of hair on the stage that appeared in real life. The long hair of those periods enabled them to wear wigs which appeared natural, while today our close cropped hair is difficult to imitate artificially. With the

aid of wigs and whiskers, actors could effectively conceal
their actual looks, while their general appearance was
not of such great importance as it is today. In former
days, also, the theatres were lighted first with candles,
later with oil lamps, and then with gas, all of which were
much softer than the searching electricity of the modern
playhouse. Defects in make-up were not as noticeable
as they are under the present lighting system.

The free use of wigs and whiskers had a great advantage.
In all plays it is essential that there be a diversity of
appearance among the characters. The audience needs
to be able to distinguish quickly one from another. In
the old melodramas, for example, when the villain came
on he was easily distinguished by his stereotyped dark
moustache. When too many of the actors came on for a
dress rehearsal, in an effort to eliminate the discomfort
of wearing moustaches or beards, the director would order
some of them to put hair on their faces. The type may
still be changed in the legitimate drama by the wearing
of whiskers because today, on and off the stage, any style
of whisker other than a simple moustache is seldom seen
on men's faces. Recourse to such a type change, however,
is seldom employed, except in plays which deal with a
former time. The law that there must be a diversity of
appearance among the actors still operates, nevertheless,
and it is in this connection that the type system comes
into play. There are other causes for the type system,
but they are not related to the present subject.

The type system is not adhered to so much in the
Continental theatres as in those of America and England.
In the Royal, and other theatres of Copenhagen, Den-
mark, the free use of wigs and other accessories of make-up

was observed. The same rule no doubt obtains in general on the continent of Europe. This may be because there is a freer use in real life of whiskers and long hair, especially in Russia, than in America and England. In general, however, it is because the Continental theatres cling more rigidly to many of the old-fashioned ways. They consider art for art's sake and do not insist on actual realism to the extent that we do. Since in the theatre one must use his imagination, anyway, they feel no doubt that this may just as well, or even better, include the art of make-up. In the New York production of *Topaze*, when an exception to the adherence to "type" was made, an actor was able to add much to the visual presentation of his part by wearing a gray wig with rather long hair. In Stockholm, Sweden, the negro characters in Marc Connolly's *The Green Pastures* were represented by the Swedish actors, who used negro make-up. This would be unthinkable in America, where many capable negro actors are now available for colored parts. In Sweden it was no doubt considered quite permissible. At the same time, it is unquestionable that American actors receive far less practice in characterization than in a former generation, since dialect parts of all kinds are generally represented by actors to whom the dialects are natural in real life.

Diversity of appearance on the stage today in America and England must be attained through actual dissimilarities in the appearance of the actors in real life. In the case of women, one may be elderly and have gray hair, another may be a blonde, and a third a brunette, in order that there may be marked differences in their appearance. Men must vary in respect to age, size, and those characteristics of appearance which are supposed, in the minds of the managers, who possess the final right of decision, to typify the characters portrayed by the actors. Policemen must be large, bankers middle aged and portly, heroic lovers tall and handsome, and so on, through an infinite variety of types more or less true to actual life.

Since the actor is chosen for a part only when he is "the type," he goes on to the stage more or less as he is, and with only the "straight" make-up used to counteract the sallowness of color which the strong light tends to cause. "Half the battle," then, consists not in having a good make-up, but in being the right type.

Since the type system is largely used today in selecting actors for parts, it is well to adhere to it as much as possible in selecting a cast for a little theatre or non-professional performance. Such adherence is rendered more necessary because most of the actors in these performances are likely to be young, and their faces therefore not so easily adaptable to character make-up.

In spite of the efforts of the managers to eliminate the necessity for character make-up entirely through the type system, there are still many times when it is necessary. At such times the operation of the type system falls to the ground. For example, an octogenarian cannot always be played by an actor of that age. Acting requires vitality and involves a nerve strain. An actor of eighty, unless he is exceptional, has long since retired, or if still playing is seen only in short and simple rôles. An important octogenarian part which required definite technique and activity to play it, would have to be placed in the hands of a much younger man. He could not be the exact type for such a part and would have to make up for it.

There are, however, occasional exceptions, where a person of advanced age plays an active part. One such exception was noted in a non-professional performance of a charming one-act play, *A Sunny Morning*, in Le Petit Théâtre du Vieux Carré in New Orleans. The two leading parts were played by a man and a woman well past seventy, who gave very artistic renditions.

Occasional parts are written for which no actual type can be found, and the managers are forced to disregard the type system entirely. The art of make-up is therefore called into use. In stock companies, the same actors must adapt themselves to a wide variety of plays and must practice make-up constantly. A discussion of character make-up is therefore worth while, since at any time the actor may be called upon to use it.

Make-up is divided into two broad classes: "straight" or juvenile, and character make-up.

MALE STRAIGHT MAKE-UP

Straight make-up is used by both men and women when they are not supposed to look differently from how they do in real life. Straight make-up tends to make the actor look younger.

Make-up articles consist of face creams, grease paints, powders, and various other accessories. The paints come in the form of sticks. There are large sticks for the body colors, and thinner sticks, called liners, with some of which wrinkles are painted. These come in all the necessary colors and shades. There are flesh colors either light, ruddy, or dark, and these are used according to the degree of color the character requires. A character supposed to be sickly or overstudious would require a light flesh, while one in perfect health would need one of a ruddier shade.

MAKE-UP

Before beginning his make-up, if the actor has an abundance of hair, he usually wears a skullcap, or ties a band of cloth about his hair. This keeps the powder when applied out of the hair. The actor should first apply a small amount of cold cream to the face, which will make the paint go on easily and smoothly. The face is then ready for the body color of the paint. A lighter shade should be applied to the forehead than to the rest of the face, for the skin on most faces is lighter where it is shaded by the hat brim.

The paint should be applied smoothly and carried to the edge of the hair, down on to the lobes of the ears and the neck. If the lobes of the ears are not touched with the paint they will probably show two white spots on either side of the face. Also, the paint on the neck must not show a sharp line of demarcation where it stops, but must be graduated off thinly around toward the back. This should be done also down the neck in front. Some careless actors let the grease paint show a sharp line of demarcation along the edges of the jaw bone, which is distinctly wrong. If the shade used is about the same as that of the skin, it need not be carried below the collar line; otherwise this should be done.

After the body color is on, carmine or maroon should be used for the cheek bones. With a little experience the actor learns which of these colors better suits his face. The color should be carried up to the temples, slightly into the outer corners of the eyes, and graduated off on the lower and outer cheek. Too much of this should not be used, for a man must not appear too "pink and white." A touch of rouge may be applied to the chin and, if desired, to the point between the eyebrows.

The face is then ready for the powder. A shade of this should be used which matches the paint, and which does not impair the work already done by rendering the face either too light or too dark. The powder is used to take the gloss off the face, a result of the grease in the paint. The face should be thoroughly patted with the powder puff; the surplus powder can then be removed with a camel's-hair brush.

The eyes may then be made up. When the eyes are large and prominent very little make-up should be used on them, and sometimes none at all. Too heavy and too dark a make-up on the eyes makes them look like "burnt holes in a blanket." The upper lids should be painted with the lake, or gray, color, which comes in the "liner" stick, and fine lines drawn along the lower rims. For dark complexions, a darker shade of this color must be used than when the complexion is fair. If the eyes are small they can be made to seem larger by extending the two lines to a point beyond the outer corners, as suggested by the diagram below:

With the little finger the upper lids may be completely covered with the paint, but it should not be too heavy on the lower rim of the eye.

Most actors use a pointed match, or small stick, with which to apply the paint when lines of any kind are desired. Sticks of soft paper can be purchased from any store dealing in artists' materials. Some actors think these are easier to use and produce better results. With the point of the stick small dots of lip rouge, or maroon from the "liner" of that color, are then applied to the inner corners of the eyes.

Cosmetics come in various colors. Matches and a candle are necessary articles on an actor's make-up shelf, and with some cosmetic rubbed on the stick and melted over the candle the eyelashes are then "beaded." After this process most of the cosmetic should be removed with the fingers. For dark complexions black should be used, but for light complexions, brown. When the eyelashes are long, dark, and luxuriant, the powder which has lodged in them need only be removed with wet fingers and no cosmetic applied.

When the eyebrows are dark and heavy they will need no make-up, but the powder should be brushed out of them. When they are faint and light, an eyebrow pencil, or the "liner" stick in the proper shade, may be used to outline them. For the lips, a lip rouge to match the general complexion is employed. Large lips require very little color. Thin lips can be treated more freely, and sometimes by means of the rouge the mouth can be given a more attractive shape. When the make-up is finished, if it is found a little too pale, it can be touched up with dry rouge applied with a rabbit's foot. In all cases the actor should consider the strength of the lights and make up accordingly. Men sometimes put brilliantine on the hair if it is dry and lifeless. In all straight make-ups, men should be careful not to look too rosy and effeminate; experience will show them what best suits their own faces.

Hands which are large and red can be whitened with a preparation applied with a sponge. This procedure should be observed particularly when white lace flows down over the hands. The teeth can also be whitened with a preparation called "tooth enamel." For rough characters, when the hands and forearms should appear dark or dirty, scene painter's umber can be applied with water and a sponge.

The directions given above for male straight make-up may be considered the "ideal," and at most are used only by juvenile characters, who, perhaps because of a romantic relation to the play, should be good looking. Actors playing elderly straight parts need to discard many of the points, such as rouging the lips, beading the eyelashes, and so on. In the present day theatre straight make-ups are simplified as much as possible.

FEMALE STRAIGHT MAKE-UP

Little need be said to the ladies about how to make up, and for obvious reasons; still, some actresses make up much better than others. While men use straight make-up only to counteract the light and, as a general rule, to look natural, women try to look as beautiful as possible. This is as it should be; therefore women need to study their faces. There are various treatments to be given the eyebrows, the eyes, the cheeks, and the lips. The eyebrows, if heavy, should be penciled as delicately as possible or not at all, and sometimes their contour can be changed; the eyes, if large or small, can be treated accordingly. Rouge can be extended over the cheeks in such a way as to counteract any depression in them, and less used in the case of prominent cheek bones. The lips can be outlined in an attractive cupid's bow, or in any shape desired. If the mouth is too large a definite shape can be painted within the natural contour.

In general, actresses use a dry make-up, which consists of the proper shade of flesh powder applied to the face after cold cream has been rubbed into the skin. The rouge is dry and applied with a rabbit's foot. When an actress' skin is not good a dry make-up is too transparent; in such a case grease paint in a light flesh color can be used. The face is then powdered, and the make-up proceeds as with men. Actresses should use brilliantine, if necessary, to give lustre to the hair, and also the white preparation for the hands and arms.

MALE CHARACTER MAKE-UP

On the next page is a diagram of the face giving the general principles of make-up for the production of age effects. The age and character of the individual to be portrayed will determine the shade to use; a ruddy shade would be proper for a healthy middle-aged man, a sallow shade for a very old man. We will suppose in this case that the make-up is for a healthy man of about fifty-five, and the actor who portrays him is young, with no natural lines. The body color for such a character may be the same as for juvenile straight make-up. A little rouge can be applied to the cheeks and chin, but not so much as for juvenile make-ups.

The eye is the most important thing to consider in aging the face. With this feature properly treated, an effect of age is immediately secured, while without such treatment an abundance of wrinkles and shadows will not give the desired effect. A glance at the diagram will show that the eye has been shaded above and below, following the general line of the eye socket in the skull. Age tends to give the eye a sunken effect, and for this purpose gray, or lake, should be used. This should be put on evenly and rubbed over with the finger, rather more of it being placed above the eye than below; it can be slightly accentuated in the

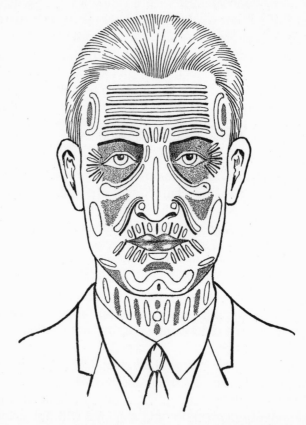

inner corners where the shading appears heavier in the diagram. The paint must not be put on too heavily, and no sharp lines should show lest the eyes look like dark holes in the face.

MAKE-UP

The student will see that this rather queer-looking diagram is marked with sharp lines, and that it has finer markings of hollow circles, oblongs, and solid shadings. The sharp lines represent wrinkles, the hollow circles and oblongs high lights which set them off, and the solid shadings depressions in the face. The drawing is meant to show the positions of the markings only, and represents to some extent the crude appearance of the face before the effects have been smoothed down and blended.

Before attempting to make up for an elderly character, it would be well for the student to examine some portrait of an elderly person. The art of painting age upon the face depends almost entirely upon the principle of light and shade. The actor paints his face in the same way that an artist paints a portrait, using the same colors, and making the same lights and shadows. Where the artist uses a brush, the actor uses the tip of his finger to smooth down sharp lines.

WRINKLES

For the healthy man of fifty-five whom we are making up, the wrinkles should be made with maroon. This is ruddy and matches the flesh color of the face. For this man, not all the wrinkles shown on the diagram need be used, and the actor uses his judgment as to those he wants. He may omit the horizontal forehead wrinkles entirely, using only the two vertical ones between the eyebrows. If the actor's face is very young, however, two or three forehead wrinkles should be painted. The essential lines for this man are the two wrinkles downward from the lobes of the nostrils, the two downward from the inner corners of the eyes, the two extending from the corners of the mouth, and the shading over the chin. Two or three "crows' feet" can be used at the outer corners of the eyes, if desired, or if not, the highlights shown directly under them on the diagram can be extended upward around the outsides of the eyes where the crows' feet on the diagram appear. If a young face has very full cheeks these can be slightly depressed, as shown on the diagram. The shading should be done with lake, as should also the shading over the chin. No more of the lines and shadows shown on the diagram need be used.

The wrinkles above and below the mouth, the depressions on either side of the chin, and the shadings in the neck and on the temples are used only in making up persons of advanced age.

Besides the wrinkles shown on the diagram, the neck can be lined for the weather-beaten appearance of a rough character. Such lines extend forward and downward on the sides of the neck from below and back of the ears.

The wrinkles in the face are best applied with the stick after it has been rubbed into the "liner." The student will quickly find that very little paint is required. In making the nose wrinkles, the student must be cautioned not to start them at the lower corners of the nose, but to carry them up and around the lobes of the nostrils, as shown on the diagram. The shading above the chin is more than a wrinkle and should be broadened to occupy the space between the bulge of the chin and the lower lip.

When all the desired wrinkles have been marked on the face with the stick, they must then be reduced from sharp lines to shadows. This is best done with the tip of the little finger. Wrinkles are only depressions in the face, broadening out as they approach the surface, and, as in painting, sharp lines should be avoided.

HIGHLIGHTS

When the wrinkles have been softened and worked down, but not spread out too much and made indistinct by the finger, the highlights can be applied. The student is asked to study the positions of the latter. On the forehead the highlights appear above the top wrinkle, above the eyebrows, and between the other wrinkles. They also appear between the crows' feet. A special point to note is that they appear *below* the lines from the inner corners of the eyes, and *above* the nose wrinkles. To bring the nose wrinkles out still better, small highlights are placed on the lobes of the nostrils. Highlights appear *outside* of the wrinkles from the corners of the mouth. To bring out the depression between the chin and under lip, a highlight is placed just under the lip, and another on the bulge of the chin, as shown. If desired, a small dimple can be placed in the chin, as shown. If the depressions in the cheeks are used, these can be accentuated by the highlights on the cheek bones. Highlights extending downward from the inner points of the eyebrows accentuate the deep shadows in the eyes where these are shown. If the nose is not prominent, a highlight can be placed on the bridge, as shown, to sharpen its line; this can be done in straight make-ups as well.

The color used for highlights comes in the "liner" in a very light flesh. This should be a shade much lighter than the body color of the face or the highlights will have no effect. The highlights should not be applied with the stick but with the "liner" itself. The end of the "liner" can be pressed flat with the fingers to make as fine a mark as is needed.

When the highlights have all been roughly applied, the finishing touches of the "painting" must have attention. Sharp demarcations must be eliminated. The tip of the little finger is best to use. On the forehead the wrinkles should be "run" with the finger to blend the highlights into them, and no sharp lines of either should be left. At the same time, they should not be rubbed too hard or they may be erased entirely. The highlights above the nose wrinkles, outside the mouth wrinkles, under the eyes, and on the chin, should be graduated off on the outside edges. It will be seen on the diagram that the highlights do not touch the wrinkles. They should so appear on the actor's face, with an open space left on the body color between the highlights and the wrinkles. Smoothing both out with the finger afterwards will erase the sharp demarcations. When the face presents the appearance of perfectly blended lights and shadows, it is ready for the powder.

Powder can easily destroy the whole effect. If it is too dark it completely neutralizes the highlights, and the make-up is spoiled. A powder of a flesh color very little darker than the highlights, or even of the same shade, should be used. Such a shade brings out the true effect of the highlights. Since the wrinkles are much darker than the highlights, the powder must be selected in the interest of the latter.

The eyebrows are then painted to match the color of the hair as a rule. When a gray wig is worn, however, a good effect is secured by making the eyebrows darker than the wig. The eyes should not be made up too "ju-

A scene from Ostrovsky's THE WOODS directed by Meyerhold in U.S.S.R.

Two styles of make-up by the author

venile," as in juvenile make-ups. They should be outlined rather more lightly with the lake, which also may be applied to the lashes instead of black or brown. The maroon dots in the corners of the eyes may be omitted. The lips need no rouge, but all paint should be removed from them with a cloth.

Characters of very old men need a lighter shade of paint. Special colors come for these make-ups, marked "sallow old men." Powder must be selected to match the make-up. For very old men the wrinkles are done with the lake color instead of the maroon; and for characters of extreme age the eyes are outlined, and the eyelashes and eyebrows painted, with white. In painting the eyebrows, the hair can be made scraggly and disarranged by rubbing it the wrong way with the paint. The highlights are made with the same light flesh, or if the face is very pale, with white; all possible wrinkles and shadows may be used.

The accompanying illustrations show the same face in two different styles of make-up. At the right the effect of age is shown without the use of wrinkles. The eye sockets merely have been shaded with lake and the eyebrows whitened. The make-up at the left is done with all necessary wrinkles and highlights.

When the complexion of a character is supposed to be very swarthy or weather-beaten, the wrinkles should be made with brown, as well as the shadows in the eyes, cheeks, and chin; the eyes also are made up with brown. The highlights should be of a darker shade than for the other make-ups described. When the character has black hair, the eyes should be made up with black.

For wrinkles, then, the actor has three colors for his

use. They are maroon, gray or lake, and brown. The actor may make black wrinkles for negro characters, but such cases are rare.

For very old characters the hands are often made up. They are given an appearance of emaciation by painting shadows with lake between the bones on the back, and highlighting the bones themselves.

The actor, with a little ingenuity, can sometimes secure any desired color or shade by blending the colors he finds on his make-up shelf. After all, this is what the painter does. The colors he has in his tubes he seldom uses raw, but mixes them in various combinations.

A cheap and effective powder can be made by the actor. This is merely precipitated chalk or talcum powder with a little powdered carmine shaken into it. The carmine should be freed of all lumps. The amount of carmine will determine the shade, and the powder can be used for all grease paints with a tinge of pink in them.

NEGRO MAKE-UP

The common make-up for a negro is done with a paste of burnt cork; this is used by the negro minstrels. A rim is left clear about the mouth to make it look larger. The cork is afterwards removed with a sponge, and soap and water. In the more artistic performances of drama, burnt cork is not as desirable as other pastes. A colored man is not always coal black, and therefore special pastes of various shades, from light brown to dark, have been prepared. If a dark brown shade is used, it permits wrinkles to be made if they are necessary. They can be made with black and highlighted with a "liner" of a lighter brown than the flesh color. The mouth, instead of showing the white of the actor's true skin, which is too light for a negro's mouth, can be enlarged with a lighter brown than the body color of the face. No powder is needed with burnt cork or negro paste.

INDIAN MAKE-UP

For Indians, a simple make-up is secured with Armenian Bole, a reddish brown clay powder, which can be bought at a drug store. This is mixed with water and applied with a sponge. A more artistic make-up is acquired with a special grease paint, which does not contain so much of the reddish shade as the Bole.

CLOWNS

These are made up with a white paste called clown white and, as we all know, the face is painted with red or black in fantastic designs. A cloth skullcap is part of the costume.

OTHELLO

There is a special color in grease paint by this name. It is a light brown, which is used to make up an actor playing the part of Shakespeare's great character, and can also be blended with lighter colors, or used pure, for Mexicans, Spaniards, or swarthy characters in general. Special powder must be used.

CHINAMEN

These can be made up with the Othello color and an application of yellowish powder which will give the yellow tinge of the Oriental skin. The eyes are, of course, made up with black. Special treatment is necessary for the

eyes and eyebrows to give the almond-eyed effect characteristic of the Chinaman. The drawing below will
illustrate it:

The light lines represent the true eye, while the heavy
black lines show where the eyes are to be lined with black.
It will be seen that the lines over the eyes extend only half
way. This gives the somewhat sleepy expression of the
Chinese face. The eyebrows are pointed downward in
the middle and upward at the outer ends. Where they
depart from the true eyebrows, the latter are blocked out.
To block out any part or all of the eyebrows, they can be
smeared with wet soap and allowed to dry before the
paint is applied to the face. A variation of the eye make-up
for Chinamen is shown in the following diagram:

In this diagram, it is seen that the eyebrows are arched
and brought down slightly at the outer ends, while no line
at all is made over the eye. Some actors playing Chinese
characters use collodion or adhesive tape to draw their
eyes up at the outer corners. The actor should try the
various methods and select that which best suits him.

PIERROT AND HARLEQUIN

In plays in which these characters appear, a departure from the usual make-up can be made by painting masks on the face either in blue or purple. The side curls over

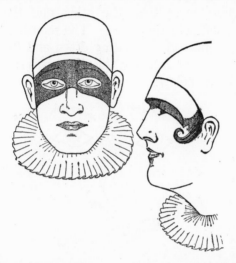

the ears are most effective. The diagram above illustrates these make-ups.

BLACK DOG IN "TREASURE ISLAND"

The make-up for this character, in Robert Louis Stevenson's famous romance, as first played, was a peculiar one, and will give an added suggestion or two to the subject of make-up as a whole. The swarthy Othello color was used as the body color. The wrinkles were made with black and highlighted with a light brown. The face was rendered as crooked as possible by distorting the nose and mouth and making the nose wrinkles of unequal length, while the front teeth were blocked out. Black hair was glued on the chest, and the second and third fingers of the left hand, which were supposed to be missing, were encased in black glove fingers, folded in on the palm, which was painted black, and tied to the wrist. One black side whisker was longer than the other and the eyebrows pointed in different directions. The mouth was painted black, with one corner pointing down and the other up. The nose was very crooked; this effect was secured in the manner shown below:

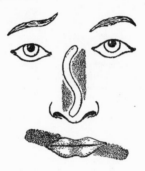

Heavy shadings of brown were painted on the right of the nose at the bottom and on the left at the top, and a crooked highlight was drawn along the bridge, as shown.

Nose Putty

Black Dog's nose appeared crooked through the illusion of paint, but theatrical nose putty is often used to gain similar effects. This is softened over a candle, becomes pliable, and is molded into any desired shape. Making a false nose of putty is a process of sculpture, and some actors are expert in this art. The regular theatrical putty for this purpose makes it no longer necessary for the actor to resort to bread dough, as in the old days, when the dough would rise during the performance, enlarging the nose to such a degree that Cyrano de Bergerac's was modest in comparison.

When a putty nose is used in a make-up it should be put on before cold cream and paint have been applied to the face. It sticks easily and is shaped and graduated on to the skin with the fingers. A little cold cream smeared on the fingers enables the actor to work the putty easily. After the right shape has been made, the nose can easily be covered with paint without disturbing its shape by smearing a finger first with cold cream and then with paint and applying the paint with the finger to the nose.

A nose can thus be made crooked, as for Black Dog, or for Quilp, in *The Old Curiosity Shop;* can be made aquiline for Jewish characters, and given a high bridge for Indians; or it can be turned up at the end. When a snub nose is made, much of the under surface of it shows, and an enlargement of the real nostrils can be painted on the putty with black.

The effect of a turned-up nose can be secured without putty. This is done by painting a shadow in lake just above the tip, and highlighting the tip and the bridge.

The effect of the high cheek bones of the Indian can be secured by molding chunks of putty on the cheek bones.

The easiest way to remove a putty nose is to run a piece of thread under it. There are other uses for nose putty; but they are exceptional, the ones mentioned being the commonest.

MISCELLANEOUS EFFECTS

The effect of missing teeth is secured in two ways. One is to cover the teeth with black sticking plaster, but in this method there is danger that the saliva will loosen the plaster. A better way is to dry off the teeth with a cloth and paint them with black grease paint. If they are thoroughly dried the saliva of the mouth will not disturb the paint.

An eye can be closed to give the effect of blindness by pasting sticking plaster over the closed lid before the paint is applied.

Eyes can be made to seem close together; this is a good point in make-up for certain comic characters. It is done by making up only the inner halves of the eyes and bringing the lines as close to the nose as possible. To make them seem far apart the process is reversed and only the outer halves of the eyes are made up. The eyebrows should be placed either close together or far apart according to which process is used, the rest of the real eyebrows being blocked out.

Very rarely the actor wants to make thin cheeks seem fuller. This can be done by inserting slices from the outside of an apple between the cheeks and the jaw. It does not interfere with the speech, but is sometimes uncomfortable. One actor who portrayed an Oriental character put hazel-nut shells into his nostrils to distend them. Half of the shell was put into each nostril, with a hole drilled in it through which to breathe.

Should the occasion present itself when the actor might wish to make up as a gold idol, the results obtained by an actor who played a god in Tagore's play, *Chitra*, may be of service. The actor made up with a ground of the Othello shade, and then powdered the face with gold dust. This can be procured at any paint store. With his finger he made a line a quarter of an inch wide down the bridge of the nose, over the eyebrows, and on the cheek bones and chin. When a spotlight was thrown on to the face it had the appearance of being solid gold.

A gruesome effect of blindness in one eye was secured in the following way: Before putting any paint upon the eye socket the actor cut out a piece of passepartout in the form of an ellipse to fit the eye socket and pasted it on. The passepartout was then painted over with the rest of the face. A streak of white on the passepartout to represent the white of the eye-ball showing between half-closed lids, and some daubs around it in black, brown, and maroon produced a startling effect.

For certain characters supposed to be simple in their natures, an effect is secured by drawing lines upward and outward from the corners of the mouth. Such characters usually being ruddy of complexion, maroon is used for this. The mouth can also be drawn down at the corners by the use of the same color. Clowns and comedians in burlesque often secure an effect of the simpleton nature by placing small black dots in the middle of their eyelids, and even by drawing vertical streaks in black from the upper to the lower lid of the eye. An effect is secured by enlarging the lower lip with maroon, while the upper lip is given little or no make-up. This is done by actors who make up for Abraham Lincoln. A wart of putty is always put on to Lincoln's cheek.

Eccles, the drunkard in *Caste*, had a putty nose which was blotched by punching little holes in it and applying various dots of maroon and brown. In this make-up the actor should avoid too obvious an effect. Freckles can be made with little dots of brown.

FEMALE CHARACTER MAKE-UP

Women never have so much occasion to use character make-up as do men. Sometimes, however, young women are called upon to impersonate old ones. Actresses should recall what was said above about the eye. When a young actress plays an old woman she had better not endeavor to use wrinkles as a principal aid. Women's faces are more delicate than men's, and make-up wrinkles are too heavy for them. A good effect of age can be secured with shadows only.

A grease paint body color is best, in case a young face is too colorful. The light flesh is used without rouge, or if the character is quite old, a sallow flesh. The shadings of lake are put around the eyes, as shown on the diagram. The cheeks are sunken, and the shadow placed between the chin and lower lip. The only wrinkles which need be used, if any, are the wrinkles at the sides of the nose and mouth. These should be reduced to shadows. The eyebrows are painted to match the wig. The eyes should not be made up much, if at all. Though actresses may use many of the aids to make-up for men mentioned in this chapter, as a general rule they are called upon only to make up "straight."

REMOVING MAKE-UP

Grease paint is removed with cold cream and rubbed off with a cloth. Some actors use cheesecloth, and others paper napkins, after which soap and water is used.

A cheaper medium than cold cream, and quite as effective, is common cooking Crisco. Vaseline, albolene, olive oil, and cocoa butter are also used.

WIGS

When a wig is worn it is an important part of an actor's make-up. It may add greatly to the effect and be a prime factor in the illusion which he is trying to create, or it may spoil the effect entirely. The treatment of a wig is a little art in itself. When a wig is made to an actor's measure he can have some surety of its suitability; when it is not he must know some of the necessary points about wigs to make it presentable. In either case, he should study the proper treatment.

A wig can be detected as such at the front where, if there is a wig band, that joins the face, on the sides at the temples, at the back where it touches the neck, and in the appearance of the hair as a whole. If these four points in the wearing of a wig are properly understood and practiced, the audience will not know the actor's hair is false.

When an actor has a wig made to order, if it is not a bald wig, but one of the variety called "dress wigs" with the close-cropped hair of modern life, it fits better if made with a wig band. This is a fine band of silk extending below the hair in front, and which is painted in with the rest of the make-up. The wig band should be as narrow as possible so as to escape detection from the front. The hair can be combed so as largely to conceal it. On the temples the wig should have loose flaps, which can be pasted down with library paste. Men's hair is clipped close at the temples, and it should not be too full there in a wig. Modern haircuts, also, are close cropped in the neck, so the wig must fit close to the neck, with the hair thinned out as much as possible and cut short. Each time the wig is worn it should be combed and brushed. We would not think of making our toilet without properly combing our hair, yet it is surprising how many professional actors put on their wigs without giving this matter any attention. The point is therefore emphasized. E. H. Sothern once called a rehearsal for four members of his company. He met them on the stage with a bucket of gasoline. He ordered them to fetch their wigs from their dressing rooms, whereupon he dipped the wigs in the gasoline to clean them (the best cleansing method for wigs), afterward put them on their owners' heads and thoroughly combed them, a treatment which they had probably not had since they had left the wigmaker's.

Wonders can be done to a wig with a comb. A young actor playing the Duke in *Twelfth Night* had a wig which, to use an expression of the theatre, looked "like the wrath of God." The wig was carefully combed by a fellow actor and after a few minutes its appearance was transformed. Wigmakers make a charge for dressing wigs, when they can generally be dressed by the owners with little time and trouble. The essential points are to clean them with gasoline and apply brilliantine to give them life, after which they should be combed and brushed.

The actor often has his face turned toward the audience. Therefore he should be especially careful about his wig in front. If he wears a stock wig which he has rented, it will not have side flaps at the temples, for these are usually made only to order. He should stick the hair down on the temples, nevertheless, and also try to make it fit close on the forehead. The actor should strive to make his wigs always snug and neat. And we cannot repeat too often: natural hair is combed; wigs should be, as well.

The Wig Band

Wigs that are partly bald have high wig bands. These come down rather far on the forehead and present a problem difficult to overcome. On prominent foreheads the wig bands often slip, disclosing the naked skin; a line thus appears between the skin and wig band which is visible to the audience. There are devices to overcome this, but they are not always successful. One is to paste a strip of adhesive tape over the joining of the wig band and the flesh. If the actor's face perspires, the mucilage may be moistened and the band slip. When the actor's forehead is prominent, the wig band should come below the point of greatest prominence in order to grip the head tightly.

Probably the best method of preventing the wig band from slipping is a false wig band. This is made of a strip of cotton or linen cloth with a selvage edge. It is tied about the forehead to extend below the real wig band, and is knotted behind. The wig is then put on and the whole painted. The false band tightens the wig, and the cotton tends to keep it from slipping. A little theatrical stickum can be inserted under the false wig band to fasten it to the forehead.

If the stickum is effective in gluing the wig band to the forehead, no false wig band need be used. If the wig is too loose, a little of its cloth framework can be sewed together on each side underneath, over the ears. When the wig band is glued to the forehead, if a narrow strip of paper adhesive tape, which can be procured in stationery stores, is pasted over the edge of the wig band and the forehead and painted in, the joining is generally invisible.

Sometimes, when the actor paints in his wig band, he finds that the general shade does not match that of his face. This is often true when he has used many wrinkles for an elderly character. The wrinkles have modified the general shade of his face. If they are of maroon, the face has been given a ruddy tinge, and if of lake, a grayish tinge. If a little of the color with which the wrinkles were made is painted on the wig band, it will make the shade of the wig band and the face correspond.

The selection of a wig is part of an actor's performance, for in his proper discrimination in this regard he shows his understanding of a character. He should choose a wig which either accentuates the qualities of his character or does not detract from them. A normal gentleman will require a wig with no eccentricities, and it will need to be as well groomed and dressy as possible, while a very eccentric character can be known as such on the actor's first entrance by a wig that has some eccentric appearance. For example, it can be parted behind, with the hair brushed forward over the ears and standing frowsily up in front. The same wig, when neatly combed and brushed in a normal way, may often serve for a gentleman of culture. Many different effects can be secured with the same wig, as with an actor's own hair, by means of a comb. In the actor's study of character he learns the many effects which can be secured with his wigs, or the various kinds of wigs to select for his parts. Wigmakers study human character in respect to wigs, so the actor should always consult the wigmaker's judgment and explain the character to him.

Oftentimes, in place of a wig, the hair may be powdered. It can be grayed with cornstarch, a little vaseline or cold cream being first applied to hold the starch. The starch is put on dry with the powder puff. When only the temples need to be grayed, this is done effectively with a clay called flake white, or even with the white clay which is used to whiten shoes. The material is mixed with water and applied with a toothbrush. A good effect for gray hair is secured with an aluminum powder; this powder can also be obtained in red, if the make-up calls for red hair.

When the actor wishes to conceal any spot where his hair is thin, he can do it with mascaro. This comes in cakes of various colors, and is painted on with a tooth-brush.

WHISKERS

These play an equally important part with wigs in a correct make-up. Moustaches, beards, chinpieces, and side whiskers are made to order by the wigmakers. All but full beards usually look natural; the latter present difficulty on account of the sharp lines on the edges. With practice, the actor can make beards for himself which have a very natural appearance.

An artificial hair called "crimped hair" is sold for the making of beards. It is braided tightly on double strings, and comes in all necessary colors. A beard should be made in three main pieces, with minor additions. When it is to be used more than once the following method is advised: The face should be painted all over and powdered in the ordinary way. Liquid fish glue is daubed on the face along the lines where a natural beard grows. A natural beard does *not* grow close to the ears, and care should be taken on this point. The glue must be carried well under the chin and on to the sides of the neck. It should also be pointed up on the cheeks, following the natural growth of a beard, or in some cases may be brought down into a low curve to the corners of the mouth, if a small beard is desired.

The chinpiece should be made first. The crimped hair is loosened from the strings and combed out on to a comb, so that the individual threads stand separate. It is easy to secure a length of three inches from the comb. When enough has been combed out, but not too much, for the beard should not be too thick, it is taken off the comb and the ends cut off where it has lodged in the comb. The chin is then daubed with the fish glue. The hair is fluffed out a bit so that it will cover the area prepared for it and is stuck on where the ends have been cut. Beards grow in two ways on the chin. They either grow solidly under the lower lip or extend upward to the lip in three points, as shown in the following diagrams:

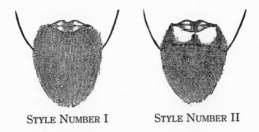

STYLE NUMBER I   STYLE NUMBER II

For genteel characters, style number two is more attractive. The chinpiece for this kind of beard is stuck on only to where the dotted line shows on the diagram. Wisps of hair are stuck on afterwards for the points. A good effect can be secured by making these points of gray, or if the beard is gray, of white, to give the beard a grizzled effect. The same thing can be done where the beard is pointed up on the cheeks. The side pieces are then put on. A small amount of hair is combed out, but *not* cut off the comb, is fluffed out thin, and is stuck on to the backing of fish glue. The actor should take care to have the tops join the real hair closely, so as not to show spaces between the beard and the hair. When the fish glue has dried, the beard is trimmed with the scissors. The edges should be trimmed off where they do not adhere to the face and are too ragged.

A beard must not be too thick; natural beards, even when never cut, flow downwards and are not bushy at the sides.

Moustaches can be made in one or two pieces. Very small moustaches had better be made in two pieces on either side of the depression in the upper lip. Moustaches which are to go with very full beards are better made in one piece; they can be tied in the middle with a tiny wisp of hair.

THE WRONG WAY   THE RIGHT WAY

One of the commonest faults of inexperienced actors is to paste the moustache straight across the upper lip. The line of the upper lip is lower on each end than in the middle, and the moustache follows its lines. The student will quickly recognize this by consulting the two diagrams above. The wrong way should be readily acknowledged.

The actor should draw the moustache *down* at the corners of the mouth, following the direction in which moustaches actually grow. When the moustache is well stuck on, the ends can be turned up in the Continental fashion, or can be made to droop in the historical "Kentucky colonel" fashion, as desired. For suggestions regarding wigs and beards, the young actor should observe people; he will thus obtain better ideas than he can get from books.

A "waxed" moustache can be easily secured by twisting the ends in the fingers covered with wet soap.

Very close cropped effects, or the effects of being unshaven, for both beard and moustache, can be secured by cutting the hair very fine and sprinkling it on the face over the glue, afterwards filling in bare spots with touches of paint. Another way is merely to paint the face with lake color, or to rub on burnt paper. A very soft lead pencil can be used, if the hair is dark enough, to outline the eyebrows, or to pencil in small side whiskers.

Beards can be made pointed, called "Van Dyke," after the fashion of the Van Dyke paintings, can be left square and full, or can be split at the chin with the scissors, parted, and shaped into two points, according to the character to be presented. When a long beard is needed, a good plan is to wet the hair after removing it from the strings, and allow it to dry. This removes the kinks and enables the actor to comb it into longer lengths.

If plenty of paint has been put on under the beard and sufficient fish glue used, the beard will come off easily. Most of the paint will come off with the beard; this, with the hardened glue, makes an excellent backing and the beard can be used again. Fish glue should not be used each time the beard is worn, for it will become too stiff. Regular theatrical stickum is sold, or the actor can make his own with equal parts of gum mastic and gum sandrac dissolved in alcohol, the alcohol being one-half of the whole.

Crimped hair can be pasted over the real eyebrows to make them either bushy or protruding, if a very heavy effect is desired.

Side whiskers are made like the side pieces of the beard. They can be cropped short, or can be allowed to flow away from the cheeks.

It is not possible to set down in writing a full exposition of the art of make-up. The points given here are meant as suggestions with which the student may start his practice. He will develop many original ideas and acquire methods which express his own personality.

EXERCISES

1. What do you understand by the "type system"?
2. What two broad classes of make-up are there?
3. What is "body color"?
4. How would you treat large eyes? Small eyes?
5. Describe the method of female make-up.
6. In aging the face, what is the most important feature of it to consider?
7. What color, in general, should be used for shadows?
8. What three mediums are used to produce age effects?
9. What colors are used for wrinkles?
10. What are "crow's feet"?
11. How would you make wrinkles?
12. What is the use of the highlight?
13. Where do the highlights go for the nose wrinkles? The mouth wrinkles? The forehead wrinkles?

14. How should the shade of the highlights correspond with that of the body color? The powder with that of the highlights?
15. What color of paint should be used in wrinkles for middle-aged men? very old men? men of swarthy complexion? negroes?
16. Make a rough drawing illustrating one method of make-up for the Chinese eye.
17. In what two ways can the appearance of the nose be changed?
18. How would you make a turned-up nose?
19. What effects would you use for an old woman?
20. What are the four important points in respect to a wig?
21. What should be done to a wig every time it is put on the head?
22. What is a wig band? A false wig band?
23. Describe the making of a beard.
24. What is a common fault in pasting on a moustache?

CHAPTER XXII

THE PERFECT ACTOR

Any actor gifted with emotional feeling, and who is able to put into expert execution all the principles that have been outlined in preceding chapters, will show an artistic completeness which will elevate him to a commanding position in the theatre. As a rule no person will go to the lengths of practice necessary to gain such results unless he possesses a natural talent for the art; and without the urge to go into the work all the practice of a lifetime will be of no avail. The musician does not seriously study the violin unless he has a love and inspiration for music; the painter does not paint unless he has a desire to express himself in painting the colors of nature. In any occupation, only the love of it will permit one to gain outstanding success.

To a person's interest and talent, years of practice must be added in order for him to acquire the technique which will direct his talent along proper lines. When an actor has done this can we say that he has reached perfection? What is a perfect actor? It is safe to say there is no such person, nor perhaps ever has been. The nearest thing we know to absolute perfection is nature herself. Art is merely an imitation of nature; and an imitation can never be as perfect as the thing from which it is copied. Horses have sometimes nibbled at stage scenery when it represented foliage, but no painting that was ever produced has deceived the human eye. No performance in the theatre is absolutely perfect. To be so, every intonation, every inflection, every emphasis, and every expression and physical movement performed by each of the actors would have to be exactly like similar expressions in real life, and such perfection has never been attained. The false can always be distinguished from the real. What we call, then, the perfection of art can only be the nearest approach to actual perfection that it is possible for imitative expression to attain.

The general estimate of many an actor has been that he was "perfect." Let us try to define the essential qualities he must have possessed in order to merit this estimate, though our idea may be at variance with others that can be offered as to just what constitutes "perfection" in the actor's art.

To begin with, much of what we call dramatic art is not art at all but nature, unless we admit that nature itself is art—which it no doubt is. Many of the qualities possessed by this "perfect actor" are not the effect of his own art, but of nature's. They relate to general appearance in physical make-up and will be touched upon in the next chapter.

The drama, and all art in general, should not be satisfied to express only the Real, but should transcend the Real and attain the Ideal. In this connection there is an incident told of a connoisseur whom a painter called in to inspect his latest work. The connoisseur examined the painting and then exclaimed, "But it is not true to nature; I never saw a sunset like that in my life." The painter replied, "But wouldn't you like to?"

The Ideal in the drama is to be found in the element of romance, which is an ideal of life; and romance always involves the element of love. The perfect actor, then, would be eminently fitted to express romance. To do this he would have to possess a face and figure that would suggest it. He would be handsome, and his appearance would have a distinct appeal to the opposite sex. His physique would be in keeping with his face, and would be filled with vitality and health. His best years of acting would be those of comparative youth, for he would have to express the romantic love interest which exists in the years of youth, though he would have to be sufficiently old for his art. He would naturally be the "hero" in all his plays.

This rare artist would have a beautifully modulated voice, rich in tone, and in which all the expressions of love and romance could be found. His diction and elocution, also, would be faultless.

The "perfect" actor would also have an almost indefinable quality which, if a definition were attempted, might be called the power of suggestion. It would rather have its expression in "undertone" than in "overtone." This undertone would offer suggestion to the audience in such a way that they would do their share in the acting with their imagination. Thus, they would not be passive for a moment. Gladstone had a saying which suggested this. He said, "The power of oratory is the ability to take up the mist from an audience and hurl it back at them in a storm."

This actor would be inherently a gentleman; and though he might not have been given a university education, or indeed any at all, his highly intelligent mind would enable him to acquire through his work and in private study a generous culture and refinement. In action and gesture he would express the utmost grace and be entirely at ease at all times, but without pose. He would make his gestures perfectly, and in all cases they would be appropriate to the mood and situations in which he used them. In addition to this, a mobile and expressive countenance would lend color and force to his words.

Since he would be essentially an actor of romance, he would be neither a tragedian nor a comedian. Instead, he would be so evenly balanced between the two extremes that he would be equally facile in the light moods of comedy and the sombre expressions of emotion. He would not reach either extreme of comedy or tragedy.

He would also be a beautiful reader. The romantic quality of his work would place him often in the field of classic blank verse drama. Good reading is a prerequisite in these plays, and the actor would illuminate his lines with a correct reading to bring out their sense, as well as with a beauty of delivery, which would impart charm. His work would be rhythmic, for he would have a perfect sense of time and an ear attuned to the slightest gradations of tone. His whole performance would be graced with light and shade, like the beautiful varieties in coloring which distinguish great paintings.

It is needless to say that this actor would be familiar with all the "tricks of his trade"—in other words, the complete artistry of dramatic technique. He might not be able to define a single principle, such as has been attempted in these chapters, but the correct expression of these principles would be instinctive with him. Finally, this actor would devote himself to the play as a concrete unity rather than to the prominence of himself alone.

We might expect such an actor to be a great artist.

This does not necessarily follow. The estimate given here is not of a great actor, but of one so rounded and balanced that no flaws could be discerned in his work. Edmund Kean, who flourished at the beginning of the nineteenth century, is said to have been the greatest actor the English-speaking stage has ever known. It was said that he interpreted Shakespeare in "flashes of lightning." At the same time, his work was very one-sided. His genius flashed up out of frequent periods of mediocrity, and then as quickly died away. This was true in passages in which he took no interest. In Othello's long speech to the senators in Act 1, Kean mumbled over the lines and was at times almost unintelligible, but at the end he electrified his audience with the flash of his genius. Moreover, he had a strident voice, which was not at all times pleasing to the ear, as well as a short stature, which carried anything but a suggestion of romance. Hamlet, in which the romantic quality is a valuable asset, was perhaps his poorest rôle. The late Henry Irving, also, though considered by many a great actor, was hampered by a nasal voice and peculiar mannerisms, the latter, however, serving rather to accentuate his genius than to detract from it.

We may conclude, then, that the great actor is not necessarily what we have defined as a perfect actor, nor the latter of necessity great. Kyrle Bellew, a fine actor of a recent day, was not a great actor, but came near to a realization of the ideal. With the exception of legs that were rather prominently bowed, but whose defect he was able to conceal cleverly, no flaw could be found in his person or his art. A diamond can be perfect without being a Kohinoor, and an actor, though he is not a superlative genius, may merit the estimate of perfection in art if he possesses all the natural graces we have described and has developed a perfect technique.

EXERCISES

1. Outline the ideas presented in this chapter as to what constitutes "perfection" in acting.
2. What do you understand by greatness in art? In what ways may an actor be great, and yet not perfect?

CHAPTER XXIII

QUALIFICATIONS FOR SUCCESS

This subject does not logically belong in a category of discussions on dramatic technique. Still it may be worth while to write a few words on the subject for the advice of those young persons who contemplate a dramatic career. The profession of acting is often a disappointing experience if the actor goes into it without discreet foreknowledge of its conditions.

A young man or woman should not entertain an idea of the stage as a profession unless he or she possesses some of the necessary endowments for success. The art of acting is not the least difficult of the arts, and is considered by many to be the hardest of them all. A smaller percentage of success is attained in the theatre than in any other profession.

Still there are many compensating advantages, and the work of the theatre is a culture in itself. Much can be said for the theatre's broadening points of view, its bohemianism, its study of human nature, and its conceptions of human life, all gained in direct contact with the work itself. But a person cannot have everything in life, and the theatre involves many sacrifices of those benefits which fall to the lot of others.

Since success is difficult to attain and the monetary returns small in comparison with other professions, the actor should first be sure that he possesses sufficient endowments to guarantee him a high average of chance for success.

Everyone who goes on the stage thinks he has a natural gift for the work. This cannot be determined without trial, so no one can deny this belief beforehand. Not even the young actor himself can actually know whether he is right in his assumption. But it must be proven, and only time and experience itself will do this.

Let us consider the things which can be known beforehand. Of these, perhaps the most important requisite is intelligence. A bright and alert mind, quick to grasp impressions, is necessary, for stupidity and dullness have no place in art, nor indeed do they bode much chance for success anywhere. An intelligent mind, supplemented with a good education, is excellent intellectual equipment. It has been said that education has no value in acting, since many great actors have been denied it. Nevertheless, these actors made a university of the world and their work, and took advantage of the education which these afforded. They may not have studied much at a schoolroom form, but from the university of the theatre they emerged educated men and women.

Many great actors of the past did not have the proper physical build for the style of work they did, but their great talents overcame this shortcoming. Then the demands along many lines were not as rigid as they are today. Good looks and good physique are a very valuable asset for success. Positive ugliness renders success difficult if not impossible. To be handsome or beautiful often means that a large part of the battle is already won. For some few, this quality has been almost the sole reason for the success which they attained. The theatre must appeal to the eye as well as the ear; and all other things being equal, the pleasing figure has the better chance. Those who play character parts need not rely so much upon their personal appearance; but as a general rule, a good physique gives the actor an advantage over those who are undersized or anæmic. The best acting requires the vitality which is found in strong healthy bodies. There have been exceptions in the persons of certain artists whose æsthetic delicacy was their principal charm. They only serve to prove the rule.

Some people will say that personality is the most valuable asset of all for an actor. Today, at least, it is most important. Until the last generation, when an actor sought an engagement the manager wanted to know little more about him than one thing. That was whether he could act. If he could the actor was engaged, and he used every accessory of make-up to look the character he represented. A tragedian might play Hamlet and appear in some rollicking one-act farce as an after-piece on the same evening.

An actor then might have said of personality, "What is that? we are actors, and our business is to appear other than what we really are." As time went on, the discovery was made that the actor could sometimes be more effective by not accentuating so much the art of seeming, but rather by having in his own personality without trying to assume it that very quality which the part required. In other words, instead of trying to assume a different person entirely, he allowed his own personality to shine through his work and invest the character he portrayed.

So comparison began to be made between the actual personality of the actor and that supposed to be characteristic of the person portrayed. If the two were in harmony, then the actor's personality "fitted" the part.

Personality, then, developed a new idea in the theatre, and it became necessary to consider still another thing in selecting an actor for a part. The last thing discovered became the first thing considered, and the actor had to have the right personality first, and second, be able to act.

But the process of development was not to stop here, and the type system was later devised; the correct type is now the first thing considered, and the ability to act the last.

At the time when this book is being written, many critics of the theatre are beginning to wonder whether the type system is not making the actor far too specialized. An incident may illustrate this. An actor was found to have a personality and physical type, and to be able to act with a quiet servility, which gave him an ideal appearance and bearing for the part of a butler. For several seasons he played butlers in different plays under the same management. One day he sought an engagement in a play which this management was about to produce, but the manager said to him, "Oh no, I can't engage you for this piece; there is no butler in it." The actor wondered whether he should have to play butlers for the rest of his life. If an actor is confined too closely to a special kind of part, he loses the opportunity to exercise a versatility he may often possess, and may even be restricted to that kind of part through his type, when in some other, to which both his type and personality are equally well suited, he might have even greater success.

Different parts require different personalities, but a

pleasing personality is most desirable for the majority of parts. Many fine actors are withheld from the highest achievement because of personalities which are more unsympathetic and repellent than pleasing. A pleasing and attractive personality is, then, of great value for success. The student knows that pleasing, and often fascinating, personalities have illuminated the work of the great artists he has seen.

Accomplishments of various kinds are very useful. The actor should know how to dance; this is of value for the promotion of grace and poise. Fencing is also good practice for the same purpose. Both are taught in the dramatic schools. Musical ability gains for many an actor an engagement, while a knowledge of languages, especially French, which is used in so many plays, gives an added advantage.

Some actors have names which do not sound well for theatrical use. In such cases they should change them for the stage. Many prominent actors with unattractive names have selected others which are euphonious and easy to remember.

An "ear" is a most important element in the art of acting. Tone in drama may be said to correspond to color in painting, and the actor's ear should be so correct that he can quickly distinguish one tone from another, and produce any shading of tone at will. The actor who cannot do this is "tone deaf." This is discovered when he gives a false reading and is not able to correct it when the right reading is given to him. For example, if he cannot distinguish the difference between "*Tell* it to me," with the emphasis on "tell," and "Tell it to *me*," with the emphasis on "me," he is tone deaf, and this is a misfortune. There are some tone deaf actors on the professional stage, but none is ever highly successful.

When all the intrinsic qualities of the man as an artist have been considered, there are certain relations of the actor to the social world which must be taken into account. The successful actor has a contact with the world and people along social lines, which assists him in his work. This is true in all lines of endeavor, but in none more so than in the theatre. A person whom it is a pleasure to meet is always at an advantage. To be a "good mixer" without being profligate of time and leisure, and to have a club where an actor can meet his fellow-actors in a common interest, accrues to his popularity and interest, if prodigality in it does not interfere with serious study and purpose.

In the theatre there is a phrase, "the ability to sell oneself." Even though an actor has talent, he may not be capable of marketing his talent to the managers. He should be a good "business man" if he would have his talent recognized more quickly than it probably will be if he possesses too retiring a disposition. To know what he can do, and then in a dignified way to be able to persuade the managers that he can do it, gives him the opportunities to exhibit his talents, when a lack of this ability of persuasion would often hold him in the background. In the theatre obstacles are many, but the great artist is he whom difficulties exalt, and for whom obstacles are spring-boards. Opportunity knocks at the actor's door often, and business ability enables him to grasp it.

As a final suggestion on this subject we must return to the first. *Vita brevis; ars longa.* "Life is short, but art is long." Some may succeed early, while others may wait years for their success, and still others find it not at all. There is generally a first reward waiting to be grasped sometime by those who have an original talent, and after this first step up the ladder of success, through conscientious effort and a serious purpose, they will come to deserve other and greater rewards.

EXERCISES

1. What three important things are usually demanded of an actor for any part?
2. What do you understand by "an ear"?
3. What is it to be tone deaf?
4. What qualifications do you think you should possess in order to succeed as an actor? Which do you think the most important?

CHAPTER XXIV

DIRECTORSHIP

I

This chapter does not attempt to offer instruction to persons in the professional theatre, for they have an abundant knowledge of play production. Its purpose is to offer suggestions to those who have little or no insight into the methods of professional directorship. Therefore an attempt will be made to present rudimentary principles of the art, so that producers in the amateur field may start at the beginning and develop their knowledge from the most elementary details.

Hitherto, the art of acting has been discussed from the viewpoint of the actor alone, who looks, as it were, "from the inside out." In this chapter, we enter upon a different function of the theatre, and consider dramatic art from the position of the person looking "from the outside in." This is not anyone who may watch a performance or a rehearsal; the one of whom we speak is intimately concerned with the performance, and more comprehensively so than any of the actors. This person is the director. While the actor is concerned only with his own part of the entertainment, the director is concerned with the acting of the whole play. The actor expresses himself through his own personal medium, but the director through the medium of every actor in the cast.

The director's position is one of perspective. Ants

[344]

crawling about upon their hill may see only the spaces bounded by their own limited horizons; but a person standing above their little world is in a position of perspective, and sees all their horizons at once. This, of course, is a more inclusive point of vantage. The director stands in a similar position.

The work of directorship is the most important in the theatre. The actors in a company can be compared to the soldiers in an army and the director to the generalissimo of that army, who directs their movements. Napoleon, for example, owed his success and fame in no way to any of his subordinates. The brains which produced the valor of his armies and startled the world were his own, though he may never have fired a gun. Argument upon this point is scarcely necessary, since it must be allowed that credit for all great enterprises should go, and generally does, to the mind that stands at the head and front of them. This is true of generals, engineers, captains of industry, and all others in the province of directorship of whatever kind, though they perform none of the actual physical labor. In the theatre, the great companies have owed their success not to any actor in them but to the directors who produced the plays. Augustin Daly's company was a case in point. It contained celebrated players, but their fame did not overreach that of Daly himself, whose genius made their reputation possible. They all had much intrinsic worth, no doubt, but during the manager's life one could not say how much of their reputation was due to their own native ability, and how much was a reflection from that of their manager. At all events the fame of Ada Rehan, his leading actress, became at his death a waning glory.

The principle of directorship easily suggests the question, What is the real secret of success in the theatre? The success of any play implies the appeal it makes to the public, by means of which profitable business is brought to the box office. When a play is produced its success depends upon a number of factors. First and foremost, success depends upon the play itself. Nothing can give lasting success to a bad play. After this, various other agents in its production are likely to claim credit. Everyone admits the value of the play as an important factor, but the manager may feel that success is due to his skillful business management; the stage carpenters may think that without its scenic production it could not have scored; the leading actor is more than likely to think it is because he has registered strongly in a fine part; and the scenic artist that the scenes are so beautifully painted. A lady decorator in a stock company was even heard to claim that the success of various weekly productions was due to her furniture and draperies! As a matter of fact, the success of any play depends upon the play, the business management, the directorship, the acting, and the scenic setting, all working harmoniously to produce a perfect whole.

Directorship should be considered as an abstract principle. When applied to the production of any one play it cannot be properly tested to prove its relative importance with other elements that make for success. When applied to the production of numerous plays, and especially with the same company of actors, it will quickly make its merit or demerit apparent. For this reason, expert directors in theatrical centres soon build reputations for themselves, and their special touch becomes known as a valuable asset for the chances of a play. Through Augustin Daly's long association with the same company of players, during which he produced very many plays, his company sprang into fame, and the abstract principle of directorship came into its own as the most important contributing cause of that success.

A director is not unlike the conductor of a symphony orchestra. He knows where the lights and shadings should come in a performance, or where the tempo needs retarding or hurrying. He knows, too, the general theme better than anyone else, and how to emphasize it to the proper degree.

"To deliver the goods" is a homely and familiar phrase in the theatre in reference to achieving success. This means simply to present a good play and have that play acted in a manner acceptable to the public. The author furnishes the play, and the director, given a competent company of actors, "delivers the goods." Many actors think that satisfying the public depends mostly upon their own efforts, but there are many instances in which companies containing fine actors have given very poor performances and not satisfied the public at all, even when their dramatic vehicles were of superior quality. A company of actors left to their own devices without a director are helpless to produce a play, a fact which proves the value of good directorship.

Let us examine the manner in which the director works. In the first place, he stands in the same relation to the actor as theory stands to practice. The person who shoots a gun aims it and pulls the trigger; the bullets fly in the direction of the aim, and hit or miss the mark according to the skill of the man behind the gun. The director is the "man behind the gun," and the actors the bullets which he shoots from it. Still there are limitations to the director's control. Further discussion on this point will be taken up later.

Since they stand in the relation of theory, and theory is far from synonymous with practice, it is not requisite that directors be expert actors. They must, however, know how acting is done; they are familiar with this point through their knowledge of the theory of acting. They need to know all the laws of acting technique as thoroughly as the actors know them themselves. The best directors are even more familiar with them than most of the actors, a point which should be stressed. Many a teacher of singing is not able to sing himself, but has complete knowledge of the technique of singing. Without this knowledge he cannot impart anything to his pupils.

True directorship involves the dramatic school principle. This is denied by many actors, for they feel it should be no one's business to show them how to act; the director's business, they say, is merely to tell them what to do with the acting knowledge which they think they already possess. The truth is, however, that the director's vision should be inclusive, and his understanding should be able to supplement the deficiencies of the actors along any line. Very recently this theory is finding support; for in a few permanent professional organizations for the production of plays dramatic classes, in which the members of the company continue to "go to school," are conducted. When an actor has been on the stage for several years he is sometimes too prone to declare, "I know my business," when he may in reality know little of the technical, scientific side of it. What he thinks he "knows" is merely what he is able to sense and feel, without which he would not have been able to act at all; since he is born with it it is not knowledge in any sense. The latter comes with study. The great Russian director and actor, Stanislavsky, began to study the art of acting about the age of ten and seems to have continued to do so ever since.

The successful director has often been himself an actor. His perspective, through which he looks "from the outside in," is all the more true if at one time he has been in a position in which he looked "from the inside out." With such a background he understands the needs of the actor and can direct him from the actor's own point of view. All directors in the professional theatre are, or have been, actors, or else have become intimately acquainted with the art of acting through study and observation. It is a singular paradox that some of the finest directors have been poor actors. Among the first was William Shakespeare, who was undoubtedly a director, but it is not recorded that he was an outstanding actor. Only theory, then, is necessary for directorship, without the ability to convert that theory personally into practice.

Acting can be divided broadly into two parts, namely, emotional feeling and technique; the actor, through his inspirations, is able to produce the emotional feeling as well as much of the technique. At the same time, the director, most of whose work is technical, suggests to the actor the correct technique in his relations to the other actors, and oftentimes in regard to his own part, as well as offering suggestions for the actor's emotional expression.

Theatre Administration

We will outline for the student the administration which enters into the production of a play. This is divided into two parts. They are:

1. The Front of the House.
2. Back of the Curtain.

The front of the house embraces:

A. The manager or lessee of the theatre. In his employ are the advertising agents, ticket sellers, ushers, musicians, and others whose work is done "out in front."

B. The manager of the company. In his employ are the director and the actors. Both managers may pay jointly the salaries of some of the workers and share in many overhead expenses. The stage hands are usually in the employ of the theatre manager.

We are not concerned with the front of the house, but with the administration back of the curtain, or the stage. This embraces broadly five separate departments. They are:

A. The Department of Directorship.
B. The Carpentry Department.
C. The Property Department.
D. The Electrical Department.
E. The Scenic Department.

The Department of Directorship includes:

1. The director.
2. The stage manager.
3. Assistant stage managers, if any.

The function of the director will be taken up in detail. The work of the stage manager is to assist the director in producing the play. He works with the property men in selecting and assembling the furniture and stage properties, and sees that they are properly arranged in the stage settings during performances. He prompts from the book of the play at rehearsals and opening performances, rings the curtain up and down on the acts, calls the "half-hour," "quarter-hour," and "overture," in the dressing rooms before the performance, and each act before it begins, as well as performing any other duty within the limits of his position. The assistant stage managers, if any, assist him in this work.

The director is the czar of all administration back of the curtain, and the other departments are subject to his.

The Carpentry Department includes:

1. The head carpenter.
2. Assistant carpenters.
3. Flymen.
4. Other men called "grips" and "clearers."

The work of the carpenters is to build the scenery from a plan called the "scene plot" submitted by the director. With the grips and clearers, who are employed usually only at performances, they also put the stage setting together, work which is called "setting the scene," and take it apart after an act, which labor is called "striking." The flymen are stationed in the fly galleries to raise and lower all scenery that hangs.

The Property Department includes:

1. The head property man.
2. His assistants.

Their duty is to gather the stage furniture and other properties shown on the "property plot" submitted by the stage manager, construct such properties as can be conveniently made, and move the properties on and off the stage at the changes made during intermissions. Properties are all movable pieces not classed as scenery, and which are handled by the actors, such as furniture, books, dishes, letters, and the like. Properties also include mechanical outside effects. These will be described later.

The Electrical Department includes:

1. The head electrician
2. His assistants.

Their duty is to place and connect all the various lights used during the performance, such as lamps, wall brackets, outside lights in entrances, and so on. The entire lighting of the auditorium and the stage is controlled from the switchboard by the electricians.

The Scenic Artist's Department includes:

1. The scenic artist.
2. His assistants, if any.

Their duty is to paint the scenery after it has been built by the carpenters. Their scheme is suggested in conferences with the director or designer, assisted by books containing color plates showing architectural and scenic designs.

Carpenters, property men, and electricians are called "stage hands," and their entire body is known as the "stage crew."

Let us now examine the appliances with which a stage is equipped. The director must be familiar with them all. They are:

I. The stage proper.
II. Scenic equipment.

III. Properties equipment.
IV. Electrical equipment.
V. Scenic artist's equipment.

THE STAGE PROPER

The Proscenium Arch is the large arch which separates the auditorium from the stage.

The Apron is that part of the stage outside the curtain between the curtain line and the footlights. In the old Elizabethan theatre, the stage consisted of a large platform which extended far out into the auditorium. All exterior scenes were played on it. At the back of this platform was an inner chamber, separated from it by a curtain which could be opened or closed. In the inner chamber interior scenes were performed. Surmounting the inner chamber was a balcony with entrances and stairs leading up to it on either side of the chamber. The balcony was used where the play called for elevations of any kind; and no doubt Juliet had her first love scene with Romeo from this balcony. As the theatre developed, all action retreated to the inner chamber and the outer stage was greatly curtailed. This was then known as "the apron." In some theatres only the rudiments of it now remain, and in the latest theatres it has been eliminated entirely, the footlights extending across in a straight line just outside the curtain.

The Flies comprise all of the space above the stage setting. This space is generally about ninety feet high and is inclosed by the tall structure which can be seen at the back of a theatre from the outside.

The Gridiron is the wooden structure just under the roof of the flies. It gets the name from its latticed construction, like the cross-bars of a cooking gridiron. From the gridiron hang the ropes with which the hanging scenery is raised or lowered.

Fly Galleries are galleries above the stage against the side walls, from which the hanging stuff is raised or lowered by ropes from the gridiron.

The Paint Bridge is a bridge high above the stage across the back, on which the scenic artist stands while painting.

The Paint Frame is a large wooden frame parallel with the paint bridge. It is suspended on ropes from the gridiron and can be raised and lowered. The scenery to be painted by the artist is tacked on it.

THE SCENIC EQUIPMENT

The Grand Drapery is the large painted drapery which hangs behind the upper part of the proscenium arch. It is sometimes cut out in the middle in the form of an arch.

The Teaser fills in the opening cut in the grand drapery. The grand drapery and the teaser extend to just below the top of the stage setting to "mask" it in. In the latest theatres there is no teaser, and the "grand drapery" is not a drapery at all but a single piece stretched across. The grand drapery received its name through being painted to represent draped folds of velvet or plush.

Tormentors are flat pieces at each side of the setting, and to which an interior setting is lashed. (See Plate I, page 378.) The grand drapery, teaser, and tormentors, form the frame for the stage setting.

Flat Piece is a piece of scenery on a frame of wooden battens. For interior sets it is fourteen or sixteen feet high and about five feet ten inches wide. (See Plate I, page 378.)

Jog is a narrow flat piece two or more feet wide, used to construct corners in interior sets. (See Plate I, page 378.)

Ceiling Piece is a broad piece of canvas on a frame hanging from the flies horizontally, and dropped on to the top of an interior set to represent the ceiling.

Return Piece is a flat piece used to extend a setting off stage, usually back of the tormentor. It is often used as part of an exterior house. (See Plate V, page 380.)

Backing is a piece of scenery generally in two hinged parts set to mask in an entrance, such as a door or window. (See Plate II, page 378.) It may also represent an exterior (Plate III, page 379), or a hallway (Plate IX, page 382).

Wings are pieces of scenery hinged from top to bottom, and standing at the sides to inclose an exterior set. They may represent woods or parts of buildings, etc. (See Plate IV, page 379.)

Borders are strips of scenery hanging on battens from the flies, and running across from right to left over the set. They are painted to represent foliage (Foliage Borders), or sky blue to represent sky (Sky Borders). The latter are used in ship and street scenes.

Drop is a full painted canvas with battens at top and bottom, and raised or lowered from the flies. It is used at the back of an exterior set (Plate IV, page 379), or may represent a hallway (Plate IX, page 382).

Leg Drop is a drop cut out in the middle, and having legs which extend to the stage on each end.

Cut, or *Profile, Drop* is a drop cut out in profile, usually representing trees, cathedral pillars, and so forth. It is always placed in front of a full drop. (See Plate VI, page 380.)

Gauze is a gauze cloth used generally as a drop in front of a scene to give the impression of fog or haze.

Scrim is a transparent cloth which can be painted like ordinary scenery. Used for dreams and visions, when figures are illuminated from behind.

Ground Cloth is a dark brown, dark blue, or gray canvas spread over the floor of the stage, and on which the setting is placed. It is used with all sets unless some special setting, such as a garret, makes it better to show the bare boards of the floor.

Set Pieces are pieces of scenery which stand separate from others, such as set houses, set rocks, and the like. They are braced and attached to the stage from behind.

Ground Row is a low strip of scenery running across on the stage from right to left to mask in the commencement of a scenic setting behind. A ground row is used in front of the river of ice in *Uncle Tom's Cabin*.

Platforms are collapsible structures on top of which flooring is placed to represent elevations.

Run is an incline extending from the stage to the top of a platform. It is used in mountain scenes and the like. Steps are used leading to a platform in interior scenes.

Doors are usually set into frames which are inserted into openings in the scenery and clamped with the edge of a hinge, the other flange of which is screwed to the door frame.

Lash Lines are lines attached at the tops of flat pieces, with which the latter are lashed to adjoining pieces.

Stage Brace is a brace made in two pieces sliding one upon the other to adjust its length, and having a double hook at the top and an eye at the bottom. It braces the scenery from behind.

Stage Screw is a large screw used to fasten a stage brace to the floor.

Lines are ropes used to raise and lower scenery from the flies. A drop has a short, centre, and long line, the long line being the one farthest from, and the short line the one nearest to, the fly gallery where the raising and lowering are done.

Sand Bags are bags of sand used to weight lines when not in use. The three lines of a drop are tied to one bag and drawn up out of the way.

As a rule, scenery is distinguished from properties as anything that requires painting by the scenic artist. Besides the parts mentioned, fences, balustrades, fireplaces, and the like are classed as scenery.

THE PROPERTY EQUIPMENT

Properties are of two kinds, namely, those which furnish a room or setting, such as furniture, rugs, and carpets, and pieces which are carried in the hands. The latter are known as "hand properties." Besides these, the appliances used for outside effects belong in the property department. Some of these must be specially constructed for theatrical use; others are the same as those used in real life.

Thunder Sheet is a piece of sheet iron about two feet by five, hanging from a rope. On the lower end is a wooden handle. Shaking the sheet gives an effect of strong peals of thunder. Distant thunder can be made by rumbling a bass drum. Pounding the bass drum also gives the effect of distant cannon.

Thunderbolt. An excellent effect can be produced with a cannon ball rolling down an inclined trough containing wooden cleats as obstructions. The ball rattles over the cleats and strikes on a metal plate at the bottom. The trough should be inclosed to prevent the ball from leaping out.

Explosion. This effect can be obtained best by shooting a double barrel shotgun into a barrel. The effect of distance can be regulated by the relative distance of the barrel from the stage.

Wind Machine is a large wooden cylinder resting in a frame and turned with a crank. Strips of wood extend along it with their edges outward. A piece of canvas attached to the frame on one side and slightly weighted on the other is placed over the cylinder. The friction of the canvas on the wooden strips produces a sound like wind.

Wood Crash is a rectangular wooden frame with slats extending from either end and meeting in the middle. A wooden bar with obstructions on it stretches from side to side between the ends of the slats. Turning the bar with a crank causes a sound like crashing wood.

Glass Crash is a box with pieces of glass rattled in it.

Lightning. This must be arranged by the electrical department. The effect is produced with two wires ending in metal rods which, when touched together, produce a flash.

Rain. This effect is produced by means of shot rolled about on a drum head. It is sometimes done with a wooden cylinder containing dried peas. The former method is the better. A visible rain effect can be produced with water running through a perforated pipe. The water must be caught in a trough on the stage. A more recent, and perhaps a still better rain effect is secured with rice. The rice is held in a canvas "cradle," as in the snow effect described below. As the canvas is moved the rice falls through perforations in a tin trough along the middle of the canvas into a tin trough on the stage. The rice falling on the tin gives a sound of rain, and a blue light directed on it causes it to glisten like rain-drops.

Horses' Hoofs. The device used consists of the two halves of a cocoanut shell. Clattering them upon a marble slab gives the effect of a horse upon a cobbled street. For a dirt road effect the slab must be covered with carpet or sacking.

Battle Shots. These can be made with two pieces of rattan. Striking the rattans on an oilcloth cushion gives the effect of volleys of shots. Single shots of either a gun or pistol are made with the true weapon.

Locomotive Effect is obtained by a bundle of wires bound together at one end, and with the loose ends struck on a piece of sheet iron. A locomotive or fire bell effect is made with the real implement.

Escaping Steam from a Locomotive is imitated by means of two pieces of sandpaper tacked on to pieces of wood and rubbed together.

Cathedral Chimes are effected by a long bar of steel hanging from a rope and struck with a stick. Dinner chimes are sounded on the true instrument.

Steamboat Whistle is a wooden or tin instrument with pipes like those of an organ. It is blown upon.

Bird Whistle is a small whistle containing water. It imitates the singing of birds.

Baby Cry is obtained through a tin instrument which, when cupped in the hands and blown upon, imitates a baby's cry.

Cock-Crow and *Cat-Meow* are generally done with the human voice. These effects are, however, somewhat dangerous to produce in this way, for if not skillfully executed, may get laughs. In such cases it is often better to omit them.

Door Bell. An electric button and battery can be affixed to a board and run with a dry battery to produce this effect. Other kinds of bell effects are made with the true instruments.

Telephone Bell. A bell is often placed in the footlights and connected with the switchboard. The audience cannot detect that the sound has not proceeded directly from the telephone.

Automobile Horn. The noise is made with the true instrument detached from the machine. A horn with a rubber bulb is most practical.

Dog Bark. This can be produced with a small can having a hole punched in the bottom. Through the hole a string knotted on the end is run. The string is rosined, and running the closed hand along it in quick jerks produces the effect of a dog barking.

Carriage Effect. Though carriages are not much used, the effect is sometimes needed in the classical comedies. It is made by running the end of a pole along the stage while holding the pole erect. It is most effectively done with a clothes wringer on which the rubber cylinders have been covered with rosin.

Door Slam is best produced with a real door. Otherwise, with a short plank having a rope at one end. The rope is held in the hands and the plank is slammed on to the floor with the foot.

Slap Stick is used in circuses and burlesque. It consists usually of two barrel staves nailed at one end on either side of an inch thick piece used as the handle.

A Flying Flag. When a flag stands on a pole next to a wing, it can be made to fly by placing an electric blower behind it back of the wing. With an electric blower, snow can be made to fly in at a door or dust across a desert. The snow is made of cut paper, and the dust is generally cornmeal.

Snow Effect is gained with cut paper cradled in a perforated canvas hung from the flies. Working one side of the canvas cradle up and down causes the paper to sift out through the holes.

Camp Fire is effected with sticks of wood piled together, with red and white electric bulbs underneath connected with the switchboard. Smoke can be produced from incense burning in a bowl back of the fire.

Fire Effects are gained by burning a powder in a pan, which is used in the theatre for this effect. It is called "red fire." The fire laws sometimes prevent its use. When this prevents the effect can be produced with a flare made by touching two carbon points in the appropriate machine.

Fireplace Effect. The effect of glowing coals can be produced with a grate filled with chunks of glass, under which are placed red and white incandescents.

Aeroplane Effects can be obtained with the motor of a motor cycle.

Lion Roar. This can be best obtained by rubbing the thumb across the head of a bass drum.

Cloud Effect. This is made with two glass plates on which clouds are painted. The plates are passed successively from one side to the other in a stereopticon lantern, which is trained on to the stage drop.

Fireflies. The effect is made with little bulbs hanging

from thin electric cords. The lights are turned on and off from the switchboard.

Crowd Effects. Any number of different off-stage effects are secured from phonograph records. These sounds may be those of shouting mobs, church choristers, dance music, and many others. Sometimes members of the company may make special records in which their own voices can be recognized.

Fog. There are two ways of producing this effect. One is with steam allowed to escape from a perforated pipe stretched across the stage in front of the action. The other is with drops of fine net. The density of the fog can be governed by the number of drops used in front of the scene.

Smoke. This effect is best produced with steam, as for fog

Waves. In *Treasure Island*, when the ship was seen rolling on the waves, these were produced with a dark blue cloth under which were stage hands whose bodies, heaving up and down, produced the desired illusion. Of course, only a night scene could make such an effect seem natural, as in this case. In old melodramas waves were also represented by strips like borders. These were cut in wavelike profile, were hung on battens by wires from the flies, and were kept slowly swinging in contrary directions. All wave effects require dark scenes.

Effects which require electrical equipment must be prepared by the electrician. They should be produced by natural means whenever possible.

ELECTRICAL EQUIPMENT

Footlights are the row of lights at the front of the stage outside the curtain. The row has lights of various colors, generally white, red, amber, pink, green, and blue; and each color is on a different circuit. In many productions at the present time the footlights are not used, but instead, spotlights attached to the balcony rail are employed. This seems to be a growing tendency in the theatre.

Proscenium Strips. (Not always used.) These are strips of lights inside the proscenium arch on each side, and standing perpendicular. They serve to increase the general flood of light.

X-Ray Border is a row of lights hanging just back of the grand drapery. It is also equipped with various colors of lights on different circuits. The footlights shine upward and the X-Ray border downward at angles of about forty-five degrees, the point of contact thus meeting the actor's face and neutralizing shadows.

Border Lights are strips of lights hanging back of borders. They are used only in exterior scenes. For interior sets, when the ceiling piece is used, they are unnecessary. Border lights are all incased in long metal troughs to reflect the light downward.

Bunch Light. This is merely a bunch of lights in a metal box open on one side and standing at the top of a metal pole. Used to illuminate spaces off stage outside of doors, windows, and the like.

Strip Light is a row of lights in a metal frame. It hangs outside a door or window, and serves in the place of a bunch light.

Gelatine Frame is a wooden frame in which are placed sheets of gelatine paper of various colors. The metal box of a bunch light has grooves at the open end. The gelatine frame is inserted in a groove to change the color of the light.

Stage Pockets are electric sockets ranged at intervals on either side of the stage just under the floor, and from which convenient connections are made.

Plugging Box is a small box which lies on the stage and is connected with a stage pocket. Connection can be multiplied from this box.

Pan Light is a bunch of lights in an inverted pan fastened under the fly gallery. It supplies light to the workers off stage in a dark scene.

Spotlight is a light from a lens used to throw a direct ray. It is often trained from the gallery.

Baby Spot is a small spotlight used to throw moonbeams, light from a fireplace, and so on. It is sometimes placed in the X-Ray border to focus light on various positions.

Electric Switch Box. Modern productions do not now always depend for effects on the regular switchboard in the theatre. "Switch Boxes" are used, which can be carried from city to city with a traveling production. Cables are strung from these large boxes to connect with the various lights, and the whole production is thus kept intact.

PREPARING THE PLAY FOR PRODUCTION

The general equipment of the stage has now been outlined, and we must next consider the manner in which the director works in preparing the play.

In the production of a new play, the director is usually able to meet and confer with the author. The original ideas of the play are naturally the author's. He has created a vision in which he imagines his characters going through the action and speaking the lines. Some authors visualize the general action of their plays very minutely.

They also conceive definite ideas of the characters as to type and general appearance. But in many cases the author has formed a mental picture of the performance which cannot all be actualized, and he is sometimes disappointed in the performance rendered by the actors. For example, an author once wrote in his manuscript a direction for a female character which read, "You come on looking as if you had just had a cup of tea." He was asking too much if he expected the actress to convey such an impression to the audience. At the same time, the author is the best judge of the natures, motives, and relationships of his characters. He has a fairly clear idea of how they should look and how the parts should be played. When the rehearsals have started, the actors themselves, aided by the director, may originate much that will change the author's original ideas. They will either disappoint him, or may even, as often happens, put so much that he had not thought of into their performances that he finds his own mental picture deficient. An actor has sometimes brought so much to a part that the author has rewritten his play and elaborated the rôle. Many good plays are to a large extent rewritten at rehearsal.

After the director has conferred with the author, he has a general understanding of the play and the motives and characteristics of the people in it. If he cannot meet the author, he must form his own conceptions while reading the play. An actor needs to work out a conception of his own part alone, but the director should have a general conception of all the characters in the cast. Sometimes the actor forms a different conception from that of the author and director, and may then talk over this difference of opinion with them. The author and director are the final judges, however, and the actor must play his part as they want it played or not at all. He may bring something to his delineation that is an improvement on what the author or director had conceived, and he must then convince them of this improvement.

The acting of a play involves three broad steps in a process of evolution. Each step should be an advance over the one before it. In each step personal ideas are concerned; they are the ideas of the author, the director, and the actor. Each succeeding step may mark a development; but on the other hand, there may be retrogression if the director and the actors fail to actualize the ideas and conceptions of the author. Such failure is often due to an over-idealized vision on the author's part, like that of the tea incident mentioned above, and is not really retrogression, for such a conception cannot be actualized. In general, however, each step is, or should be, a step forward. An expert director, after absorbing the author's ideas concerning the play and its characters, uses his own creative imagination to improve upon them if possible. At rehearsals these combined ideas are presented to the actors, who elaborate upon them when they can with their own inspirational sense. The final development of the dramatic structure then culminates in the actor, but always within the limitations set by the director.

By the very nature of his work, the director is creative along with the author and the actors; all work creatively in that evolutionary progression we have mentioned. The author does not always have as great a technical understanding of the theatre as the director possesses. When the director receives the play from the author's hands, he is likely to find many flaws in its construction which render it, in the form in which he has received it, not completely adapted to production. He must then supplement its deficiencies with his own ability along technical lines.

One director said at rehearsal that he had read and studied the play thirty or forty times during his summer vacation. It was a play of foreign authorship, and he had not been able to confer personally with the author. He desired to understand thoroughly the psychology and motivation, as well as the personal characteristics, of the different characters so as to acquire as perfect a vision as possible of all their relationships to the play as a whole. It can be said from this that the director should study the play as completely as possible before the rehearsals begin.

A play may seem effective when it is read, but when rehearsed many maladjustments in lines and business may be apparent. The director must then make adjustments in places which contain technical shortcomings. This does not mean rewriting the entire piece, for it is assumed that before a play is produced it is considered worthy of production about as it stands. Only such changes need be made as render the play practical and effective in production. An example may be cited in the case of a symbolical one-act play. The author was unknown to the director, there was no copyright, and he took what liberties he chose with it. In the first place, he found the title unsatisfactory, since it was unattractive and lacked an appeal. He therefore changed the title to one which was succinct and embodied the idea of the story. The author had described the costuming of the piece, but the director found that a better symbolism could be suggested by changing the colors and design. He changed some of the hand properties, also, to suggest a better symbolism. Several of the actors found their speeches clumsy and difficult to deliver. The director then changed the wording of the speeches, while retaining the author's sense, so that the actors could speak them with fluency and ease. In one scene, the director found a breach, or "hole," in the dialogue, where the idea should have been bridged from one section to the next. Some lines were necessary to form the necessary bridge in order for the dialogue to flow smoothly from the one idea to that which followed. The director turned author and wrote these lines. At the end of the playlet, the lines and action finished abruptly and lacked any suggestion of climax, either in words or ideas. A writer rounds off a sentence with appropriate words, or a chapter with a closing idea, and the end of a play should be gracefully rounded off with some climactic idea, or at least brought to an end in such a way as to indicate definite finish. This playlet ended but did not seem to be finished. The director therefore devised some business in pantomime and tableau, since the nature of the play permitted such treatment, and thus rounded out the end properly. Throughout the piece he introduced many bits of business which had not been implied by the author nor suggested by the lines.

In producing this little play, much, then, lay in the hands of the director along the line of creative imagination. Some authors are willing that any change, interpolation, or modification be made in their play when they have faith in the director, for their principal desire is to see the play succeed. Other authors feel so sure of their own expertness that they will not permit a line to be changed. Both author and director may go to extremes. On the one hand, an inexpert director will often cut out so many of the author's lines, and tamper so heavily with the business, that an absent author may return to find his play stripped of its finest points. This is notedly true in the motion picture field, in which authors have found their scenarios greatly changed in production. On the other hand, authors who insist upon the virginal productions of their manuscripts meet many failures thereby. Even Shakespeare's works cannot all be produced in their entirety, as some of the lines have no bearing upon the story.

Within limitations, therefore, the director must be permitted some liberties in respect to rearrangement or elimination of the author's lines, or, for the sake of technical requirements, he should be allowed to introduce his own should the author not be present to write them himself. Sometimes the director will say to an author, "We need another line here to take this character off," or will suggest that there are too many lines in a given situation. The elimination of lines and business is easy, and there is a wide tendency toward this in American productions. It is far more difficult to elaborate upon the work of an author by creative interpolation of lines and business.

After all, the purpose of play production is to give the best entertainment possible, and even the classics have not escaped free treatment at the hands of directors. Augustin Daly's old prompt book of *The School for Scandal* reveals that this producer took many liberties with the established script. Interpolated bits of business for comedy effect, and many insertions of what are known as "gag lines" occur. Some of the lovers of the classics, who hold them to be inviolate, would resent such freedom with crystallized classic drama. But Richard Brinsley Sheridan was long dead when Mr. Daly produced *The School for Scandal*, and could not object if he would. However beautiful an antique may be in its original condition, any device to render it still more attractive should not be amiss. Mr. Daly made minor modifications even in Shakespeare's comedies, and introduced business and short lines here and there to produce more rounded effects. The director must use his discretion in this respect. A director in New York City once ludicrously distorted a Shakespearean play to suit his whim because he aimed at displaying original ideas.

Some directors have the habit of making speeches to the actors. These are often tedious and not always pertinent to the matter in hand. Speeches, however, can sometimes accomplish much which might otherwise require specific detail in direction. A director of an amateur group found a short speech very effective in this way. At the final rehearsal of a playlet he had been called in to "whip it into shape." The actors were young, but were playing mature characters. Their movements were too youthful. A short speech to the assembled company, in which they were told to "add twenty years to their lives" in maturity of movement and action proved immediately effective to all concerned.

Working Out the Manuscript

In preceding paragraphs we have anticipated somewhat in explaining the director's method of progress. Most of the rearrangement and interpolation of lines and business, or their elimination, does not occur until the director gains a perspective of how the play is shaping itself at rehearsals. In fact, the final "carpentry" of a play usually takes place while the play is being rehearsed, for before rehearsals are called, the director can only study and work out his manuscript to the best of his ability.

The manuscript submitted to the managing producer by the author is extremely deficient in the matter of stage business, relative positions, stage settings, and the like. The average author is satisfied to indicate, for example, that an act takes place in "John Brown's library," that John Brown is seated at his desk when the curtain rises, that on certain lines other characters enter, and that on other lines they go off. Some authors work out more of the mechanical details of action than others do; but after all, such a task is the work of the director. When the author says John Brown is seated in his library he may describe his idea of how the library should look, or he may say nothing about it. He may say, "Daughter Alice" comes in from the street, but may not indicate where the street door is located in the set. Some one else enters "from the dining-room," but no mention is made of its location. In reading the act, the director may have learned no more about the set than what is indicated here; but he knows that it represents a library, and that this library has an entrance to the street and a door leading to the dining-room. His technical work begins practically with the stage setting.

CONSTRUCTING THE SET

The work of determining what the setting shall be proceeds simultaneously with that of working out the technical business of the action. A mechanical method is used for working out action which is more or less popular, and is perhaps the most effective. As the director reads the script, he visualizes the actors' movements and relative positions as they speak the lines. In many scenes a number of actors must be on the stage at the same time, and the director's memory cannot retain a mental picture of all their positions at once. He therefore takes a large sheet of paper, on which he draws as much of the embryo setting as he has thus far established in his mind, and moves checkers or pieces of paper about with the names of the characters written on them to indicate the actors' movements. In this way he knows at all times just who is on the stage and what their positions are.

We have supposed that an act is in a library, and that John Brown is seated at his desk. The director may then surmise that the desk will be most conveniently placed at centre, and thus he places it. Very shortly he may discover that the placement of some other piece of furniture makes it necessary to move the desk over to the right or left. Before he has worked out the whole act, however, he will know definitely just where his desk is to be placed.

The director has also been told that John Brown's daughter comes in from the street. His first conclusion may be that this entrance is best placed at the back, and perhaps through a centre arch. The dining-room, from which some other character is supposed to enter, he places for the time being up at the right. If Daughter Alice has to go to a window and say, "Why, it's begun to rain, father," the director knows there is a window in the set, and must find a place for it. Later, if she says she is going to her room to change her things, a door must be placed leading to her bedroom. As the dialogue proceeds, the director may find that the positions of the actors render it more convenient to reverse the positions of Alice's exit door and the window, or the window and the dining-room door.

He uses the same method in respect to the furniture. If a character should sit, on a certain line, he places a chair or sofa in some open space for him to sit on; if he goes to a bookcase and selects a book, the bookcase must be created and an available space allotted to it. By the time the director has worked out with his checkers, or squares of paper, all the relative positions and movements of his characters, he has also drawn a fairly complete diagram of the setting. The entrances, windows, arches, and probable staircases which he has placed on his diagram are those essential for the action, as well as special furniture which the characters are actually to use. When this is done the diagram may be submitted to the scenic designer and artist.

When we said the director was czar of all operations back of the curtain, only the dramatic acting of the play was implied. The director is not always responsible for the entire scenic and decorative production of the play. In large productions, the director needs only to supply sketches showing what openings and essential furniture he requires. These sketches are then given to scenic designers and decorators. The former produce the architectural designs for the sets, after which they are built by the carpenters and painted by the artists, while the latter decorate them with furniture and draperies in the proper period and style.

MARKING THE MANUSCRIPT

While the director is working out the action, he makes memoranda of it in the manuscript. He does this in various ways and as simply as possible, with merely the idea of remembering the movements. For example, a character is to enter at the left upper door. The author has written simply, "Brown enters." The director writes after these words, L. U. The two letters indicate "Left Upper." Two characters are standing at centre, and one may need to cross to the right on a certain line. The director writes after the line, X. R., which is the abbreviation for "Cross right"; and where the author may have written simply, "He goes out," the director follows this with R. I., if the character goes off at right first entrance.

These are the simplest of his markings; others are more complicated. In a certain place, several characters may be on the stage at once and their various actions may be more or less simultaneous. The director will then make a small diagram in the margin to illustrate their actions. Below is an example:

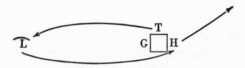

The small curve indicates a sofa at the right; the square, a table at the left; the letters, the initials of the characters; and the arrows, the movements which they make. Thus H leaves his seat and goes to the left upper door; L comes over to take his place at the table; while T rises from the table to go and sit on the sofa just vacated by L. G remains seated.

At intervals the director also must make in the margin a memorandum of the relative positions of the actors on certain lines. To do this, a memorandum something like the following may appear:

```
            G H
   S        L  M        B A
```

The left of the stage would be the right of the diagram as it appears here, and vice versa.

When the director has gone over the entire script in this way, having determined the general design of his sets, and marked the movements and relative positions of the actors, it is in condition to be used for the rehearsals. While the rehearsals are in progress, the director is able to see his visualized theory put into practice and he will probably find it necessary to change many of the movements and positions. Many of them can be improved upon. The movements already marked are only rudimentary and are merely to establish the actor's relative positions from speech to speech. At rehearsals, great elaboration on these movements will need to be made. A character may be marked in the script to X. R. (Cross right) but nothing further marked as to what he does after crossing. At rehearsals, the director may develop various movements and actions for him in that position, independent of the other characters.

Other markings must be made in the script for use during the performance of the play. These markings are for the use of the stage manager in ringing the curtain up and down and in attending to various outside effects.

These effects are quite as important as the lines and business of the play and must be delivered on cues with the same promptitude. For this reason, precaution must be taken, and a red pencil, the markings of which easily attract the eye, is called into use. Since the stage manager must attend to these effects, the director often leaves the work of indicating them in the script to him.

Suppose that on a cue a doorbell must be rung outside the entrance at the centre. In the script, about half a page before the cue for the ring occurs, the stage manager marks in the margin in red pencil, READY DOOR-BELL R. If, at that place in the dialogue, he is on the other side of the stage, he has plenty of time to get around to the position to ring the bell, and the red marking warns him that it is coming. He underlines the actual cue for the bell with the red pencil, and marks in the margin, DOOR BELL R. He also anticipates the curtain cue in the same way, with READY CURTAIN, and CURTAIN at the end.

These precautions avoid the likelihood of mistakes in producing outside effects too late or not at all. When outside effects are missed, or the actors and the audience are allowed to wait for them beyond "the psychological moment," the result is sometimes more ludicrous than the forgetting of lines. When red markings have been properly worked out in the script, the audience does not suffer the absurdity of hearing someone say, "There's the bell and it's John; I know his ring," when they have heard no bell at all.

A word should be said here about a common device which enables an actor to see what is going forward on the stage while he is outside waiting for his cue. Sometimes his entrance cue is not a spoken line but some bit of business performed on the stage. He must then see this business. In order that he may do so, if the set is a "boxed" one and therefore inclosed, a small "peek-hole" is cut in the scenery, outside a door, for example, through which he can watch the business and therefore come on at just the right time.

SCENE, PROPERTY, AND LIGHT PLOTS

Besides the scene plots, property and light plots must also be developed. The property plot is worked up during the rehearsals. The stage manager sits at the prompt table with the director and works out a list of the furniture and other properties required for the production. Later, the list is given to the property men. The separate pieces are grouped under the acts in which they are used. The director, the decorator, and the stage manager, may all be concerned in visiting warehouses, furniture houses, antique shops, department stores, and the like, for selecting the properties for the play. All the lighting effects throughout the play are indicated on a light plot for the use of the electricians.

II

When the director has completed his preliminary work on the manuscript, he is ready to bring the play into rehearsal. For many reasons, the actual furniture and properties that are to be used at the performances cannot be used at the rehearsals. The hand properties would be in the way of the actors, who, at early rehearsals, need their hands for their parts Ordinary chairs and tables can be used and entrances indicated with chairs. Chairs placed side by side serve for a sofa.

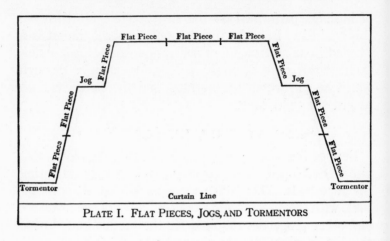

PLATE I. FLAT PIECES, JOGS, AND TORMENTORS

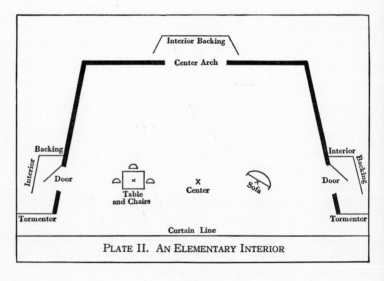

PLATE II. AN ELEMENTARY INTERIOR

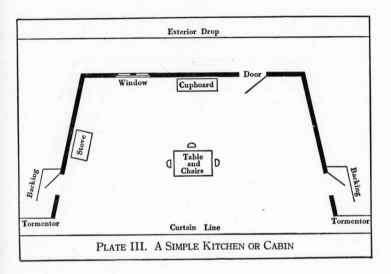

PLATE III. A SIMPLE KITCHEN OR CABIN

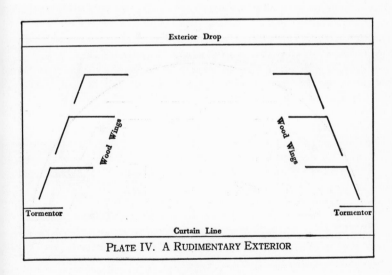

PLATE IV. A RUDIMENTARY EXTERIOR

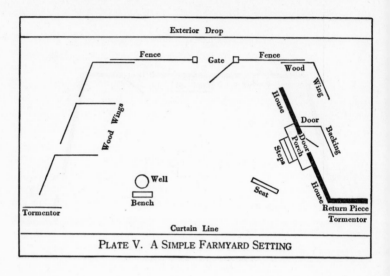

PLATE V. A SIMPLE FARMYARD SETTING

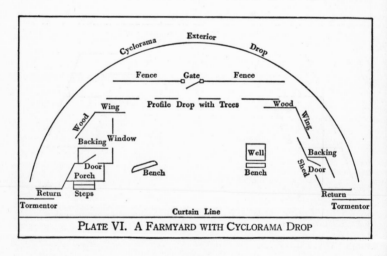

PLATE VI. A FARMYARD WITH CYCLORAMA DROP

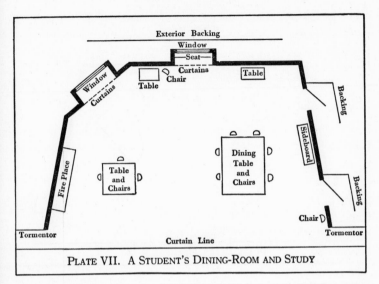

PLATE VII. A STUDENT'S DINING-ROOM AND STUDY

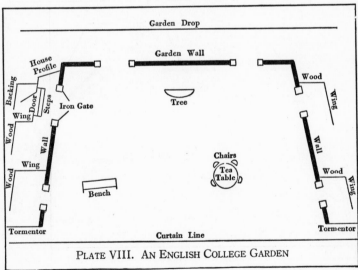

PLATE VIII. AN ENGLISH COLLEGE GARDEN

TECHNIQUE IN DRAMATIC ART

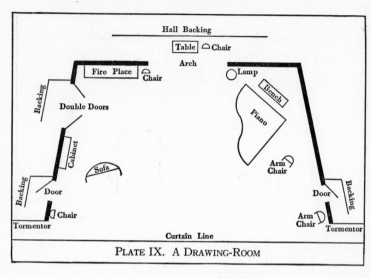

PLATE IX. A DRAWING-ROOM

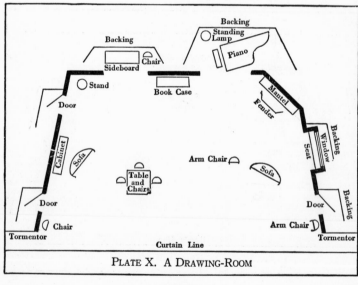

PLATE X. A DRAWING-ROOM

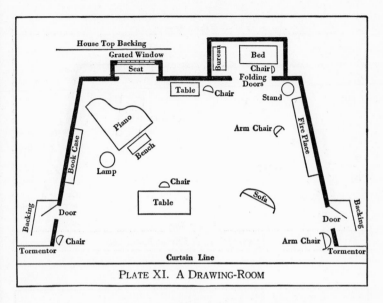

PLATE XI. A DRAWING-ROOM

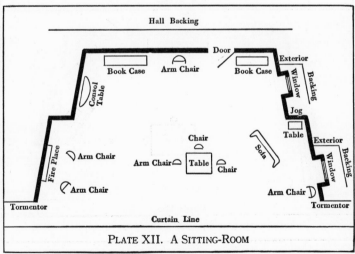

PLATE XII. A SITTING-ROOM

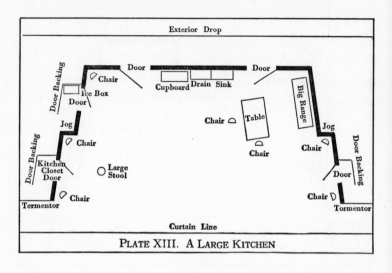

PLATE XIII. A LARGE KITCHEN

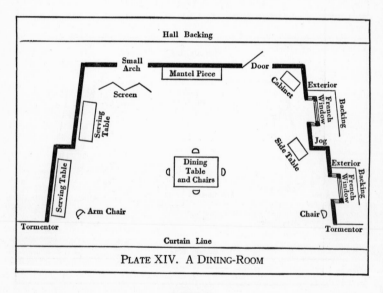

PLATE XIV. A DINING-ROOM

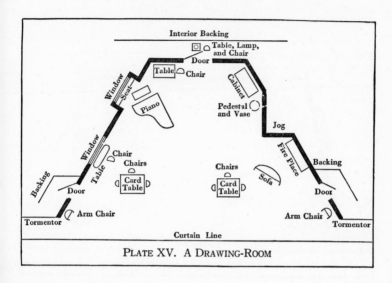

PLATE XV. A DRAWING-ROOM

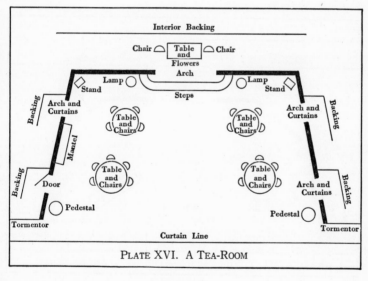

PLATE XVI. A TEA-ROOM

TECHNIQUE IN DRAMATIC ART

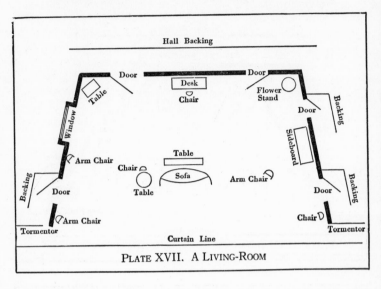

PLATE XVII. A LIVING-ROOM

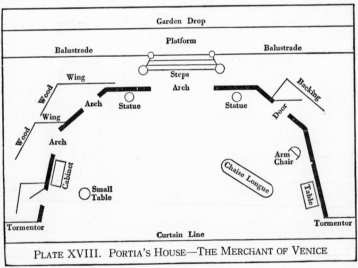

PLATE XVIII. PORTIA'S HOUSE—THE MERCHANT OF VENICE

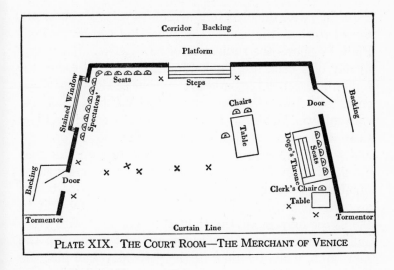

PLATE XIX. THE COURT ROOM—THE MERCHANT OF VENICE

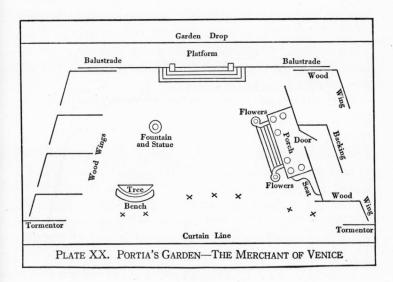

PLATE XX. PORTIA'S GARDEN—THE MERCHANT OF VENICE

In the pages devoted to diagrams of settings, some are drawn to show the simplest settings that can be devised. Plate IV shows the rudiments of an exterior. It consists merely of a back drop and side wings. Plate II shows a somewhat elementary interior. This setting has three entrances. A full stage setting usually has three or more for convenience. However, at times there are exceptions. The three entrances enable different characters to come on and go off simultaneously without meeting one another or clashing in their action, and also give a sufficient number of exits into various parts of a house for use in any play not too complicated. For example, the exit to the street may be at the right through the centre arch, and to other parts of the house at the left through the same arch, while the door at the right may lead into the bedrooms, and that at the left into the dining-room, kitchen, and servants' quarters. Such a set might be used as the living-room in a simple comedy. In the old days, when traveling companies did not carry their own scenery but relied upon that which the theatre supplied, this set was called a "centre door fancy."

Plate III shows a modification of this setting used as a kitchen, or cabin. At least three entrances are still necessary here, but the entrance at the back is shifted to one side and a window is added. Plate V shows an elaboration of Plate IV, in which a fence and gate are placed across the back and a house at the left, the whole to represent a rudimentary setting of a farmhouse. Plate VI elaborates this setting still further and employs a cyclorama drop, besides which a farm shed is seen at the side opposite the house and a cut drop across the back.

Plates IX, X, XI, XII, XV, and XVII show various

designs in sitting- and drawing-rooms, from which the amateur director can gain suggestions for scenic design and furniture arrangement. Plate VII offers a suggestion for a student's dining-room and study, and Plate VIII shows an English college garden. Plate XIII gives an idea for a large kitchen, and Plate XIV for the dining-room used in the same play. Plate XVI shows an arrangement for a tea-room in a hotel. Plates XVIII, XIX, and XX were copied from Augustin Daly's production of *The Merchant of Venice*.

FURNITURE PLACEMENT

The student is asked to consult Plate II. He will find three crosses marked on the diagram. The one marked "centre" is in the middle of an imaginary line drawn from side to side. The other two crosses are midway in the distances on either side of the centre cross. A table and chairs are placed over the right-hand cross, and a sofa over the left-hand one. The distance, therefore, between the sofa and table is twice that between these pieces and the side walls. As the centre is the most important spot on the stage, there must be sufficient playing space at and near that position. When the distance from right to left is divided in the manner shown, it renders the furniture symmetrical with the set. These two pieces must not be placed too close together, because so doing would limit the playing space at centre. At the same time, they must not be placed too close to the side walls, because the symmetry would be disturbed, and also characters would find difficulty in getting between the furniture and the walls. This is a simple point, but is often violated in non-professional performances. On a large stage, if the central space were very wide by reason of furniture placed too far apart, the actors would be made uncomfortable, and the action retarded because they would have so far to go from one side to another, before the movement could be completed. At the same time, the symmetry of furniture placement should not be so exact and even as to seem rigid. The same thing applies to character distribution. It should be understood that the principles outlined here are the standard ones, and that from them any graceful modifications may often be made.

It will be seen that a person coming on at one door down stage and walking across to the other would not greatly deviate from a straight line. Furniture should be placed far enough back so that the actors, in coming on at right or left first entrance, do not have to walk in a curved line around the furniture. Such movement would interfere seriously with their action, when they should make it straightforward and definite. At the same time, the furniture should not be placed too far back. If it is, the actor is too far from the footlights and his effects are weakened. If the student will observe the settings in a professional theatre he will find that a sofa and a table are to be seen in almost every living- or drawing-room set. These two pieces of furniture, placed as shown in Plate II, offer the most primitive arrangement of furniture possible. Primitive as it is, it remains the basis for some of the most elaborate settings that can be made. This rudimentary method of placement, plus the playing space which it allows, affords accommodation to a full cast of actors in the average comedy. All at one time, three persons can sit at the table, and two or three on the sofa. Three can stand at the centre, while two couples can stand at extreme right and left. In Plate V, the same primitive method is used in placement for an exterior set, showing a well and bench at one side and a seat at the other.

In Plate XI, the table has been shifted a little toward the centre out of its symmetrical relation with the sofa, in order not to be directly in front of the piano. Plate III shows a table and chairs at centre and a stove and cupboard. It will be seen that the table is set far enough back to allow a straight line between the two doors down stage. Other furniture might be added to this set, but the three pieces shown are the ones with which the action would be most concerned.

Plate XVII shows a sofa at the centre. In the act of the play from which this setting was copied, the sofa was the most important piece of furniture in the room and was therefore placed at centre intentionally. The act was the last in the play, and the death of the leading character took place on the sofa. There is abundant playing space in front of it. A simple rule for furniture placement is that there should be sufficient room between the various pieces at the centre, around them at the sides, and between them and the footlights.

Furniture is of great assistance to the actors, but easily becomes a hindrance. There must not be too much of it, nor must it be too large. Amateur productions are often given on small stages. Since the size of the stage cannot be increased, the furnishings must be governed accordingly. One director had a fetish for decorating his sets very elaborately and without regard to his playing space. He used large handsome sofas, elaborate library tables, massive armchairs, and various lamps, stands, and other pieces, all of which were very handsome, but too large and

numerous for the rather small stage; the actor had difficulty in threading his way about in the furniture jungle.
The actor must receive first consideration, and a surprising amount of his effect depends upon his furniture. If a
chair is too low, a character who tries to sit upon it with
graceful dignity may find himself awkward when he descends much too far.

Furniture should be selected with two important principles in mind. One is that it should be convenient and
useful for the actor, and the other that it should possess
symmetry and fitness in regard to the space. The selection
of furniture in respect to period and design belongs to the
department of the decorator, if one is employed, and we
are not concerned with this phase here. The director
should see that on a small stage the furniture is not too
massive, but that on a large stage it is massive enough.
A grand piano is almost always in the way in a small
setting, but is a great assistance in filling up space when
the stage is large.

In decorating a stage, as well as in acting, the principles
of embellishment and eliminating non-essentials should be
practiced. It must be decided whether a setting should be
elaborately decorated, or whether the furnishings should
be sparse. This must be left to the decorator. David
Belasco believed in decorating a scene with the minute
details of real life and showing the various accumulations
gathered by those settled in one place. Other directors
think all this minute detail distracts attention from the
actors themselves. For instance, they do not approve of
a highly figured wall paper, for the actors might not have a
high enough relief against such a background. A profusion
of pictures and various objects also distracts the eye. As

a simple rule, the decoration should not be too obtrusive nor should it be too meagre. .

When some piece in a production, whether a piece of scenery or one of the properties, .has been placed in a setting and it is finally decided to dispense with it, it is "killed" and is then "dead." When some small property must be found concealed in some place on the stage, such as a book behind a sofa pillow or a letter under a rug, it is placed there before the curtain rises and is said to be "planted."

Front scenes are represented with a drop running straight across from right to left first entrance. Such a scene often looks bare, but can be relieved with a piece of furniture or two. If there is a dark change for a front scene, the stage hands can easily place the pieces of furniture correctly by counting the number of steps they take in the dark, from the side to the correct position. Scene II, Act I, of *The Merchant of Venice*, shows a hallway in Portia's house. This is placed in I. Its flat bareness is relieved with a small seat placed over at right centre. The seat also breaks the monotony of a whole scene played standing. In *Julius Cæsar*, Act II, Scene I, the hallway in Cæsar's house can be decorated with a Roman chair at one side, balanced at the other by a pedestal and statue.

All good directors are particular regarding the placement of the furniture. It is first studied to achieve the most artistic arrangement, or relation of one piece to another, and then as to its exact set of positions. To insure these positions at all performances the stage hands are required to mark with chalk on the groundcloth or carpet the various places where the pieces are to be. When a change of furniture is to be made in the dark, the marking is done with luminous paint. The same system is pursued with the scenery.

A point of some importance should be mentioned here. Mirrors are frequently used, but they should not cast a reflection. When placed facing the audience, the attention is seriously distracted if the audience see themselves reflected in the glass. If they reflect the actors on the stage, they distract their attention from their work. To avoid this, the mirrors can be glazed effectively with soap or painted with silver.

The Fourth Wall

Besides having a strong relation to acting technique, the fourth wall sometimes plays a part in regard to furniture placement. Such times are not very frequent, for dramatic action and relationship are usually confined to the three visable walls of a stage setting. At times, however, the suggestion of the fourth wall is effective in the arrangement of furniture.

In Chapter VI, a phase of this treatment was cited from the plays *Julius Cæsar, Treasure Island*, and *Sherlock Holmes*. Sometimes furniture is effectively placed when ranged against this fourth wall. In *The Passing of the Third Floor Back*, much of the dialogue in the first act takes place before an open fireplace. This fireplace is represented by a grate and andirons placed at centre just inside the curtain line. Facing the grate are two armchairs. The probable reason for this position of the fireplace is that the dialogue which takes place before the fire is very effective; and the placement enables the characters to keep their faces largely toward the audience. In *Fanny Haw-*

thorne, also, which in England had been called *Hindle Wakes*, a fireplace was used in this way with a soft red light in the footlights to give the effect of glowing coals. The fireplace thus placed enabled the actors to play an important scene facing the audience. In *The Inspector General*, a play done by the Yiddish Art Theatre in New York, a setting was observed to have a small table and two chairs placed at the curtain line, the chairs with their backs to the audience. During the action, several characters at different times sat in these chairs. This variation in furniture arrangement is not often practiced; but when it is it is usually effective if there is logical reason for it.

Some modern theatres have their stages broken up with cross-sections, which can be raised from beneath to form platforms, or lowered to give passageway into basements and the like. Any elevation in a setting adds variety to its appearance, and also lends dignity to much of the action. For example, the balcony scene in *Romeo and Juliet*, in which Romeo reaches up to the embrace of Juliet, fosters the impression that Romeo seeks to attain that which is difficult of attainment. The two levels of action also impart variety and color. Dignity of action is secured in the picture of a person descending a long flight of stairs. In Shakespearean drama, platforms are frequently used to give variety of level, for such variety suits the dignity of this class of drama. In some productions of the "advanced" theatre this principle is carried to extremes, as when, in a certain production of a Shakespearean play, most of the stage was occupied with a huge flight of stairs. These could not be struck for a change of scene, so all the exterior scenes had to be played in front of the staircase. When not overdone, different levels, produced with stairs, balconies, or platforms, offer variety to the aspect of the setting and color to the action. Different levels are also very effective in scenes employing crowds. Any large number of people on the stage looks much larger and more massive when they are distributed upon different levels rising toward the back. When they are all on the stage level, the effect is foreshortened and the crowd does not seem so large.

DIRECTING THE REHEARSALS

We shall suppose that the first rehearsal of a new play has been called. Different directors employ various methods in launching the rehearsals. One method is for the author to read the play to the company. Perhaps quite as effective a method is for the actors, while sitting about in a circle, to read the play themselves, each one reading his own part. In some cases, this preliminary is dispensed with and the company plunges immediately into the rehearsals.

At rehearsals, each actor should provide himself with a pencil with which to mark into his part the directions for movement when they are given to him. The director must now move the actors about to correspond with the movements he has marked in his script. At rehearsals, it is the duty of the stage manager to mark into the manuscript any new business developed by the director. After the play has been produced and all business set, a new manuscript is usually made. Since much elaboration must be made at rehearsals, some directors develop practically all their action here, not having used the checker method beforehand. Still, the director can often obtain better results if he has meditated upon the action at leisure with his dummy actors, and has made his rudimentary outline.

During the first rehearsals the actor, not having yet committed his part to memory, must hold it in his hands. George Arliss said on one occasion that the actor should hold his part lightly in his hands. Since tension is a great enemy to the art of acting, even this little expedient is of value at rehearsals to promote relaxation and ease. It tends to develop the habit of relaxation at actual performance.

A new development in the theatre is the belief that the actors should be allowed to find their positions at will through their own impulse. It is thought that their mood of the moment will determine their positions better than a director can do it for them, and that prearrangement on the part of a director cramps their impulse and disturbs the mood and its logical expression in action. There is something to be said on each side. When an actor is alone on the stage he does not need to consider his relation to others, for no one else is present. A director will often say to him, "Do whatever you like, the stage is yours." But in ensemble relationships directorship becomes more involved. Actors might be allowed to find their positions at will, and up to a certain point this would seem natural. Suddenly, at some point, when a number of persons were on the stage, one character might need to whisper something to another, and the whole process would be awry if these two persons were at that moment on opposite sides of the stage. Then steps would have to be retraced and the two actors would have to correct their impulse to move, for example, into opposite corners and go instead where the director needed them for the whispered colloquy, whether this accorded with their impulse or not. One actor, under a stress of mood, had a strong impulse to cross to the opposite side of the stage when the director needed him where he was. The actor was not able to adjust his impulse and mood to his required position.

Again, actors who are allowed to move at will according to their impulse, many times feel no impulse at all and remain where they are. The performance then lacks variety of action, as there is little variation in stage pictures and groupings. In a performance when this lack of variation was noticed, the fault lay with the director, who was either incompetent or too great an advocate of this method. Most of the time the characters were stretched across the stage almost in a straight line, and seldom moved excepting to come on or go off.

In Russia much more time is generally devoted to the production of a play than in other countries. Fifteen or more months in all have been known to be used. Most of this labor is of an educational nature and concerns the historical background of a play, the costuming, the customs of the time of the play's locale, and the most intensive study of the characters. The great director Stanislavsky is noted for his work in all its phases. Since he devotes much time to rehearsals, his general method is to allow the actors to find their positions at will. This is continued with very many changes and new trials until the stage pictures are pleasing to him.

A character in crossing from one position to another may often place himself directly in front of another character standing farther up stage. It is the duty of the actor to be seen as well as heard and understood. Therefore, he should not allow himself to be hidden, but should move aside to an open space where he can be visible. He may do this without being directed to do so, and may make his action coincide with that of other characters.

A skillful director can so visualize the natural impulse for action that should go with various lines that an entire performance will be lighted and shaded with an infinite variety of movement and action, all fitting correctly into the moods of the actors. Suggesting some action to an actor often imparts to him the impulse needed to perform it.

As a concession to each method of production, we may say that the actor should be given as much freedom as possible, but must not overstep limitations in his relations with the others.

Rehearsing a play progresses along the three lines which correspond to the three sides of the human trinity, namely, the physical, the mental, and the spiritual or emotional. If the director is thoroughly familiar with his actors, his main business at the first rehearsals is merely to lay out the mechanical movements which he has marked in his script. Movement and action are the physical aspects of a performance, and the director does not at the first rehearsals expect the actors to put full expression into their lines. When an actor whose work is unknown rehearses in a New York production, he is usually expected to suggest what he will do with his part at the first rehearsal, and this often takes him at a disadvantage. An actor cannot act his part with real effect until he has studied and pondered upon it. An incident occurred which illustrates this point. An actor was called on the telephone by a dramatic agent and told to go immediately to a certain theatre, where rehearsals of a new play were in progress and actors were being tried out for parts. He did not ask for any details, but went immediately to the theatre, where he found other actors waiting. Some of these were sent away, being told they were not "the type," but this actor was asked to remain. In a few minutes a part was put into his hands and he was ushered on to the stage. He took a quick glance at the part, which seemed to be a Mr. Somebody-or-other who was making a call at the residence of another person, but the actor had no time to find out what he was supposed to be talking about. Therefore, he could not deliver the lines with any intelligent effect, nor accompany them with appropriate action. In a few minutes the end of the scene arrived and the actor made his exit. The part was taken from him and he was told that he was "too English." He turned to another actor who was standing by and inquired, "What kind of play is this?" The actor replied that it was a Southern play entitled, *The Mountain Man*, and that the characters needed Southern accents. This actor was an American and had acted successfully in Southern dialect. Many managers assume that Americans speak with a sort of twang, and because this actor's speech was somewhat pure and free from local mannerism, he had been taken for an Englishman and therefore was not suitable to the part.

DISTRIBUTION OF CHARACTERS

This principle corresponds exactly to that of furniture placement, in respect to symmetry. The furniture does not move, but the actors do. To counteract the shifting movements of the actors there must be an effort to keep the groups which come together at different times in symmetrical relationship to one another and to the setting. As the focal point is the centre, when action is at centre it should be balanced as evenly as possible on either side of that point. A person alone on the scene cannot observe this balance, for balance requires two or more people. When a number of persons are on the stage, they should observe the principle of balance.

Two persons may have a scene while standing at centre. They must then observe balance in respect to the central point. They proceed to a sofa at one side and sit, and they no longer observe symmetry in respect to the stage, but naturally sit symmetrically in respect to the sofa. The only reason for rendering this relationship unsymmetrical might be that they were lovers and consequently sat close together. Symmetry and balance should be observed, then, not only in regard to the stage setting as a whole, but in respect to various pieces of furniture, such as sofas or tables, when characters are grouped about or on them.

Sometimes, in the matter of grouping, the furniture may play an important part when it breaks up groups by causing the actors to be distributed about it. When they are thus separated from one another, a huddled appearance is avoided. Directors often vary the positions of the actors by having consecutive scenes of a similar nature played in different parts of the stage. Also, very important scenes are often brought forward instead of being played too far back.

The curtain rose on the first act of a play, disclosing a poker game in progress. The table was at one side, and all the characters on the stage were seated at it. In this position, the principle of grouping balance could not be observed except in respect to the table. One or two characters left the table, and the principle became operative. They might have sat in the corner close to the table, but the principle of balance made it advisable to carry them over to the other side of the stage, and this was done. Fluidity of human motion prompts us to seek open spaces. By the same principle, also, when the shifting of relative positions brings one actor in front of another, the one behind should move to one side or the other to find an open space where he can be completely seen by the audience. The only exception is when groups of characters stand at the back.

In the melodrama, *Cornered*, the curtain rose disclosing a sofa at one side, on which was a sick woman, and surrounding her were relatives and the doctor. A butler was often brought into the scene, but his position was always at the other side of the stage. He stood in that position during many speeches, while dialogue progressed among the characters near the sofa. The butler was the only character who could be spared from the vicinity of the sofa, and he was used to balance the grouping in so far as possible. In this way, one character at the side, if he is prominent enough, can balance an entire group on the other. For example, Shylock, in the courtroom scene, because of his importance, balances the entire assembly.

Very often a group of characters standing have shifted too far to one side. The director will tell them to dress the stage. Some of the actors will then move deliberately to the side that has been left open. Such direction is somewhat faulty. As a matter of fact, "dressing the stage" should never be necessary in this sense. Every movement the actor makes should have a purpose. If it is a definite action, that purpose is understood by the audience; if it is indefinite, the purpose is only in the mind of the actor and no meaning is conveyed to the audience. If an actor moves to another position merely to dress the stage because the grouping is unbalanced, his action shows no definite purpose and has no dramatic meaning. The technical principle mentioned in Chapter II, in which a character makes room for another entering the scene, uses the principle of dressing stage, but rather in the sense of *keeping* it dressed than in righting a symmetry once disturbed. The movements given to the actors should always take them to positions which preserve the symmetry automatically.

Classic drama generally has larger casts than modern plays, and more people are often on the stage at a time. The art of balance grouping is called into play when "extra" people are used in palace scenes and the like. Since many persons have to find room, all open spaces are used, with the result that the characters flow, as it were, into positions which balance from side to side. Plate XIX, which represents the courtroom scene of *The Merchant of Venice* has the grouping at a certain point indicated by crosses. It will be seen that those on the scene are about equally balanced on both sides of the central point, if the group of spectators in the right upper corner can be counted as one. Plate XX represents the setting for the last act of this play, and the crosses mark the grouping when the curtain falls.

Directions for the actor's movements should always correspond to the impulses in his lines. The director may tell him to rise on a certain line and cross the stage; or he may direct him to sit, on a certain line. Actors often move, rise, or sit, on lines that are not the logical ones for such actions, whereas lines preceding or following are the logical ones. The director should be careful that in directing an actor to move, he has selected that line which will give the actor the most logical impulse.

If the director is familiar with the actor's work and knows him to be suited to his part, it is usually advisable to give him at the first rehearsals merely the outline of his movements and general action, and wait until he has begun to develop his characterization for himself before beginning the intensive work of molding him into the finer points of his portrayal. David Belasco was noted for the fact that for several days he gave no directions to the actors beyond the rudimentary action we have described. He really sought for ideas from the actor. He knew that an actor could often supplement the ideas of the director and thus make a further step in the progression of ideas. He therefore waited to see what the actor would do with his part through his own initiative. This freedom of treatment on the part of the director imparts many ideas to him which he has not himself thought of. When these ideas are consistent, he elaborates upon them to round them out with better effect. When they are illogical or incorrect, the actor is restrained; but throughout, the actor often reveals much along some line in which he can most effectively be directed. The actor's business is to put into a part the best he has in interpretation and development; the director's to see that he does this within technical limits. This illustrates the limit that must be put upon the director's control, which was mentioned further back.

The actor has an individuality, and this should not be hidden. He has also inspiration, which enables him to do many things without being told. He may be asked to convey certain ideas, but should be allowed to do so with his own personality. If directed too closely he may make the mistake of copying the exact method of the director and thus lose the distinguishing method of his own quality. In many cases he needs to be told only what to do and not how to do it. A director used to hold the actors too closely to his own method, both in action and delivery of lines. As a result, the whole performance seemed to be a symposium of his own characterizations, or at least as he had visioned them. One actor showed how the director himself might have played a detective, another how he might act as an old man, and so on.

It is equally harmful for an actor to copy too closely a performance from another actor whom he succeeds in a part. If he watches the actor's performance night after night while he is rehearsing to appear in it later, he may often absorb, in addition to the business and technique of the true character, the mannerisms of the actor himself as well. These are rather a hindrance than an asset in his performance and do not fit his own personality. The actor, then, must not be robbed of his individuality; and at all times he must be made comfortable. Business must always be adjusted with the principle of comfort in mind.

After the outline of mechanical action, the mental and emotional sides of acting must be given attention. The mental side has been described already in relation to reading. This verges quickly into the emotional side, which rounds out the performance with the right expression and feeling. In this phase of the work the director is often prompted to say, "Make more of that," or "That is too strong," or else to tell someone to express such and such an emotion on some special line. From previous chapters the student can readily see the multitude of principles in which the actor may need direction.

A custom in Continental theatres may be termed that of "moving backgrounds." Perhaps the first example of it in America was seen in the performances of the Moscow Art Theatre in New York. They are mentioned in another chapter. In a play at the Royal Theatre, Copenhagen, Denmark, the principle was observed. In one scene a large number of people were on the stage, among them many extra people. While the principals were in action at the front, the human backgrounds were always in motion. This might be called a diffused ensemble effect. Our method tends toward focus on central points, as mentioned in another chapter; but here the motion and shifting of placement relationships seemed quite natural, and was certainly most effective. In our productions, if characters not participating in the dialogue are close to the footlights at one side or another, they are expected not to distract by action or pantomime from the focal points of attention. If they do nothing at all, they tend to look stiff and un-natural and may better be moved up stage. In the Danish production a young man and woman were observed sitting together at right and well down stage. They were at the time "out of the picture" and were taking no part in the audible dialogue. Yet for a considerable period they maintained an animated conversation in dumb show, laughing and chatting as naturally as they might have done in real life. At the same time, many "extra" characters moved about in the background; so the action of the couple mentioned, even though their position was at the front, could have been considered part of this background. It is the opinion of many that the art of Continental theatres is in many respects superior to our own; and it seems to be our tendency in recent years to imitate the Continental technique of moving backgrounds.

ENDS WHICH JUSTIFY THE MEANS

The purpose of the director is to get results, and he should get them in any way he can. In motion pictures, the actors sometimes have to exhibit little initiative. The director usually visualizes the business of the entire play. He then gives to the actors most, if not all, of the movements they are to make and the moods they are to register. The actor often does not know the complete story of which he is a part. We have seen that in the spoken drama the actor has some latitude and initiative; but in both fields the director, in the final analysis, may use whatever means he can to secure the effects he seeks. A story is told of a motion picture director who was unable to secure an effect of great fright from the star actress in a picture he was directing. She was to walk toward the side wall of the setting, and at that point was to be startled so by some imaginary sound that she would show great fear. The actress was unable to produce this effect. The director secretly instructed the property man to station himself back of the setting with a loaded shot gun. He then directed the actress to try again, and the camera man "shot" the picture. When she reached the side wall the director snapped his fingers, the property man shot off the gun, which was then close to her ear, and her fright was realistic in the extreme.

A director producing a play with amateurs was able to secure an effect in a similar way. Some characters were cast away on a desert island and had lighted a beacon fire, the flare from which they hoped would attract attention and bring about their rescue. One of the actresses needed to give frequent starts at certain fancied noises. She had only the words of the dialogue as cues for these actions, for there were no real sounds. She felt she needed an impulse for the starts, and could not make them when no impulse was given. At the rehearsals, to create an impulse, the director pounded with a stick when the actress was to make her starts, until she was able to produce the effects without this mechanical aid.

Technique in which time is involved can often be aided by counting. A director often tells an actor to make a certain number of counts before proceeding to his next action. In an amateur performance, a character had to cross the stage, look off stage over the shoulder of another character and then exclaim, "It's the rescue ship—Thank God!" When we peer at an object in the distance we generally require a pause before we are able to recognize it. The actor spoke his line immediately on reaching the other man's side. Correction failed to secure the right result even when the actor was told the principle. Finally, the director instructed him to wait at the other's side until he had counted four before speaking his line. This produced the right effect. In another case, a character who had gone off at a door to inspect the room beyond returned immediately. This did not present the illusion of his having made a sufficient examination. The director told him to remain off stage while he counted five slowly.

The duel between Tybalt and Mercutio in *Romeo and*

Juliet was once treated with the use of counting. The actors found they could not make the duel appear convincing, and their movements did not coincide and dovetail correctly until they spaced the movements with certain counts between passes.

In all these cases, the actors may or may not have really felt the situations, but if the effect appeared correct to the audience it did not matter. To be effective, results must be produced with the correct technique. An actor cannot completely feel his situation unless he is technically correct in its production; conversely, any mechanical means used to establish the correct technique will assist the actor materially to feel his situation.

GIVING A PERSON A SCENE

The first discussion under this heading refers to a practice which from time immemorial has been familiar in the theatre. It is called "getting up stage" and is now used metaphorically in the theatre, and even in real life, to mean haughty, proud, and overbearing. Its origin is this: The actor wants to keep his face toward the audience as much as possible. It helps his performance if the audience can see his expression frequently. It is a general law in the theatre that actors standing together should place themselves on a line with one another, neither one being above or below. They then stand half turned toward each other and half toward the audience in the "standard" position described in Chapter II. In this relative position the chances of each actor are equal, and none has the advantage of the other. Unfair actors sometimes violate this rule. Many an actor who wishes to take advantage of his colleagues and allow his face and expression to be seen with greater ease will retire up stage so that he is above the line on which the others stand. This forces them to turn their backs partly toward the audience, while his own face is seen more fully. If he has control of the play's production, he will often place himself at centre in the "up stage" position, while the other characters are partly turned away from the audience on either side. Since their faces are turned away, attention is detracted from them, and as he is turned more fully to the audience, this makes their disadvantage an advantage on his side. Such a position gives him the scene, but is not always for the good of the play.

A person should be given a scene only at times when interest must be focalized in certain places. The director must discriminate as to when they occur. The lines of one character are often extremely important, while those of another can easily be subordinated. If one character gets up stage and speaks unimportant lines while another delivers vital lines with his back toward the audience, this is distinctly wrong. The actor is not the one to judge. The director should know when lines may be delivered with the actors on a line together, and when one actor, for the greater effect of a scene, should be a little above. The director, like an umpire at a game, should not consider any one actor's advantage, but the best effect of the whole.

One instance was noted in which a maid servant was called to her mistress' side and severely reprimanded. The servant had but one or two short lines, while the mistress had several long speeches. Yet the actress with little to say stood several feet above the other, who, with her face turned away from the audience, was trying to be effective in some important lines. The director had failed to notice and correct the fault. Actors, if given too much latitude, are not always exact in establishing their relative positions, and directors should control these movements.

Many plays contain dinner scenes in which some of the characters are placed with their backs to the audience on the down stage side of the table. Those thus placed are usually of lesser importance in the scene. They may have little to say, while those on the other side and at the ends carry most of the dialogue. In A. E. Thomas' *Come Out of the Kitchen*, in a scene of this kind which used four people, the persons on the down stage side had a great deal of dialogue, and the person facing the audience had not as much to say, but had to produce much comedy effect in the business of gourmandizing his food. This business was considered of prime importance and was given the position in which it could be seen. When a *tête-à-tête* chair is used, the person with the more important lines would naturally be placed in the position facing the audience.

From the foregoing paragraph we find that one way of giving a person a scene is to get down stage and leave him up stage alone. This process was once reversed in an unusual way to achieve the same result. A method was used similar to the photographic process by which the central figure is thrown into high relief, while the background is blurred out, thus producing focus of attention on the principal. Arthur Hopkins, in his production of *Richard III*, felt that Richard should have a focal prominence in certain scenes, and that his grotesqueness and villainy could appear effective against a background out of which he stood in high relief. When the actors had scenes with Richard, they followed their natural instinct to come on to a level with him and came down to his side. Mr. Hopkins said, "Get back, gentlemen, get back," until he had forced the actors to form the "blurred" background which he desired. Richard, of course, did not turn away from the audience to address them, but kept his face to the audience and spoke more or less over his shoulder. This method may have been devised, also, to project the hauteur and superiority of Richard, whereby the courtiers did not intrude too familiarly upon his presence. No argument is offered for this method, and it is very unusual.

Since the centre is the point on the stage of greatest interest, giving other characters a scene often involves going out of centre, and in taking up the interest once more, returning to it. In *The Admirable Crichton*, a character had been the guardian and protector of others in the play, and was brought to account for fancied shortcomings in his guardianship. He stood at centre and defended himself with a long eloquent speech. This position gave him the centre of attention and the scene was his. At last the arguments of the others went against him and seemed to prove him guilty. With a few more words he went to one side and turned his back to the audience. This acknowledged his defeat, and the others, who had now dominated, moved into centre and thus took the scene to themselves. By a sudden turn in the story, the position of the character was vindicated. He then moved back into the centre, from which he once more asserted his dominence and command. A familiar situation is found in *Richelieu*. The minister's position is lost unless certain documents proving the treason of his rival, Baradas, are immediately delivered to him, and he has sent a messenger to procure them. While he waits anxiously, and the king meanwhile is hearing the accusations of the treacherous Baradas, he sits at one side, deserted by the courtiers and surrounded only by his friends. At the crucial moment the messenger arrives, puts the packet into Richelieu's hands, and he springs up and advances to the centre. From there he shows the documents to the king and the rival is led off to prison. In Richelieu's defeat the scene belonged to the others, but in his triumph it was his, and he went into centre to reclaim it.

In *Laugh, Clown, Laugh*, with Lionel Barrymore, a scene was played on either side of a table. When the scene started, both men were on the same line and their chairs were slightly turned toward each other. After a little the scene became somewhat intense, and the interest centred more in the lines of Mr. Barrymore than in those of the other actor. There was a break in the scene, when the other rose and performed some action. When he sat down again he switched his chair about so that he was partly turned away from the audience. This served to focus attention more completely upon the star, who from then on delivered some very important speeches.

This technique placed the other actor somewhat out of the picture. Getting into the picture enables an actor to take some part in a scene, while getting out of it gives the scene to some one else.

It is always well when one person is to dominate a scene, if there are several actors on the stage, to have him stand at the apex of a triangle with the apex up stage. In this way the actor will be talking almost directly to the audience without seeming to do so. In order to give him perfect dominance, the other actors must stand motionless, and of course with their backs partly toward the audience.

Giving a person a scene involves, also, the principle of distance. The plate of a camera takes in only what the focus can embrace. Other objects are "out of the picture" by being far enough away on either side not to be included in it. The focus of attention at certain points is supposed to embrace only certain persons at one time. Other persons must not intrude upon that focus, just as, when outdoor scenes are snapped in the motion pictures, observers are kept away from the focus. To give another actor a scene, one must keep off at a sufficient distance so as not to intrude upon the focus of attention. A simple rule is that a person who has the scene must not be crowded. When one person's back is toward the audience, he need not pay so much attention to the law of distance as when his face is visable.

ATMOSPHERE

A book could be written on this subject alone, but only a suggestion or two will be attempted here. "Atmosphere" has some relation to directorship along the lines of acting technique, but a more vital relation to that branch of the director's work which does not apply to the individual actor. The actor, then, is not always concerned in the production of atmosphere. Atmosphere more often relates to the setting in which the actor is placed.

It might be differently defined by people of the theatre. We shall define it here as of three kinds.

These are:

1. Scenic atmosphere.
2. Individual personal atmosphere.
3. Collective personal atmosphere.

The figurative atmosphere of the theatre is a suggestive atmosphere which we feel; it is, of course, received from the agencies used in producing it. In the theatre, it is a factor in making the scene seem real to our sense.

Scenic Atmosphere: It is not always enough that the scenery be adequate in painting and design. Many natural touches can be imparted to give it a sense of realism. This quality of atmosphere can often be promoted through the sense of smell. When we are in a forest, nothing more completely gives us the impression of woods, trees, and the essence of nature than the delicious odor of pine needles under our feet. When we visit a rose garden, the incense of the petals delights our nostrils; we instantly sense the true atmosphere of our surroundings. In the theatre, atmosphere can be created in a forest scene if the stage is decorated with real evergreens, the odor of which is carried out to the audience. Leaves gathered in the woods and sprinkled on the stage may carry their odor to the audience, and also, since they are real and not painted, an atmosphere is carried through the sense of sight as well. We never smell Chinese punk without receiving a suggestion of Orientalism. In Oriental scenes, directors have often arranged contrivances to carry the odor of punk and incense over the footlights. A flag made to fly with a blower creates an impression of a windy day. When cut paper is dropped from a snow-bag to represent snow, the atmosphere of cold is often so realistic that an audience will feel inclined to wrap their cloaks about them. In a dramatization of *The Garden of Allah*, the sand-storm, which was produced with powerful blowers and cornmeal, imparted an atmosphere that was most realistic.

Varied effects of atmosphere are secured with lighting. The pale light of the moon suggests an atmosphere of stillness and romance. The amber light of an autumn sun gives an atmosphere of lengthening shadows and a dying day. A streak of light stealing through the bars of a dungeon imparts an atmosphere of chill loneliness and despair.

The atmosphere of sound is equally effective. The tinkling bells of sheep in the distance suggests the peaceful atmosphere of the pastures; while bird whistles occasionally sounded in an act present an impression of light-heartedness and romance. The Forest of Arden in *As You Like It* lends itself splendidly to such treatment. With bird whistles and sheep bells, the mood of the play is appropriately suggested. In the drama, *My Son*, distant fog horns blowing on a foggy night off the coast created a weird illusion.

The ticking of a clock helps greatly to create atmosphere. For example, it can be used effectively in a farmhouse kitchen to create an atmosphere of homelike peace and quiet. This general atmosphere would pervade an entire act. At some dramatic moment, however, when the dialogue ceased in order to make way for some important dénouement, the silence, marked only by the ticking of the clock, would create a strong element of suspense. In a remarkable play by Lord Caldron, called *The Little Stone House*, the clock plays a very important part during the many pauses in the dialogue, when its ticking makes the pauses eloquent or heightens their suspense. The opportunities for atmosphere in varied effects are countless, but these few examples should suffice to suggest the method.

Individual Personal Atmosphere: A definition of atmosphere in a figurative sense is given by Webster as "moral atmosphere." This kind of atmosphere is the impression imparted to us by an individual's personality. Each person is surrounded by his "aura" or, as it is more simply defined, his personality. The actor carries this suggestive aura, or personality, in the mood in which he enacts a scene. On some one of his entrances, his "atmosphere" may be immediately suggested. It may be an atmosphere of great joy or of deep sadness. In the rôle of Manson in *The Servant in the House*, the actor needs to carry always an atmosphere of spirituality. Hamlet is pervaded with an atmosphere of sadness and melancholy. The Stranger, on his first entrance in *The Passing of the Third Floor Back*, immediately projects an atmosphere of mystery, benevolence, and the spirit. Individual personal atmosphere must then be understood to be the impression obtained from any pervading mood of a single person.

Collective Personal Atmosphere: This is the general atmosphere or impression created by a number of persons. When the curtain rises on an act, we may receive the atmosphere of the scene from the scenery and its accompanying effects alone. Again, that atmosphere may be supplemented by effects proceeding from the actors themselves. One scene in Augustin Daly's production of *As You Like It* disclosed the banished Duke and his followers outside their cave in the forest of Arden. Atmosphere has its function, and in order that its impression may fully register, a moment or two should elapse before the dialogue begins. This scene, therefore, gave the audience a picture of woodland peace before the dialogue began. Some of the foresters were chatting at the table where the evening meal was about to be served; two were sitting on the ground engaged in stringing their bows; some others were at one side playing a game resembling our mumblity-peg; while one or two others were dozing at the back. Two foresters entered with a sapling on their shoulders, from which hung the carcass of a newly slain deer, and accompanying them were two hunting dogs. They proceeded into the cave with their prize. All this was atmosphere, and it was created before any of the dialogue was spoken. It served to give the audience the correct mood and impression of the scene which was to follow.

At the rise of the curtain on the first act of *The Merchant of Venice* in the production by Mr. Daly, the trading life of the Mart in Venice was produced. Any market place is a hum of business, and Mr. Daly sought to convey this impression. As the curtain rose, various groups of nobles, citizens, merchants, water carriers, and flower girls passed in and out and mingled together. There was then a procession accompanying the Doge in state across the square. Antonio and his friends did not enter and begin the dialogue until this moving tableau had been shown.

Mr. Daly was criticized, however, when, to create atmosphere, he brought on some street urchins in Act III, Scene II, to tantalize Shylock and pluck at his gaberdine when he was frenzied at the news of his daughter's elopement. Atmosphere has great value and effect, but must not detract from important scenes. In David Belasco's production of *The Auctioneer*, with David Warfield, there was a street scene backed by a department store entrance. Supernumeraries were made to pass and repass, some of them coming from the store and others entering it. Their action was controlled so as not to be done while important portions of the scene were in progress. Supernumeraries offer the commonest means for the production of collective personal atmosphere and can be used in many ways for this purpose. The commonest places for the production of this kind of atmosphere are at the beginnings of acts.

OUTSIDE EFFECTS

Outside effects are most important. When properly produced they do much to create illusion, but when improperly executed easily become ludicrous. Care should be taken that they do not "imitate nature abominably." At final rehearsals the director should be careful that they sound exactly like the noises which they are supposed to represent; if they do not, they vie with the comedians in getting laughs. It is not enough that they be heard by the actors only; they should be distinctly heard by the audience as well. At the same time, they should not be too loud or they may drown the voices on the stage. When rain and thunder are produced off stage, the dialogue may not be heard if the effects are too loud. Heavy peals of thunder should be made on definite cues in the dialogue, and then made to subside during succeeding speeches. Prolonged effects should also be managed with judgment. They should not be continuous or without regard to the quality of the scene in progress, but should be regulated by the changing moods of a scene. For example, in dialogue of volume and excitement these effects can be heightened, for the actors' voices will rise above them; but when the mood changes and the voices are more subdued, such effects must be modulated as well. In certain quiet and impressive sections of a scene, the effects should be discontinued for the time being. The quality and volume of the effects must depend on the director's judgment.

A serious defect in outside effects is to jumble them. Like the actors' lines, they should be clear-cut and distinct. They should not be mixed indiscriminately with the lines any more than the lines themselves should be jumbled together by the actors. Effects, like lines, should be produced on cues, with due regard to the psychological moment.

A scene in the second act of *Othello* will illustrate this. Iago has entered upon his villainous plot and has made Cassio drunk. Cassio and Montano engage in a duel. Their friends take sides and there is a general fight. In the excitement, Iago speaks in an aside to his accomplice Roderigo,

> IAGO: Away, I say; go out and cry a mutiny.
> > (*Roderigo goes off to ring the alarm bell. Iago then continues:*)
> > Nay, good lieutenant—alas, gentlemen!
> > Help, ho!—Lieutenant—Sir,—Montano,—sir;
> > Help, masters! Here's a goodly watch indeed!
> > > (*Bell rings off stage.*)
> > Who's that which rings the bell? Diablo, ho! (*Bell.*)

The town will rise; God's will, Lieutenant, hold! *(Bell.)*
You will be shamed forever. *(Bell.)*
  (Enter Othello and attendants.)
OTHELLO: What is the matter here? *(Bell.)*
MONTANO: Zounds, I bleed still; *(bell)* I am hurt unto
  death. *(He faints.)*
OTHELLO: Hold for your lives.
IAGO: Hold, ho! *(Bell.)* Lieutenant, sir,—Montano—
  gentlemen,—*(bell)*
  Have you forgot all sense of place and duty? *(Bell.)*
  Hold! the general speaks to you: *(bell)* hold, for shame.
  (Bell.)
OTHELLO: Why, how now, ho! from whence ariseth this?
  (Bell.)
  Are we turned Turks, and to ourselves do that
  Which heaven hath forbid the Ottomites? *(Bell.)*
  For Christian shame put by this dreadful brawl! *(Bell.)*
  He that stirs next to carve for his own rage
  Holds his soul light; *(bell)* he dies upon his motion.
  (Bell.)
  Silence that dreadful bell! it frights the isle
  From her propriety—*(Bell.)* *(An attendant goes off.)*
              What is the matter, masters? *(Bell.)*
  Honest Iago, that look'st dead with grieving
  Speak, who began this? on thy love I charge thee.

It is seen that the sounds of the bell come in on definite cues, but so frequently as to appear to have no
regard to the lines. At the same time, the lines and the
bell sounds are clear-cut and distinct from each other.
This effect is a little difficult and requires rehearsal,
for the bell must come in quickly on each cue so as not
to halt the lines, nor yet drown them by ringing simultaneously. The bell does not stop until the line after the

departure of the attendant. It would take him a moment or two to stop it.

A simple series of outside effects occurs in *Richelieu*, and the stage manager must take care to reproduce the effects with truth to life. Richelieu sits alone in his chamber and fears that a net of conspiracy may be closing around him. He says:

> —e'en now
> Thro' the chill air the beating of my heart
> Sounds like the death-watch by a sick man's pillow.
> > (*He rises.*)
> If Huguet should deceive me—
> > (*He hears distant sounds of horses' hoofs and listens.*)
> > > Hoofs without!
> > (*The hoof beats grow louder, and stop. There is a slight pause, then a sound of a heavy bolt being drawn, and clanking chains.*)
> The gates unclose—
> > (*There are then sounds of steps approaching the door.*)
> > > Steps near, and nearer!
> > (*The door is burst open and Julie de Mortimer, his ward, rushes in.*)

These effects must be produced on the exact cues and should correctly imitate the sounds as they would occur in real life. When some outside effects are thus produced, they are eloquent in inspiring dread or tense expectancy.

CURTAINS

The management of the curtain should be governed by the nature of the entertainment. Farce is quick and brisk; emotional drama is ponderous and slow. Sometimes the curtain must be fast or slow according to the kind of picture or situation it is to reveal or shut out. Curtain action is of three kinds, namely, fast, medium, and slow.

There is never any occasion in farce for a slow curtain. This would defeat the idea at the start. The commonest curtain action is medium, and it is the one always used when no other specification is made. As a general rule, a play starts with a medium curtain. None of the story has been told, so the curtain cannot be used to accentuate suggestion in any way. On a succeeding act, however, when the story is under way, it may be necessary to register some impressive idea. This may be done on some beautiful scenic effect. For example, the dawn may be seen breaking over the distant hills. A slow curtain rising upon such a scene will emphasize the idea of the slowly breaking day. A rising curtain may have medium speed, but should never be quick. A lover, for example, might very slowly open a case containing a necklace for his sweetheart so as not to dazzle her too quickly. So, also, scenes which have the surprise of a special beauty are often more effective when disclosed with a slow rising curtain.

In *Hamlet*, on the death of the Prince, the final curtain is always made to descend slowly. To use a quick or even a medium curtain on this scene would seem like throwing the Prince ruthlessly into his grave. His spirit has slipped gently away and the curtain should fall in the same way, like the slow and mournful steps which are to follow him to his tomb. In general, slow descending curtains foster a note of sadness and should not be used when joy and laughter bring the curtain down.

Since the action of farce is more or less swift, a quick descending curtain is sometimes necessary when the action at the end of an act is especially rapid or climactic. A curtain may sometimes be too rapid and shut off too quickly action which the audience should fully grasp and understand. Fast or slow curtains must not be used indiscriminately, but only when a special need arises from the situation. A quick curtain must not be too quick, and a slow curtain can sometimes be made too slow.

Curtain cues should be anticipated, especially on slow curtains. The stage manager generally takes a cue several words from the end on which to press his button. The curtain must also be "warned" several speeches ahead in order that the flyman may be ready on time.

One director had the custom, especially in farce, of ringing the curtain at such a time that at the final word the curtain was not more than ten feet from the stage. The anticipation had to be correctly timed. In *The Unknown Soldier* the last act began with a prayer. To give the audience the effect of hearing the prayer only from the middle on, the actor began to speak before the curtain left the stage and continued as it rose.

ACTION ON CURTAINS

The common treatment in respect to the end of an act is to have the actors hold the picture during the second curtain and the applause which accompanies it, and on the third curtain make their bows to the audience. Holding the picture on the third curtain often looks stereotyped and unnatural, and is usually not done. In a company with a star, the number of persons on the stage is usually narrowed down on succeeding curtains, and the star takes the last one alone. In well-ordered performances the curtains are rehearsed as well as the play; the number of persons for each curtain is designated, and they have their allotted places in which to stand. They take these places quickly, if they were not on the stage when the curtain fell, and thus do not delay the rise of the curtain. This would weaken the applause, and good showmanship demands that there shall be as much applause as possible. The stage manager often makes out a list indicating just what characters shall appear on each curtain. When they know where they are to stand, they avoid a huddled appearance, as well as a scurry to find places. These successive curtains for applause are named "calls."

Another method of treatment on the second, and sometimes the third curtain, is to present a moving tableau showing some further development of the action that took place at the end of the act. This treatment can be used only when the situation permits it, yet sometimes it is the most logical to employ. For example, at the end of an act, a young soldier bids goodbye to his mother and rushes off to his company. The second curtain shows the mother at the door waving her hand after him. The curtain remains up while she comes slowly to a table, picks up the portrait of another son who has lost his life in battle, looks at it, and then falls weeping into a chair. Many elaborations on previous action can be made on second and third curtains. The presentation of immovable tableaus on successive curtains was an old-fashioned method, but is not now so popular.

Some theorists in advanced ideas in the theatre do not believe in curtain calls between acts. They think these calls take the actor for the moment out of his character and thus destroy his illusion. When the play is over, however, they permit calls after the final curtain. Even when calls are allowed between acts, if a "dead man" is on the stage at the end of an act he should surely not rise and take the call, but should quickly leave the stage after the picture and before the curtain rises for the call. It tends to destroy the illusion, also, if a favorite actor gets out of his character by bowing in acknowledgment of a "reception" from the audience on his first entrance. In the best productions no flowers are sent over the footlights.

LIGHTING

This subject embraces one of the most important principles in the production of modern plays. In the present day theatre more attention is being paid to this element in play production than formerly. This is due to the rapid strides that have been made in scientific methods of applying electricity. Many uses are found for this medium which were denied the old theatre, when only gas, and even the earlier candles, were employed. By means of new inventions for distributing electric light, the possibilities in its use have been increased, so that today producers can illuminate their stages with effects that imitate nature closely.

Light is one of the most potent bearers of illusion in the theatre. It gives a final touch of effectiveness, but at the same time is much abused.

It is a question as to how much latitude may be employed in exact imitation of nature, and how much regard must be paid to what we term stage license. The audience comes to see as well as to hear, and much of this involves watching the actors' faces. In many situations of real life, human drama is played in little light or none at all. These scenes, if transported to the stage, would require some light at least; though even in the theatre scenes are sometimes played in darkness. Striving too closely to imitate the exact conditions of nature sometimes defeats the best effects of the theatre.

People in the real world move in a constant play of shadows. Shadow, therefore, is considered a natural quality of lighting in the theatre. But shadow can sometimes be carried to extremes. This might be true in broad comedy and farce which, more than any other kinds of drama, require an abundance of light. Therefore, directors should use discrimination in the lighting of a play; for although the lighting should be made to conform to nature as closely as possible, it should not defeat stage license and rob the audience of the best visual effects of the actors themselves.

Many experiments have been made in recent years with overhead lighting. Since the light of the sun comes from above, it is believed that light should do so in the theatre. Some producers therefore eliminate the footlights and direct the light only from the borders and various "spots" overhead. Still, science tells us the earth reflects the light of the sun. The footlights may serve in a measure to imitate this reflection. Therefore, many of the methods of overhead lighting without counteraction from the footlights are not always true to nature after all. This is a point which every producer must decide for himself.

David Belasco produced a play in which he dispensed

with the footlights altogether. Instead of these he had special spotlights which he trained on the actors, and each character, according to his general position, had a different light, either from above or at one side. This was all right so long as the actor remained in the light, but when he moved out of it his face was in shadow and his effects were weakened.

In another play the first act was played in a drawing-room, and afternoon tea was served. The footlights were cut out, and the only light was supposed to come from some drawing-room lamps. These left most of the stage in shadow, and the effect would have been gloomy even in a real room. The dialogue of this act was light and airy, but the actors' faces were often in shadow, which did not serve to heighten their effects. The ultimate failure of the play might have been foreshadowed by the gloom of its first act.

For purposes of this discussion we will declare ourselves in favor of footlights as a necessary adjunct to stage lighting. By the mere fact that real light can come from every direction save out of the earth by reason of reflection and diffusion, light coming from the footlights can produce a natural effect. In imitation of nature, therefore, light on the stage may be made to come from any direction save out of the floor itself.

The method and effect of lighting are governed by the author's story. The lighting must be regulated in respect to the story's geographical situation, whether in the cold regions of the north or in the heat of the tropics, the season of the year, the time of day, and whether the scene is in the house or out of doors. Next, the lighting must be further governed by the nature of the play.

The closet scene in HAMLET by the Montreal Repertory Theatre.
Verticality concentrates the action of the players

HENRY IV played in the Elizabethan style against the natural architecture
at Dartmouth College

Composite photograph of scenes from PEACE ON EARTH showing thoughts in the prisoner's mind. A Theatre Union production at the Civic Repertory Theatre, New York City

It may be a story of tragedy, of melodrama, of mystery, of love and romance, or of hate. The method of lighting, as it accords with the nature of the story, establishes an atmosphere which suits the moods of the various scenes. The demand of the theatre in respect to lighting is varied, and no two plays require exactly the same system.

A recently developed system of lighting might be termed the "spot light system." In *Peace on Earth* it was effectively employed. For all scenes the play had a cyclorama drop backing of black velvet. Within the cyclorama were several platforms on different levels. These were painted black. In the last act the action was cut up into very short scenes, which were played by single characters or small groups on the different levels. The leading character stood as a prisoner in a cell below. The other characters, and the little scenes they played, represented merely the thoughts passing through the prisoner's mind. The stage was dark, except for the light in the prisoner's cell; and as the various scenes, or "thoughts," were enacted, spotlights were thrown on them out of the darkness. As the lights changed quickly from one scene to another, this method vividly presented the effect of rapidly changing thoughts in the prisoner's mind.

The two most important sources of light are the footlights and the X-Ray border, with the addition of the proscenium strips when these are used. The proscenium strips may be equipped in the same way as the footlights, with lights of various colors. Besides these mediums, light comes from the other borders, bunch lights, or strips in entrances, spotlights trained from the borders or from the sides above, sometimes a spotlight from the gallery, a spotlight from a fireplace, and various lamps and wall brackets on the stage.

Real lamps on the stage would not in themselves throw sufficient light. The light of the lamps can be supplemented with stage lighting so as to give an effect such as these lamps would give in the narrower quarters of real life.

The different circuits in the footlights are used in various ways. White expresses the frank, broad light of full day. Blue gives the cold pale light of night. Moonlight requires blue. Red gives a light of warmth. It must be used in the light of a fireplace, or for any conflagration. Green is ghastly and may be used for mystery or any scene of ghastliness and dread. Amber and red are used to express a setting sun. They have a glow of warmth, and may be employed when the sun has ceased to shed the white light of its zenith and imparts the ruddier glow of its setting at late afternoon. Pink light is soft. Like the color in the cheeks, it expresses youth and tends to eradicate age. It may be used to express the feminine softness of a lady's boudoir, when the lamps are subdued with pink shades and the light is softened. The lights are usually blended in the "foots" and borders. Pure white would be too white, would kill color, and produce ghostlike effects in make-up. Tests for the right color of lights should be made at the dress rehearsal, and the proper blendings made.

The footlights kill the shadows cast by the overhead lights, and thus produce a balanced light. Sometimes the lights at the ends are extinguished so as not to illuminate the outside of the proscenium arch. This should be darkened with the auditorium, so that all the lights will be concentrated on the stage. The lights in the X-Ray border are of the same colors as those in the footlights, and are arranged in circuit units to match the units in the footlights. These units are laid out in combinations evenly distributed throughout their length, so that the lights can be directed from either side or the middle. Baby spots can be attached to the pipe of the X-Ray border and equipped with gelatine mediums of any color. Individual spotlights can also be trained from any place in the footlights. This was done in *Rip Van Winkle*, and the spotlight was trained on the dwarf's face at the moment when Rip caught sight of it. The "spots" in the "foots" give special illumination on any scene or character. The use of a spotlight in the gallery, when it is trained on a performer in vaudeville or musical comedy, is familiar.

A well-equipped stage has a dimmer, or reducer, controlling all the circuits. By means of this the light can be reduced in volume without being changed in direction. "Strips" and "bunches" in entrances kill the shadows and illuminate the exterior. These, also, may have color mediums when some special light is desired.

THE SOURCE OF LIGHT

Light is the greatest enemy or friend of facial expression. If the actor's face is too much in shadow, his expression is greatly hampered; but in comedy, if his expression is illuminated with sufficient light, his effects are enhanced. Much of his effect in facial expression may depend upon the source of light. A light coming from only one side may distort his expression, and thus tend to ruin his effects. The effect of such lighting can be tested with an ordinary full-face bust. If it is placed in darkness and a spotlight trained on it from one side or another, the appearance of the features will be distorted in such a way that the nose and mouth will seem twisted to one side. The effect is normal only when the bust is given an even light from all sides and above.

Scenes in daylight, and especially those out of doors, imply sunlight. The source of the light is determined by the time of day. If it is midday the light is overhead; and since in midday there are few or no shadows, the light may be evenly distributed. If it is late afternoon the light should be stronger at one side in order to cast shadows, and the amber mediums should be used in the bunches in the entrances. Afternoon light must not, however, be too sombre nor the shadows too deep, or they may detract from the expression; some modification in the lighting should be made in order to observe the necessary stage license. The light of the moon can be made to come from any side, and is produced with a spotlight with a blue medium, elevated, to correspond to the real moon's direction. A bull's-eye lantern in the hands of a burglar in the dark creates a true illusion in whatever way it is directed. When a lamp is used as the only illumination on a scene, it should be the only source of light beyond the necessary artificial lighting to distinguish the actors. Its effect is perfect when, for example, it weirdly lights up the faces of thieves gathered about it in an underground den.

When we take a snapshot of an object out of doors we stand with our backs to the sun. The light then travels over our shoulder upon the object we are photographing. This principle is not practiced in the theatre, but in the opinion of many it might well be. This is a most effective method to employ in al fresco performances when they are given at night. Strong lamps are directed on to the scene from behind the audience. These lamps illuminate the trees and greensward as well as the actors, and the light from them is sufficient. This method would have a disadvantage in an interior theatre unless the light were neutralized by lights from the stage; for without the latter the light at the back of the audience would throw the actor's shadows on the back wall. Natural effects can be produced by combining the stage lighting with other light from the back of the auditorium.

As a general rule, the actors themselves should not cast heavy shadows, if any at all. These tend to distract attention from their work or expression. Scenery, however, is rendered more effective when it casts shadows, and by the shadows which are cast the source of light is most easily indicated.

The Moods of Light

Lighting should be made to correspond with the character of the play and its moods. It assists the actor materially to express these moods. The bright light which is required in farce corresponds with the brightness of the entertainment. Farce played on a gloomy stage is invariably killed, for the actor's facial expression is most valuable in this class of drama. Scenes of romance are not so effective in broad full light. The moon has always been associated with romance. Performances in Shakespeare's time were given in the afternoon, but the poet would no doubt have rejoiced if he had had our theatre with its lighting system, by which the true illusion of the moon in *Romeo and Juliet* could have been effected. This was denied him, for though the actors played in broad daylight, the lines asked the audience to suppose that Romeo and Juliet were making love in the light of the moon. In other scenes, also, Shakespeare's lovers often meet in the moonlight. Jessica and Lorenzo in *The Merchant of Venice* present another case. We associate fairy tales and their elves, pixies, and sprites with moonlight. *A Midsummer Night's Dream* is an example. Daylight is too matter of fact for such romantic scenes, while the falling shadows of dusk, or the rays of the moon, give it its proper setting. Mystery thrives in shadowland and darkness. Mystery melodrama usually has comedy and drama in alternate scenes. It therefore requires darkness and light alternately. The light needed for melodrama is very complex. A groan, a scream, or a shot, is most effective in the dark and inspires dread; but in the light it would not be so gruesome. Joy suggests light, but sorrow or sadness, darkness. This may be the reason that a room of death is generally darkened. Death scenes are more effective when played in a subdued light. Camille should not die in bright sunlight. Her death expresses tragedy, and tragedy is not friendly to the brightness of the sun.

A general law regarding lighting is that it should correspond with the mood of a scene whenever possible; bright light should be used for bright and happy moods, and sombre or subdued light for the darker ones.

The principles hitherto outlined in this book are strictly those put into practice in the professional theatre. They have been designed for suggestion not only to the professional actor, but to all amateur and non-professional actors in general who engage in the acting of plays. There are many methods used in play production which do not need to be employed by professional actors because the skill of their experience renders these methods either entirely unnecessary, or if necessary at all, then not in so intensive a degree. Non-professional actors, through comparative inexperience, oftentimes require an intensiveness of direction and the use of certain mechanical methods to secure results, which professional actors of long experience might find irksome or unnecessary. For the benefit of non-professional groups in the theatre we will mention in this place certain methods in direction which have been tried and found effective for particular groups in this class.

One of the most important qualifications of a director dealing with non-professionals is the ability to keep matters harmonious between his staff and his cast. Many non-professionals try to give the name of artistic temperament to that which is only temper. A. T. stands for asinine "tommyrot" as well as artistic temperament. The former might be more common even in the professional theatre if commercial organization, and the necessity of earning a living on the part of the actor by holding his engagement, did not render it more or less prohibitive. The director should always be the final arbiter, and non-professional actors should learn, as professional actors do, that plays can best be put on by one and not by many.

The director of non-professionals requires intensive rehearsals of his cast. One director of a little theatre, noted for its smooth and "professional" performances, after a careful first reading of the play, would have long discussions in "open forum" with his cast, in which opinions were exchanged regarding the play, scene by scene and part by part. Then, as the play went into rehearsal, the director would call scene rehearsals, in which the actors would go over each scene so many times that the "dovetailing" was complete. He would tell his actors that a performance was like a string of beads, each scene perfect in itself, but depending upon the entire string of beads, or scenes, for real beauty.

When possible, the director should adopt the following procedure during the last week of rehearsals: Suppose the play is to open on a Monday night. Then on the preceding Wednesday let him have a property rehearsal; on Thursday, a property and furniture rehearsal; on Friday, a property, furniture, and scenery rehearsal; on Saturday, a property, furniture, scenery, dress, and make-up rehearsal. If the full dress rehearsal is not as smooth as it should be, the director can call a "line" rehearsal again on Sunday and keep the people only a short time. It is well, however, to have a day's rest between the final rehearsal and the opening performance. This period of rest is given also in the professional theatre. The non-professional actor is not so well trained as the professional in "waiting for laughs." Therefore, in a non-professional production, it is well to invite a small picked audience to the dress rehearsal. In this way the actor will learn where his responses come in laughter or applause, and will then see how to time his "waits."

It is well when working on a long play to spend perhaps a little more time on the last act than on the others. Many directors neglect the last act and think it will "carry itself," the results proving disastrous sometimes. Nothing is more amateurish than a draggy last act.

In respect to the principle of Eliminating Action, which was treated in Chapter XVI, the following method, which was used by one director of a non-professional group, was found effective, as applied to the whole performance, in eliminating unnecessary actions. He inaugurated what he termed "pantomime rehearsals." At these rehearsals the actors went through their parts whispering the lines, but using all the gestures and stage business worked out in earlier rehearsals. A small group of spectators, to whom the play was entirely new, were invited in to witness the rehearsal. They made notes on action not quite clear, and at the close of each act these notes were discussed. All action and business adjudged unnecessary were eliminated. As the season progressed, these "pantomime rehearsals" became less necessary. A suppressed method, corresponding much to this "pantomime" method, is often practiced by professional actors at rehearsals. It gives practice in reserve force. This practice should not be continued to include the last rehearsal, for then the acting should be "just as at night." From this "under tone" of acting the actors easily build up to the true pitch. Some may think that overacting can be easily toned down; but overexpression is a habit with many actors. A truer theory might be that acting can be more easily "toned up."

In respect to make-up, a prominent director of a Little Theatre group gives the following advice to his actors: He says, "The first essential before making up is to set your palate as the painter sets his. Keep the grease paint clean and the powder dry. Purchase a tin make-up box and keep the make-up articles in that. The make-up mirror should be properly lighted. The best light comes from bulbs set into the wall on either side of the mirror, or hanging from above close to these positions and on a level with the face. Lay a towel on the shelf and spread out the grease paint to the left, then the 'liners,' and then the high light sticks. Next, the powder puff, the rabbit's foot, the can of powder, and the can of cold cream. The bottle of stickum should be kept tightly corked. With your palate properly set you are ready to begin the process of make-up."

Many fine character actors are very disorderly with their make-up shelves, but it is well for the beginner, at least at first to heed the above advice.

Non-professional actors, and even professional actors, often ape other actors who have portrayed certain characters, instead of going to life itself for their pattern. This was very evident in a Little Theatre Tournament held in New York City. There was not enough originality or individuality expressed.

THE DRESS REHEARSAL

The play should be so well prepared that when the dress rehearsal takes place it should proceed as smoothly as a regular performance. It requires all the scenery, properties, lights, costumes, and make-up. Its purpose is to acquaint the actor with all of the accessories beforehand and his relation to them throughout the play. The director should not interrupt the dress rehearsal, no matter what hitches occur. This is necessary in order that for the first time the actors may sense the uninterrupted flow of the performance and get the "feel" of their scenes, without breaks. Some directors, while watching this rehearsal, have a stenographer at their side, to whom they give notes on matters to be corrected. When an act is finished the actors are called on to the stage, the stenographer reads the notes, and the director makes the necessary suggestions regarding the actors' performance or costumes.

It is an infallible law that one can never count on anything that has not been rehearsed. The old line, "I won't do it now, but it will be all right at night," has become a traditional joke. It is also an exploded idea that a shabby final rehearsal predicts a good first performance. Through their tension and anxiety on the first night the actors can correct some of their mistakes of the final rehearsal. Still, the only real guarantee of a "perfect" first performance is a dress rehearsal that proceeds without a hitch. The best directors postpone their opening, if necessary, until a smooth dress rehearsal has been secured. An important word to the director is this: "Too many cooks spoil the broth." The director's word should be law. Many performances are bad when directed by more than one person because the direction has not conformed to one consistent scheme. Whatever flaws the direction may contain, consistency in one method should always be employed.

Amateur actors do not realize that they are capable of giving a better performance of a play than, in the modesty of their inexperience, they believe possible. Three things are necessary. The most important thing is capable direction. Far more bad performances by amateurs are due to the directors than to the actors in the cast. A study of these chapters should make that apparent. Next, it should be realized that acting is work—interesting work, however, and not play. With this in mind the actors should, first, attend all rehearsals promptly, and second, thoroughly know their lines. With these three features well attended to, they will be gratified with the results.

A word in conclusion: The student who studies this chapter with a view to perfecting himself in play production may feel that certain necessary hints and instructions are lacking. He may want to know three things: How shall the actors be told to move about? What shall they be told to do? And how shall they be told to do it? The first two questions can be answered only by the play to be produced. They shall move about as the lines in the play suggest. The impulse of the actor, as well as the judgment and discretion of the director, should be brought to bear to make all movement logical and natural. They shall do what the lines of the play suggest, as well. How they shall perform whatever their parts require is sufficiently answered in the technique outlined in previous chapters. The director should be familiar with that and see that the actors carry it out correctly.

EXERCISES

1. State in a few words why directorship is important.
2. What factors make for the success of a dramatic production?
3. Of what is acting composed?
4. How is theatre administration divided?
5. What are the five departments employed in the production of a play? What is the function of each?
6. Describe the old Elizabethan stage.
7. What three classes of stage equipment are there?
8. Describe the three broad steps in the evolution of a play's production.

DIRECTORSHIP

9. Mention a few things the director may do to improve the play as the author has written it.
10. In what may the director be permitted license, and in what does he sometimes go to extremes?
11. What is meant by "constructing the set"?
12. What is "marking the manuscript"?
13. What are the stage manager's markings in the script?
14. How few entrances should a full stage setting usually contain?
15. Describe the correct positions for a sofa and a table on either side to express symmetry.
16. Give three important rules for furniture placement.
17. In what way can furniture hamper the actor's work?
18. Mention some way to use "the fourth wall" in furniture placement.
19. Wherein lies an advantage in various levels on a stage?
20. If you were producing a new play, what would you consider the best method to pursue at the first assembling of the company? Give your reasons. At the first rehearsal? Your reasons.
21. Devise a situation showing grouping balance. Illustrate by diagram.
22. What can you say about impulse in respect to action?
23. How closely do you think an actor should be directed?
24. What is giving a person a scene? Give an example.
25. Describe "getting up stage."
26. Where is the apex of a stage triangle?
27. What is "atmosphere" in the theatre? What kinds are there? Give examples.
28. How should outside effects be managed?
29. When would you use a medium curtain? A slow curtain? A quick curtain?
30. What is meant by "overhead lighting"?
31. What features in a play govern the system of lighting?
32. Explain the uses of the various colors of lights.
33. Why do Romeo and Juliet make love by moonlight? What kind of light does melodrama often require?

CHAPTER XXV

PUBLIC SPEAKING

The market is abundantly supplied with books devoted exclusively to this subject. They give a more comprehensive review of the art than can be attempted in a single chapter. Much can be said about public speaking if all its phases are covered, but we shall touch upon only a few of them here. Public speaking involves the limitless possibilities of how and what to say in original speech, as well as how to speak the words of others. This book has been devoted to the art of saying the words of others in dramatic form. In this chapter, we shall point out some of the contrasts and similarities in methods employed by the actor and by the public speaker, and shall give suggestions only on the delivery of public speech, exclusive of elements pertaining to its construction.

A broad generalization can be made regarding public speech in contrast to acting. The actor works in a separate world, which is that of make-believe; but the public speaker works in the same world with his hearers. The actor talks *toward* and *for* his audience, but the public speaker talks *to* them. This difference in relationship requires a distinct difference in attack. In our delineation of dramatic technique we said the actor should talk toward his audience, but should not step out of his own world and talk *to* them. But the public speaker is in the same world with his audience and this is just what he should do. The actor should not look any one of his audience in the eye but the public speaker needs to look directly at his audience collectively. An audience looks *at* the actor, who is supposed to be oblivious of their existence; but they look *to* the public speaker for the reception of his ideas.

For this reason, there is a much closer bond between the speaker and his audience. A distinction should be made between the public speaker and the "reader," or reciter. The latter is more or less in the position of the actor, and in reciting some dramatic poem requires much of the same detachment. The public speaker is, strictly speaking, a person who delivers, or gives the impression of delivering, original ideas.

PERSONALITY

A pleasing personality is as valuable an asset for a speaker as for an actor. He should inspire his audience with confidence on his first appearance, for he wants to impart to them a pleasing expectancy of something to their interest. A forbidding personality and a sombre expression would defeat this purpose. He intends, perhaps, to present a series of arguments, to make a plea for some charitable movement, or to swing opinion along some social or political line. He must present his ideas, of whatever nature, to the intelligence of his audience. An unpleasant personality would cause him to lose ground instead of gaining it. What is known as "the confidence smile" often discloses its falseness to those who analyze correctly; still, an easy smile at the beginning of an address establishes a pleasant atmosphere for what is to follow. Many speakers put their audience in good humor with a comical incident or story at the beginning of their discourse.

SUBJECT MATTER

Many novices in public speaking are appalled at the thought of addressing an audience. They fear they will stumble over their words or be unable to select the right ones, or that they cannot hold attention for any length of time. They do not realize that one secret of successful speaking lies in having *something to say*. One cannot interest an audience without having something definite to say to them. The actor has learned his lines and therefore has certain definite ideas to deliver. This gives him confidence—unless he should forget the lines. The public speaker should be sure of what he is to say, whether it be a discourse composed of his own ideas or a speech he may have committed to memory. He can have confidence in himself only in this way, and impart the same confidence to the audience.

OPENING ATTACK

The first thing the public speaker needs to do is to get attention. How shall he do this? Surely, if he cannot secure the attention of his audience, he cannot get the confidence in his address which he requires. In the first place, if he has confidence in himself he will not be afraid. Fear is the worst of enemies to any effort on the public platform, and the actor or public speaker with stage fright is lost. The speaker should advance easily and naturally to the front of the platform and show by his movements that he feels at home there. There should be no awkwardness or tension in his posture. He should express relaxation and ease in his position before beginning his address. Expert public speakers do not plunge immediately into their discourse, but make a slight pause in order that the audience may get a full sight of them before they begin. The speaker comes forward with a pleasing expression as if to say, "Here I am, I hope you like my appearance and that you will assent readily to my addressing you." He looks pleasantly over his audience and waits until they have settled in their seats and he thinks he has their full attention before he speaks. If he has notes and a reading desk before him, he may, without nervousness, arrange his papers on his desk and otherwise get ready for his delivery in a quiet, unobtrusive way.

POSTURE

Like many young actors who have difficulty with their hands, the novice in public speaking may have the same difficulty. Ease, grace, and naturalness of posture imply repose. If the novice is not certain of his bodily repose, he may devise beforehand a method of posture with his hands which he can assume at the beginning of his address. This idea recalls the case of a young speaker who was not always easy with his hands, but was clever enough never to allow himself to look awkward. Whenever he found his hands in the way he folded his arms. His direct intention in this action and the reason for it were not apparent to the audience, and looked natural. It was much better than the obvious refuge from awkwardness of putting his hands in the pockets; this reveals its reason in many cases. Inexpert speakers often put their hands in their side pockets; but this expresses a careless unconcern which might defeat their purpose, namely, to establish intimate contact. To fold the arms across the chest would be equally wrong. The arms thus placed might seem to express a barrier between the speaker and his audience, when a flow of magnetic contact should exist betwen them. A dignified speaker would never place his arms akimbo. Respectful dignity is necessary at the beginning of an address, and none of these postures is dignified. The expert speaker, like the expert actor, would not think of his hands at all, but the novice is more than likely to betray awkwardness in posture at the opening of his address, and should guard against it. Three easy positions for the hands might be,—letting them hang at the sides, holding them easily in front at the waistline, or placing them behind. Female speakers often fold their hands in front at the waistline as they begin their discourse. A reading desk often acts for the speaker like furniture for the actor, and helps him to appear at ease at the beginning if he places his hands upon it from behind or stands with one hand upon it at the side.

An upright position, in which the body is planted fairly well on both feet, but not stiffly, or with one knee slightly bent, helps the speaker greatly to acquire repose. By no means should the speaker stand like a soldier; there is no posture more formidable than this to detach one thoroughly from his surroundings. One has only to watch a company of soldiers standing or marching erectly and with eyes front to realize this. The soldier's position is not relaxed, and the speaker's posture must be. In this relaxed position, the speaker stands in repose and breathes easily and naturally before beginning to speak. This can be called release from tension.

MANNERISMS

An instructor in public speaking found that many of his pupils had a peculiar habit. The public speaker needs to get to his audience with his ideas, and to do this he gets as close to them with his body as good judgment will allow; he will often walk close to the front of the platform when he wishes to stress a particular point. The pupils referred to had a habit of drawing back upon the first words of their discourse. They did this so perceptibly with their heads and shoulders that their feet had to follow to restore their balance. The reason was only too evident. It was due entirely to fear. The novice who attempts a public speech has undertaken a definite task, and having entered upon it, should not draw back either figuratively or literally. If he does, he is like a soldier flying from the enemy. Instead of drawing back from his audience as he begins to speak, the speaker's movement would be logical if he took a step toward them. A speaker who uses a reading desk after arranging his notes, if he has any, often walks around to the side of it and toward his audience, before he begins to speak.

In the easy and reposeful posture we are describing, all mannerism or unnecessary action would naturally be avoided. Since the speaker is concerned with a flow of ideas from his own mind to that of his audience, thought only is involved, and the body must not intrude upon and distract from it. The speaker should assume an ease of posture that will suppress too much action of the body, except when the body can be made to aid in enforcing ideas. Certain positions for the body and hands are assumed, not with the idea that these members shall be noticed, but that they shall not be noticed at all. The speaker is dealing with ideas, and the body must be as unobtrusive as possible. A stiff, ungraceful posture would call attention to the body immediately. Drawing back in the manner just described, shifting on the feet, fumbling with the lapels of the side pockets or with the watch-chain, would distract a necessary attention and might shatter the confidence of the audience, for they would think the speaker was nervous and afraid.

To Be Seen, Heard, and Understood

In Chapter III, sufficient has been said about magnifying the voice; this would be for the public speaker simply throwing his voice to all parts of the auditorium. For the actor it is somewhat more complex, as described in that chapter. The speaker cannot register his ideas unless his audience hears them. Nothing is more irritating than to miss half of what the speaker says, and nothing can more effectively remove attention from the listener and convert the auditorium into a sleeping room. It is only necessary to be a guest at some luncheon of a Rotary or Kiwanis club to secure a concrete example of inexperienced public speaking. At such a luncheon visiting guests are introduced by their friends among the business men and are expected to say a few words. On one such occasion the majority of the speakers showed shyness, mumbled their words, and spoke in such low tones that they could not be clearly understood twenty feet away. The inexperienced public speaker, especially if he is self-conscious or afraid, seldom or never speaks loudly enough. He will do well to make trial of projecting his voice before an event, stationing a friend at the back of the hall, so that when he delivers his address he will be sure that he can be heard and understood.

Speaking on the stage or platform involves three important elements in delivery. Besides magnification, or voice projection, they are pronunciation and enunciation. The last two are different things. Pronunciation is that quality of speech in which we utter words with the correct vowel sounds, either long or short, and give correct emphasis on certain syllables according to dictionary rules; enunciation has reference to utterance which is clear-cut and distinct in both vowels and consonants.

No person should attempt public speech unless he gives close attention to these three principles. The speaker, like the actor, must be seen, be heard, be understood. Nothing should be necessary to say about pronunciation. A dictionary is to be found in any intelligent home. Noah Webster spent ten years in compiling his first dictionary and left a valuable contribution to the American people. His authority is accepted. The person who addresses an audience should be certain that he gives all his words correct pronunciation by dictionary standards. The art of perfect enunciation is more complex and should be established through practice and habit.

There is a wide tendency toward careless enunciation among all nations. Its principal cause is vocal laziness However, this can be overcome with conscientious practice; and the person who studies the subject of public speech should be willing to give the matter that practice necessary to render his speech easy, graceful, and coherent.

Though pronunciation and enunciation are different principles, one verges into the other in the utterance of vowel sounds. For instance, when the dictionary gives the sound of long *o* with a dash above it, we know it is sounded like *o* in "lone." In the word "pronounce," the dictionary places this dash above the first *o*. Yet many persons utter the word as if it were spelled "pruh-

nounce." They generally say "dooty" for "duty,"
"dook" for "duke," and "Loocy" for "Lucy," in all of
these leaving out the sound of u. Through sheer laziness
in lingual action, they may also say "attemp to" for
"attempt to," "gen'lmun" for "gentleman," "unough"
for "enough," "judgmunt" for "judgment," "one o'
them," for "one of them," and so on. Thus slurring
the vowel and consonant sounds not only makes the discourse difficult to understand, but renders the speaker
unattractive, manifesting as it does the fact that he does
not possess cultured speech.

As a remedy for faulty speech, the speaker is recommended to read aloud for practice the address which he
is to deliver, or any well-written passage, and to do this
in respect to the syllables and not the words. Let him
proceed slowly through the selection, paying no attention
to reading and expression, but with the mere idea of
pronouncing correctly and enunciating clearly and distinctly each separate syllable. Practice in this work will
soon render his diction correct, and a pleasure to the ear.

Pronunciation is really an easy matter. The trouble
with people who have difficulty in pronouncing unusual
words is that they try to pronounce a word all at once.
In discourse, as well as in most situations in life, a person
should do one thing at a time. Sometimes, when facing
a new word, he flies at it all at once and tries, as it were,
to swallow it whole. An actress was reading her part at
rehearsal and came to a scientific word which was strange
to her. She stopped and said, "Oh dear, I can't say that
word." The director probably could not either, for he
did not offer a pronunciation, and the rehearsal continued.
The word occurred in the speech of the next actor to speak.

He had never seen it before, but with ease he read, "That's what we scientists call Butterflies. I've had to neglect the Lepidoptera these last few years, my dear." The actress facetiously replied, "Oh, just like that!" This is really an easy word to pronounce, for its syllables are simple in construction. It was only necessary to divide it into its syllables and pronounce them one at a time. A general rule for syllable construction is that each syllable must have a vowel or vowel sound, and this sound ends the syllable. The division is usually placed after the last vowel in the syllable, whether it has one or more vowels. When two consonants come together, the division is placed between them. Thus, Lepidoptera would be divided to read, Lep-i-dop-te-ra. An exception is made in the first and third syllables, which end with consonants instead of vowels. The emphasis follows the rule of the Greek language, which, in words of more than three syllables, places the emphasis on the antepenult, or the third from the end. A simple word to the student on these points is—consult the dictionary for pronunciation, and for enunciation don't be lazy.

DELIVERY

Talent in acting and public speaking is not interchangeable. The fact that a person is a good actor, and is therefore used to appearing before a public, does not imply that he is a good public speaker as well. On the other hand, a good public speaker might not be a good actor. Some of the same principles are included in both arts, but the outstanding principles in each art are more or less unrelated. For instance, in learning the lines of others, the actor has no experience in devising his own. The speaker's art is narrative, descriptive, argumentative, and persuasive. The actor's art may be all of these at times, but above all it is imitative and emotional. These last-named qualities have little relation to the art of public speaking. The actor who attempts public speaking is often ineffective, for he cannot use the principal means through which his art operates, namely, imitation and emotion. In this work there is no opportunity for him to act, and as a result he becomes conversational, colloquial, and colorless. This is not true of all actors, for some of them make excellent public speakers, but it is the general rule.

In acting, the actor uses light and shade to break and vary his delivery, in which pauses, variation in emotional feeling, interspersed physical action, and his relation to other characters, tend to interrupt its even flow. The speaker, on the other hand, is left to himself and must preserve a smooth flow of delivery without interruption from outside agents. Where the actor's delivery is imitative and emotional, the speaker's is more elocutionary and declamatory. The actor, in recitation, tends to act instead of describing, declaiming, or reciting.

Again, the actor works in the conversation of everyday life, while the speaker does not often employ it. The latter must use a rhythm of delivery more or less measured. While the feeling of the actor is inspirational, emotional, and impulsive, that of the public speaker is calm and calculated, except in special moments of stress; and his delivery should have measure and fullness of expression. He has calculated what he has to say, and delivers his address with the assurance of knowing just what he shall say next. The actor must present the illusion that all his thoughts come to him on the spur of the moment; he must therefore be spontaneous in the delivery of his lines. The speaker, on the other hand, should give the impression of being ready with all the topics of his discourse. He then approaches his task calmly and with assurance, and delivers one topic after another in a flow of rhetoric somewhat measured and exact.

FACIAL EXPRESSION

The face reflects the emotions, and emotion is more a quality of acting than of public speaking. Therefore the speaker's work does not call for so constant a play of facial expression as the actor's. Still, an expressionless face in the public speaker would seriously hamper his effects. Many times he must express the moods of his sentiment or feeling. His expression should follow the changes of these moods. After presenting some forceful argument he may say, "Am I not right?" or, "What do you think about it?" He could gain no assent from his audience if his face maintained a blank expression. In such questions, the speaker and actor might act the same. They would perhaps make a gesture of appeal and ask the question with their eyes and whole expression. Public speaking, like acting, requires the use of all mediums to register its effects; and an expressive face does much to give force to the ideas.

READING

After all that has been said in former chapters about reading and expression, it is scarcely necessary to state that correct and eloquent reading is a necessary element of good speaking. The speaker cannot get his ideas over to his audience unless he interprets his sense with a reading that makes his meanings clear. What we understand as reading involves interpreting the written thoughts of others. A person who expresses his own thoughts usually reads correctly; but faults are apt to occur when he interprets the written thoughts of others. When he says what he means, only correct reading will make it mean what he says. This is instinctive, however, and the principles of expression have been established through original thought. When the speaker has occasion to express the thoughts of others, he must be careful to translate the ideas embodied in these thoughts correctly to his audience.

MOVEMENT

This is extremely important. No good speaker stands still throughout a whole address. To do so would be monotonous and would injure the effect of his talk. The speaker is free to move how and when he will. There is no exhibition more subject to monotony than a public speech, and the speaker must guard against this in every possible way. He can secure variety in several ways. He may express it in his general reading and delivery, by showing as much light and shade as his subject will permit, though he may gain it in movement as effectively as in any other way.

We have often seen a public speaker, when he has finished some topic in his discourse, and before he passes on to a new idea or topic, take a few steps to another part of the platform. While he does this he may be collecting his thoughts for what he shall say next. Such movement spaces his delivery, and while he changes his position, the audience has time to digest the idea which he has just finished and prepare themselves for the next. This interim in his speech is a breathing space. We all know the tantalizing monotony of water falling drop by drop repeatedly at regular intervals without a break. It is maddening to a sensitive ear. The speaker must break his discourse with an occasional movement of the body and a pause in his delivery so that the flow of his ideas may be spaced and may not become monotonous.

Two speakers delivered "papers" from manuscript on the same platform behind a reading desk. The first placed both hands on the desk and kept his eyes constantly on his manuscript without changing his position, except to turn the leaves. His unvaried position did not permit of any pauses or variety in his delivery, and the effect was naturally monotonous. The second speaker, though he could not move away from the desk because he had to read his manuscript, expressed variety in his delivery nevertheless. At times his hands rested on the desk as he read. He would often catch a sentence ahead at a time with his eye. He then raised his eyes and delivered the sentence to the audience. On changes of topic, the reader made a pause which he punctuated with a physical movement. He sometimes took his hands off the desk and let them fall at his sides. He moved slightly on his feet and perhaps took a step backward. After this pause and movement, which allowed the audience a breathing space and also indicated a new attack, his eye caught the next sentence. He spoke it toward the audience with his eyes away from the paper, and with an entirely different expression and tone to introduce the new idea. His hands were sometimes behind him and sometimes folded in front. As he was reading from manuscript, little or no gesture was possible, but he could establish variety of movement nevertheless. The first reader, who had never taken his eyes from his manuscript or changed his position, appeared as though he were reading aloud to himself. The other's method established contact with his hearers and took them into his confidence.

A speaker who uses notes in his address finds that they prevent freedom of movement to some extent, unless he holds the notes in his hands. The necessity of referring to them is some advantage as it gives the audience a pause and a breathing space. The speaker without notes or manuscript has the whole platform for his movement, and by making free use of his whole body in movement and gesture, can make his talk more effective. He may walk from side to side or forward and back. If he has a reading desk, he may sometimes lean easily upon it at one side.

Movement, excepting that of gesture, should not take place in the midst of a concrete idea. It should be rather a punctuation between separate thoughts. It may be made simultaneously with some new idea or appeal in order to emphasize it, as when a person says, "Now we ask your coöperation in this matter." The speaker may move a little to another side and make a gesture toward the audience with both hands to enforce his appeal. As a rule, the speaker should introduce bodily movements as spacings between his ideas.

Movement will become monotonous if the speaker changes it in a regular and unvaried way. Some speakers run from one side of the platform to the other at regular intervals and arrive at about the same spots each time. Such movements are stereotyped if there is no variation in them. This regularity in the movement develops the same feature in the delivery, and the whole effect is monotonous. A young minister was observed to have but two movements for his hands. Their general position was on either side of the pulpit. At times, he let one or the other fall at his side, but in a few moments it went back again to the familiar place.

Suppose a student in a public speaking contest has committed his address to memory and in some unfortunate moment forgets what to say next. When an actor forgets his lines and "goes up," as it is called, he knows certain tricks of his trade by which he can cover up his lapse of memory. One familiar method is to repeat his last words, during which he has time to think for the next. The repetition helps to reëstablish connection with the forgotten line. If it does not come, then his fellow-actors know he is "up" and may be able to "jump" to their next speech. When he forgets, the actor "fakes"; that is, he devises some words of his own which bear upon the idea; and the other actors, hearing the strange words, learn his situation and come to his rescue. The public speaker has no one to assist him and must save himself as best he can. The novice in public speaking often does the very thing that gives his predicament away. He stands stock-still and looks down at the floor. Nothing can indicate his mistake more surely than this. The speaker has the whole platform and may move about on it at will. If he forgets his next line, he can easily cover up his defect by moving to another position. If, then, the line does not come, he can resort to a repetition of his last one to get his connection. If still it does not come, he must jump to something he can remember. By no means must he expect the forgotten line to spring out of the floor. The words are the essence of thought, and that is around him on a level with his head. Whether a speaker forgets or not, looking down is not a good practice, for it breaks the intimate connection which he wishes to maintain with his audience. He must look at them if he is to keep this unimpaired, except when he may be engaged in descriptive or dramatic illustration.

The speaker often makes a grave mistake as a result of committing a speech to memory. He may deliver it too fast. When he has learned the words of his address, he becomes in a way like an actor delivering the lines of someone else. He must be careful to present the illusion that the words of his talk are spontaneous and thought of for the first time, although the flow must not be impaired. When he knows instantly each sentence which is to follow the one before it and, because of this knowledge, runs swiftly through his discourse, there may be two bad results. One is that he fails to space his ideas in the various ways described above, and the other that the ideas tumble so swiftly from his lips that the audience have not time to fully digest them. The speaker should pretend to deliver all his ideas as if he were thinking of them for the first time, and must observe all his rules in order to accomplish this end.

GESTURE

Little need be said about this. The student may consult what was said of gesture in Chapter VII. In dramatic recitation it is often used profusely, but in public speaking it is tempered to the nature of the address. The same rules apply to it in this art as in acting, the only difference being that while in acting gesture is used more to illustrate and enforce emotion, in public speaking it is used to enforce ideas. For example, if the speaker uses a gesture in a strong appeal to his audience, he may make it in the same way that one actor would to another, but in a slightly modified form. In public speaking there is not so much occasion for the dramatic and sometimes exaggerated form of gesture that is used in drama. In the latter, one is always an actor; while in the former, the speaker must be careful never to go outside of himself. He should so restrain his gesture as always to preserve his dignity of address, never verging on the territory of the actor, who often loses himself in an excess of emotion. In public speech, then, gesture should be such as to convey correctly ideas in the descriptive, narrative, and argumentative manner of this art; and the speaker should be careful to maintain his personal contact and not become like the actor through an emotional detachment.

To sum up, the speaker needs personality, expression, good diction, variety, ease, and eloquence. Above all, he must strive to avert monotony, which renders any speaker's efforts void.

EXERCISES

1. Mention a difference between the method of the actor and that of the public speaker.
2. What do you consider one requisite for confidence in public speaking?
3. If you had to deliver an address, what would be your way of presenting yourself before you began to speak?
4. Name some postures which you consider wrong in a public speaker.

5. What mannerisms can you mention that would be bad for public speaking?
6. What three things are necessary in order to be understood clearly? Define them.
7. What are outstanding qualities of acting? Of public speaking?
8. Were you reading your manuscript, what movements could you devise to relieve monotony of posture?
9. What would you do if you were to forget what you were to say next?

CHAPTER XXVI

SUGGESTIONS FOR TEACHERS

Actors generally learn all of their technique through direct contact with the theatre. To use a term employed in the colleges, we might call this the laboratory method. It is distinct from theory and is completely practical. In colleges, textbooks present the theory and it is worked out in practice in the laboratory. Textbooks on acting technique are, of course, never used in the professional theatre; practice alone is supposed to be a sufficient medium for the actor's development. In very recent years, however, this idea has been modified in some quarters. It is supposed that the actor may not "know his business" perfectly merely because he earns his living in the professional theatre. Just as a doctor or a lawyer may continue to study, the actor as well can profit by doing so. Studios are established in connection with professional companies, in which the actors continue to study along with their professional performances.

In a textbook on the art of acting, a student can gain very many ideas on acting technique, but however successful the attempt may be to explain the laws of technique, no student can become proficient in it by merely studying the book. One actor was heard to exclaim, "You can't learn acting from books!" This is quite as true as the statement that you cannot learn to play the piano from books, yet books are written on the art of the piano. A person learns to play a musical instrument only by practice, but he gets much of the theory of music from books. The same should be true of acting. In the final analysis, however, the actor, like the musician, must have practice in order to perfect his technique.

How shall the student proceed with his study of acting and how shall the instructor impart to him a knowledge of its technique? This can be done through the laboratory method in the same way that an instructor oversees the experiments of his students in chemistry or physics. The stage of any theatre is a laboratory in which the actor gains his practice. Therefore, to teach technique, the instructor should have a stage upon which the students can gain practice as the actor does.

All the principles described in these chapters have been observed in professional experience. Many of the examples cited are reproductions of scenes and sections of dialogue that have been done in the professional theatre. They were acted just as they have been outlined. The purpose of the student is to learn to act in a professional way; if he can reproduce these scenes with the correct technique described, he arrives at a close copy of professional acting and is, in technique at least, "professional" in his method. To do this, he requires a stage and rehearsal as any professional actor does.

By a stage we simply mean any space approximating that of an ordinary theatre stage. The professional actor has to have no more than this and needs only a space equal to that which he is to use at performances, and on which he can get his relationships to other characters. The space is laid out with one side indicating the audience; the director's table faces the improvised stage; and chairs and tables are used to indicate necessary furniture and entrances. These simple arrangements fully equip the student's "laboratory."

At the beginning of his career, a young actor learns much by watching the work of older actors. It is not ethical in the professional theatre for anyone but the author, director, stage manager, or manager, to occupy chairs facing the stage at rehearsals. The actors must find their places off stage at the sides, and they need not watch the general rehearsal unless they wish. In the school of dramatics, however, it is valuable for the students to watch and study all operations on the stage. For that purpose, it would be well for the class to be ranged in positions facing the stage in front so that they can be made to pay attention to all practice. The professional actor is supposed to know his technique, and rehearsal is for the purpose of having him use it in different situations. The student, on the other hand, is in class to learn this technique, and can do so largely by observing his fellow students. When he is himself called on for practice, the others watch him in turn. In this way, comparison and criticism can be made, and the student learns not only from his own practice but from that of the whole class.

THE PHYSICAL ELEMENT

Of the three sides to acting, namely the physical, mental, and emotional, the first one the instructor should consider is the physical. This relates to movement and action. The student would naturally be directed to read Chapter II in which the first topics are embraced under this principle, or as much of the principle as would form practice for the first class day. The first topic in the chapter gives directions on how to stand. The student would note the marks giving the relative positions of two persons standing together. He might even practice these positions in company with a fellow-student. Taking the next topic, he might go through the movements by himself on how to turn, using some space in his own bedroom as an improvised stage. He could practice the directions on how to make an entrance and an exit with his own bedroom door. In this way, he would have studied his lesson at home and could come to class the next day prepared for recitation. In the class, then, the lesson could be taken up with these movements, and in sight of all the students, each student could be directed to illustrate the various pieces of action. If some bit were wrongly executed, it could be submitted to the rest of the class for criticism.

If the three topics mentioned were the subject for the first day's lesson, they could all be combined in practice. For example, two students might be placed standing in the centre of the stage. Any playbook could be given them and some dialogue selected which would logically permit of the action that was necessary. Reading this dialogue would accustom them to speaking together in the standing position. One might then be told to cross to the right and make his exit at a door. In the absence of a real door, the student could easily indicate the action of opening and closing it in pantomime. He could re-enter the imaginary door with the correct action, advance to his companion at the centre, assume the proper "standard" position, and at the same time observe the principle of distance. The two students might then be placed in various positions so as to give each one practice in how to turn. In fact, all the movements described under these topics could be worked out in actual practice by the students.

These first principles are extremely elementary and simple, yet an actress with some years of experience was seen repeatedly to turn about in wrong ways, and the director often reproved her. She had not had the advantage which the student possesses of direct coaching in these simple principles. The class might master the business of these rudimentary actions in a single period.

When the subjects of definite and indefinite action were reached, the scene between Dr. David and Dr. Harrison could be enacted. The stage could be set in the manner described in that chapter. The students could hold their textbooks as if they were parts in the play and read the lines. The student who read the lines of Dr. Harrison could illustrate the movements in definite and indefinite action which accompany these lines, and the class meanwhile could be asked for criticism of the work.

The centre of the stage would need attention. One of the first things the student needs to learn is to find this centre easily. Several students might be ranged in and about the central point and various movements be made to change their positions. The students would then be expected to dress the stage in order to keep the groupings balanced. They would give room, make way for others, and "take over" to one side or another. This would accustom them to adjusting their positions to whatever movements were made. A little further along in the course, one or more students might be told to commit to memory Hamlet's soliloquy after the players' scene and reproduce the action given in respect to the centre of the stage. This would be excellent practice in reading and delivery as well.

The student should be checked at the very beginning of his study from all tendency toward mannerism. Foot and head movement without a reason is the commonest of all. This should be treated under the subject of repose. The instructor might give two students some dialogue to read and have them deliver this in a standing position, paying attention to the head and feet to avoid movement of these members. On lines of special stress, the head and feet tend to move. Dialogue containing stress and feeling would be best for this practice. Some of the students might even be directed to learn certain selections to be delivered in absolute repose. Special credit might be given to the student whose delivery was of the highest proficiency in ease of posture and free from these mannerisms.

Some of the European violin virtuosos have, in their youth, practised for weeks or even months with a bow without rosin. They were permitted to make no sound until their arms, elbows, and fingers were accustomed to holding the bow in the right position. This is physical action in respect to the violin. The amateur needs a longer time to become proficient in a play than a professional actor. By far the most important reason for this is that the amateur is not familiar with the technique of physical action and movement. The student will expect ultimately to appear in plays. When a child studies the piano he expects to "play pieces" as soon as possible. A conscientious teacher will not allow the child to plunge into pieces until he has mastered some of the five-finger exercises.

Physical action and movement are the five-finger exercises of acting. Many a director in amateur theatricals finds his progress severely hampered because the actors do not even know how to move from one place to another. No rehearsals of even the shortest plays should take place until the students are proficient in all the principles of movement of every kind about the stage.

THE MENTAL ELEMENT

When the student has mastered the principles of mechanical action, he is ready to take up the mental side of the work. There is infinite scope in this, as well as in the emotional side, which should come later. He should learn how to pitch his voice. Should an auditorium be available, the class might stand on the stage while the instructor went to the back of the auditorium, and one after another they might read passages from some book or play and throw their voices so that the instructor could distinctly hear. This would give them practice in magnification of tone. At the same time, they could be restrained from seeming to make a special effort to talk too loud. For practice in talking off stage or with their backs to the audience, they could turn their backs while they read, or could go into some corner out of sight. In this way they would secure the exact pitch of voice for any situation and learn to get the right "feel" of the auditorium and the audience.

There is wide scope in reading for the development of variety of rendition. This subject might be given separate attention without consideration for physical technique. Classes might be held for the sake of reading alone, or this subject might be combined with the principle of magnification. For purposes of reading, selections from Shakespeare's plays would be valuable. While one student read a passage, the class and the instructor might take notes on the method, and criticism might be passed on the rendition. It is often difficult to arrive at Shakespeare's sense, and examination of these passages would be good practice in finding the correct readings to convey it most correctly.

In the reading class there would also be excellent training in the expression of variety. As in public speaking, some passages might require pauses between ideas. These would express something in the way of light and shade in the expression. Tempo and rhythm would also play an important part in the work of reading. Criticism could be offered as to whether a selection was read too fast or too slow, whether it was uneven and broken in its flow, or whether it proceeded with a smooth delivery and expressed a pleasing rhythm.

As gesture relates principally to the actions of the hands, it is of course a part of movement but has a mental connection as well. Since most young actors are awkward with their hands, they should give gesture considerable attention. Whenever a student makes a gesture, the instructor should see that he makes it with a purpose and gives correct illustration of what is meant by it. He should also make it well or not at all. After reading the chapter on the subject of gesture, the student could practice the various gestures by himself. In the class, various students might be called on for illustrations by means of gesture of different emotions and situations. Passages might be given them which contained opportunity for gesture, and they might be asked to read these passages with a view to elaborating them with appropriate gestures. Some stress has been laid on the "long arm movement." On certain gestures, there is no time when it is not the most graceful. On other gestures, stretching the arm to the full length would be unnatural and "theatrical." These are the small, intimate gestures which are naturally restricted by small spaces. For example, a gesture toward an object at a distance would often permit of the long arm movement; but toward something close to the body, only the small or "short arm" gesture would be logical. The student would be taught to discriminate between the different kinds.

The law of attention is concerned with the mental side of acting and not with the physical or emotional. Little or nothing could be imparted on this subject by class drill. It could be practised only in actual performance, and attention should be given to it during the production of plays. Suiting the Action to the Word, like gesture, is mental as well as physical, for it is the "reading" of action. There is abundant opportunity in this subject for direct practice. The many examples that are given in the chapter on this subject might all be reproduced. There are the examples: "I am going to leave your house this very minute"; "I am your humble servant"; "I command you to leave this house"; "I'm so tired I must sit down and rest"; and many others. The directions are simple, and in one or two trials the student could execute the necessary gestures perfectly.

As a test for the student in deciding whether to use action or gesture simultaneous with, preceding, or following words, the instructor might parcel out lines which required some accompanying action and ask the student to decide what gesture or action he would use to accompany them, and how the actions should be made. Chapter XVI, also, entitled "Points in Action," contains more examples which the student might actually rehearse. Where lines or any sections of dialogue are not given, these could easily be devised by the instructor, the main idea being that the student should portray the technique as described.

Throughout the course, and especially in the production of plays, the instructor should see that the students coöperate with one another. It must be evident from reading this entire treatise that we consider coöperation a star feature in dramatic technique. Let some student, sitting at a table with another, read some selected passage. Let the other devise logical occasions when the statements in the speech should register upon him. Let him see how many reactions he can make to the speech and at the same time avoid distraction of interest from the reader. Let the practice be in reaction, but let the reaction not be so broad and insistent as to become distraction.

The Emotional Element

The Fourth Wall, Comedy, The Pause, Climax, Tempo and Rhythm, Light and Shade, and occasional examples in other chapters, come under this heading. These are more effectively practiced in the rehearsal of plays. Still, in some examples, treatment could be applied in class practice. In the fourth wall principle, the student might be given direct practice in keeping his eyes off the audience. Two persons might be stationed on either side of him while he stood in the centre. One person might speak to him from one side and he might look at that person.

The other would then speak and he would turn to him, being careful not to let his glance rest upon any of the space in front. This has no relation to emotional principles, but the following has: Let a student read or recite some passages and decide when he might look directly at the person he was supposed to be addressing, and when there would be occasion for revery or detached thought and it would be logical to look front. The same kind of practice might be given in finding logical pauses between ideas in any selected speech. The chapter on Comedy is well supplied with examples in which the student might be drilled. The more subtle principles, however, would be more easily practiced in rehearsals of plays.

In motion pictures and the best of Continental theatres there is a "make-up man," who oversees the make-ups of the actors. Since every actor cannot have the advantage of the service of a make-up man, and since, which is more important, making up is part of the art of acting, the actor should study it as an integral part of his work.

The class in make-up would be of great interest to the student. The instructor should see that he did not overload himself with a lot of unnecessary make-up articles. The longer an actor stays on the stage, the fewer of these he seems to need, and some old actors have been known to reduce their make-up supply to a single stick of grease paint, a can of powder, and a can of cold cream. The tendency of the amateur is to overdo everything in his make-up,—eyes too black, face too red, wrinkles too heavy. The first make-up would of course be the "straight" make-up, and the first operation, putting on the body color. The student should be cautioned to use as little as possible to get the right effect, and the instructor would see that he had applied the body color perfectly before putting on any rouge. These two operations might be enough for the first day's class. Another day might be devoted to completing the make-up. When character make-ups were considered, the first day's practice should be confined to body colors, shadows, and lines. High lights would best be reserved for subsequent classes.

When instruction was given in play production, the student should himself learn to instruct. He would first thoroughly absorb the contents of the chapter on that subject, after which he could be set to certain drills upon it. One drill might be oral, upon all the parts of a stage, the scenery, and the lights, in order that the student should thoroughly know the terms for the appliances with which he has to work. A certain scene, or an act from some playbook, could then be given him. He would first construct a setting in which this scene or act should be played and then work out the business for it, writing his markings for movement, and marginal notes for the groupings. In class, he would direct this scene with some of the other students. Meanwhile, the others, who had been given the same task of preparing their books for direction, would consult their own work for comparison. Discussion of the various methods might follow, and the interchange of ideas would broaden the general understanding.

In examining the student the teacher could give him credit through both the laboratory method and that of oral or written examination. By the laboratory method credit could be issued from day to day on the work done in class practice. Then at the end of each semester, and at the other regular times for written examinations, the students could be examined from the questions at the ends of the chapters. Passing in both branches of the study would prove his efficiency in both the theory and the practice of the work. Fifty per cent of credit could be given for each.

The instructor must be thoroughly familiar with his subject through a study of the book, and have its principles at his finger tips in order to teach it competently.

A Little Theatre director, who conducts classes in Play Production in the summer months, has found the method of giving "laboratory performances" most effective. The pupils are given a play to study in class. They read and discuss it from all angles. Then, after the cast is selected by the class, a reading rehearsal is called. The instructor helps the class in working out the "business," and the cast then walks through this "business." The play is then handed over to the assistant director, a member of the class, and the rehearsals are called. One week after the first rehearsal with the assistant director, the play is produced for a laboratory performance. Property masters and costume mistresses have been appointed, and the play is produced in detail. A picked audience is admitted, who bring with them pencils and paper. At the end of each act the members of the audience hand in criticisms, which must be honest and constructive. Results from this manner of instruction have been most successful.

What kind of plays should the student first attempt? The natural answer to this is, The easiest possible. Emotion is the hardest element in acting, for it transcends technique. The student needs first to become proficient ın his technique before attempting plays with any great demand on the emotions. For this reason, it would be best to attempt first colloquial and conversational one-act plays. Many of the "intellectual" plays of which we have spoken are effective and "showy," and their general effect overbalances the artistic effort necessary in the actors. Intimate comedies in this class, however, can be found which are suitable.

A narrower dividing line exists between the amateur and professional actor than is generally supposed. There are some poor professional and many good amateur actors. The difference lies only in professional experience and knowing some of the "tricks." "Professionalism" may involve only the knowledge of how to speak loud enough, getting on and off, picking up cues, turning about, getting from one place to another, getting accustomed to an audience, learning the lines, and, in the final analysis, getting paid for the work. There are even some "professional" actors who know little more. The actor who said, "You can't learn acting from books," referred to the soul of acting. But the principles, the technique of these principles, and the "tricks of the trade," can be imparted by word of mouth or printed in books, and acquired by the amateur as well as the professional actor.

INDEX

INDEX

Bellew, Kyrle, 335.

Bernhardt, Sarah, and dramatic schools, 4; her use of the fourth wall, 86; her gestures, 95; starts by her, 140; her artistic falseness, 230.

"Be seen, be heard, be understood," 127.

Beyond the Horizon, by Eugene O'Neill, 28.

Bird whistle, 359.

Black Dog in *Treasure Island*, a make-up for him, 315.

Booth, Edwin, in *Hamlet*, his traditional business, 7.

Border lights, 363.

Borders, 355.

Bowing, the method, 168.

Breaking Point, The, by Mary Roberts Rinehart, 28; a curtain speech in, 121; finding the objective in, 123; a climax in, 188; example of distraction, 267.

Breaking the position, for a laugh, 119; for applause, 120.

Breathing, in the old plays, 164; examples of, 162, 163, 164.

Breathlessness, 239.

Bunch light, 363.

Burlesque, its purpose, 113; its nature, 243.

Butlers, occasions for anticipating cues by them, 41; the fourth wall principle in respect to them, 42.

C

Calls, 424.

Camille, lighting in, 434.

Camp fire effect, 361.

Carpentry department, 351.

Carriage effect, 360.

Cathedral chimes, 359.

Cat-meow, 359.

Ceiling piece, 355.

Centre of the stage, its relation to acting, 19.

Character comedy part, its nature, 244.

Character part, 244.

Charley's Aunt, 114; element of surprise in, 227.

Chinaman make-up, 313.

Chitra, by Tagore, the make-up for a gold idol in, 318.

Classical music, the pause in relation to, 130.

Classic drama, its nature, 6; balance in, 403.

Clear-cut action, while reading a newspaper, 234; in *Adam and Eva*, 234.

Climax, 180; by orators and ministers, 181; in public programs, 181; in vaudeville, 181; in *Hamlet* and *Othello*, 182; in *The Merchant of Venice*, 183; its nature, 183; in the old melodramas, 184; in *Macbeth*, 184; respecting the delivery of lines, 186; how to produce it, 186; in melodramatic speech, 187; in *The Breaking Point*, 188; in *Common Clay*, 188; in *Rip Van Winkle*, 189; in *Adam and Eva*, 190; in relation to reading, 190; in *Nothing but the Truth*, 213.

Cloud effect, 361.

Clown make-up, 313.

Cock-crow, 359.

Collective personal atmosphere, 417.

Comedian and the telephone book, 106.

Comedy, its true ideal, 107; its technique, 118; the kind of play, 242.

Comedy drama, its nature, 242.

Comedy part, its nature, 244.

Come Out of the Kitchen, by A. E. Thomas, the dinner scene in, 411.

Comic opera, its nature, 243.

Common Clay, by Cleves Kinkead, pause in, 138; gesture in, 171; climax in, 188; tempo in a comedy line, 204; eliminating action, 233.

INDEX

INDEX

Entrances and exits, how to make, 38.

Enunciation in public speaking, 448.

Escaping steam from a locomotive, 359.

Explosion, 358.

Eyes, in respect to attention, 68; making them up, 302; effect of blindness, 319.

Eyes of Youth, The, light and shade in, 210.

F

Facial expression in public speaking, 453.

Fading into motion, 221.

Famous Mrs. Fair, The, 44; a pause in, 136.

Fanny Hawthorne (Hindle Wakes), the fourth wall principle in, 394.

Farce, its nature, 242.

Fashion, aside speeches, 90.

Faversham, William, his technique, 47; a remark on magnification, 61.

"Feeding," in vaudeville acts, 278.

"Feeding" a laugh, in *It's a Boy*, 110.

Female character make-up, 320.

Female straight make-up, 304.

Finality, 149.

Finding the objective, needs for, 46; in comedy, 122; in *Othello*, 178.

Fire effect, 361.

Fireflies, 361.

Fireplace effect, 361.

Fiske, Mrs., climax by her, 186; her method of acting, 246.

Flat pieces, 354.

Flies, 353.

Fly galleries, 354.

Flying flag effect, 361.

Focalization in photography, 285.

Focalization of interest, 284.

Focus of attention, 67.

Fog, effect of, 362.

Footlights, 362.

Forgetting in public speaking, 457.

Forgetting lines, 142.

Forrest, Edwin, in *Macbeth*, his traditional business, 7.

Fourth wall principle, occasions for using, 88; in relation to a fireplace, 93; in relation to furniture placement, 394.

Freckles, making them up, 319.

Front scenes, the manner of decorating, 393.

Furniture placement, 389.

G

Gagging, 293.

Garden of Allah, The, atmosphere in, 416.

Gauze, 356.

Gelatine frame, 363.

General business, or general utility part, its nature, 244.

Gérôme, his style, 258.

Gesture, in motion pictures, 97; different kinds, 97; in Continental theatres, 102; the purpose of, 102; suiting the action to the word, 103; of command in relation to words, 168; in relation to suiting the action to the word, 169; on important ideas, 169; in public speaking, 458.

"Getting it over," methods in burlesque and vaudeville, 87.

Getting up stage, 409.

Giving a person a scene, 409.

Glass crash, 358.

"Going stale," 115.

Goldfish, The, arrested action in, 230.

Golfer, a simile, 76.

"Good ear," 341.

Goodwin, Nat, in *Why Marry?* 109; his technique, 125.

Grand drapery, 354.

Grand opera, its nature, 243.

Gridiron, 353.

Ground row, 356.

INDEX

Grouping, of two or more persons at centre, 22.

Gypsy Trail, The, the fourth wall principle in, 93.

H

Hamlet, climax in, 182; Hamlet's mood, 252; the grave-digger, 259; atmosphere in, 417; the final curtain, 423.

Hamlet's Advice to the Players, 166, 289.

Hamlet's second soliloquy, light and shade in, 216.

Hamlet's Soliloquy on Death, 20; the fourth wall principle in, 89; its reading, 148; the relation of tone to, 149.

"Hand properties," 357.

Hatton, Frederic and Fanny, 77.

Heavy part, its nature, 244.

Highlights, 309.

Hokum, its definition, 240; in *Twelfth Night,* 240.

"Holding the picture," 108.

Hopkins, Arthur, 411.

Horses' hoofs, effect of, 359.

How to commit lines to memory, 56.

How to kneel, 266.

How to stand, 17.

How to turn, 35.

How to walk, 225.

I

Ibsen, Henrik, 10.

"Illusion of the First Time," 117.

Illusion of unconsciousness of what could not be known, 237.

Improvisation, 252.

Impulse for movement, 397.

Indefinite action, its nature, 26; its relation to fading into motion, 222.

Indian make-up, 313.

Individualism, 271.

Individual personal atmosphere, 417.

Ingénue part, its nature, 244.

Inspector General, The, 285; the fourth wall principle in, 394.

Intellectual plays, their nature, 10.

In the Next Room, by Eleanor Robson and Harriet Ford, 249.

Intonations in dialect parts, 156.

Irving, Henry, 236, 255; his defects, 335.

It's a Boy, the dancing doll episode, 110.

J

Jefferson, Joseph, in *Rip Van Winkle,* 159.

Jog, 355.

Julius Cæsar, shouts in, 39; the mob, 74; the fourth wall principle, 85; Antony's oration, 198; ad libitum in, 237; a front scene in, 393.

Juvenile part, its nature, 244.

K

Kean, Edmund, his observation of drunkenness, 248.

"Killing" a property, 393.

King Lear, 251.

Kinkead, Cleves, 171.

L

Lady of Lyons, The, by Bulwer Lytton, 196.

"Landing" a line, 79.

Lash lines, 356.

Last Supper, The, 85.

Laugh, Clown, Laugh, giving a scene to another actor in, 413.

Laughing, the method of, 238.

Leading part, its nature, 243.

Le Gallienne, Eva, 246.

Leg drop, 355.

Legitimate drama, its nature, 6.

INDEX

Light, important sources of, 429.

Light and shade, in nature, 207; among characters in plays, 209; between contrasted conditions, 209; in *The Eyes of Youth*, 210; between serious and comic elements, 210; in *The Merchant of Venice*, 210; in reading, 211; in *Nothing but the Truth*, 213; in *Rip Van Winkle*, 215.

Light comedy, its nature, 242.

Light comedy part, its nature, 244.

Lighting, 426; in *Rip Van Winkle*, 431; in *Romeo and Juliet*, 434; in *The Merchant of Venice*, 434; in *A Midsummer Night's Dream*, 434; in *Camille*, 434.

Lightning, 358.

Lion roar, 361.

Little Stone House, The, by Lord Caldron, atmosphere in, 416.

Little Theatre director, method of teaching play production, 473.

Little Theatre tournament, 438.

Locomotive effect, 359.

Lombardi Ltd., by Frederic and Fanny Hatton, 77.

Lytton, Bulwer, 196.

M

Macbeth, climax in, 184.

Macready, William Charles, his pauses, 130.

Madonna Enthroned with Saints, The, by Raphael, illustrating the law of attention, 69; light and shade in, 208.

Magnification, 61.

Make-up articles, 300.

Male character make-up, 305.

Male straight make-up, 300.

Mannerisms, 238; of a New York actress, 264; in public speaking, 446.

Marking the manuscript, 374.

Marquis, Don, 172.

Mary the Third, 44.

Meanest Man in the World, The, by George Cohan, action preceding speech in, 175.

Meissonier, his style, 258; his painting, 285.

Melodrama, its nature, 241.

Melodramas, old, reaction in them, 277.

Mental element in teaching, 467.

Merchant of Venice, The, magnification in, 63; its construction, 183; light and shade in, 210; stage settings, 389; a hallway in, 393; groupings in, 403; collective personal atmosphere in, 418; lighting, 434.

Metropolitan Museum of Art, The, 69, 208; paintings in, 259.

Midsummer Night's Dream, A, lighting effects, 434.

Milne, A. A., 37, 235; a comedy line by him, 153.

Miracle, The, in New York, a pause in, 136.

Mirrors, their treatment, 394.

Missing teeth, make-up for, 317.

Model of a German village, 283.

Monologists, 277.

Moods, 254.

Moods of light, 433.

Moscow Art Theatre Company, 259, 283; their technique, 49.

Mountain Man, The, 400.

Moustaches, how to make, 327.

Movement in public speaking, 454.

Movements of the head and feet, faults of making, 54.

Moving backgrounds, in the Danish Theatre, 406.

Moving tableaus, 425.

Mr. Pim Passes By, by A. A. Milne, 37; a trick exit in, 235; its mood, 254.

Mrs. Wiggs of the Cabbage Patch, pauses in the rôle of Stubbins,

INDEX

in *Mrs. Wiggs of the Cabbage Patch*, 281.

Reading, intellectual interpretation by means of, 146; its definition, 146; of comedy lines, 147; of parentheses, 150; light and shade, 211; in public speaking, 453.

Rehan, Ada, 345.

Release from tension, in public speaking, 446.

Removing make-up, 320.

Repose, its nature, 52.

Return piece, 355.

"Reverse physical action," an example of, 25.

Revue, its nature, 243.

Rhythm, its relation to tempo, 193; in dancing and poetry, 195.

Richard III, grouping focus in, 411.

Richelieu, giving an actor a scene in, 412; outside effects, 422.

Rinehart, Mary Roberts, 28, 121.

Ringing the curtain, when to do so, 424.

Rip Van Winkle, action preceding speech in, 172; climax in, 189; light and shade, 215; eliminating action in, 233; Rip Van Winkle's voice, 260; spotlight, 431.

Rising, the method of, 228.

"Rising inflection of phrasing," 187.

Romantic drama, its nature, 241.

Romeo and Juliet, the mood, 254; the balcony scene, 395; the duel, 408; lighting effects, 434.

Run, a, 356.

S

Sand bags, 357.

Scenic artist's department, 352.

Scenic equipment, 355.

School for Scandal, The, produced by Augustin Daly, 369.

Scrap of Paper, A, use of the fourth wall in, 91.

Scrim, 356.

Secret of success in the theatre, 346.

Seen, heard, and understood, in public speaking, 448.

Selection of furniture, 392.

Self-consciousness, remedied by breathing, 160.

Servant in the House, The, individual personal atmosphere in, 417.

Set pieces, 356.

Seven Ages of Man, The, in *As You Like It*, its reading, 148.

Seventeen, by Booth Tarkington, 112.

Shakespeare, William, as an actor, 349.

Shakespearean drama, breathing in respect to, 165; incongruous poses in, 265; platforms, 395.

Shakespeare's plays, the parts in them, 250.

Sherlock Holmes, the fourth wall principle in, 85.

Shylock, balance by him, 402.

Siddons, Sarah, in *Macbeth*, 7; her reaction, 276.

Side line action in *Hamlet*, 286.

Simultaneous action, 281.

Singing, the use of breathing in, 161.

Sistine Madonna, The, 208.

Six Cylinder Love, 78.

Slap stick, 360.

Sleeping palace, 107.

Slow curtain, 423.

Smoke, 362.

Snow effect, 361.

Social drama, 242.

Society drama, its nature, 242.

Sociology, its definition, 270.

Solar plexus, gesture in relation to it, 97; its relation to breathing, 160.

Sothern, E. H., as Shylock, 71; his treatment of wigs, 322.

Sothern, the elder, cause of his fame, 251.

"Speaking front," 78.

INDEX

Speaking off stage, 39.
Speed, 202.
Spotlight, 364.
Spotlight method, 284.
Spotlight system, in *Peace on Earth*, 429.
Stage brace, 356.
Stage equipment, 353.
Stage manager, his outside effects, 376; how he makes the property plot, 377.
Stage pockets, 364.
Stage screw, 357.
Stage whispers, 64.
Stanislavsky, 10, 259.
Star part, its nature, 243.
Star system, 271.
Steamboat whistle, 359.
"Straight" and "character" parts, how to distinguish, 33.
Strange Interlude, by Eugene O'Neill, asides in it, 90.
Strip light, 363.
Struggles, 230.
Studio work, 227.
Subject matter in public speaking, 444.
Suiting the action to the word, one method, 25; examples of, 167; finding the objective, 177.
Sunny Morning, A, played in New Orleans, 300.
Surprise, in the circus, 226; in *Mrs. Wiggs of the Cabbage Patch*, 227; in *Charley's Aunt*, 227.

T

"Tag," the, 121.
Taking stage, methods of doing so, 22.
Talma, 247.
Tarkington, Booth, 112.
Teaser, 354.
Telephone bell, effect of, 360.
Tempest, Marie, her "illusion of the first time," 159.

Tempo, its relation to rhythm, 193; in farce, 201; its relation to climax, 203; in a speech from *Within the Law*, 205.
Tension, relation of the solar plexus to, 115.
Terriss, William, 255.
Theatre Administration, 350.
Thomas, Augustus, trying out a play, 276.
Three Live Ghosts, a pause in, 137.
Three Musketeers, The, by Alexander Dumas, 271.
Thunderbolt, 357.
Thunder sheet, 357.
Tone, cumulation in, 126; tone and inflection, 149; sustension of, 152.
Tormentors, 354.
Traditions of the old school, 5.
Tragedy, its nature, 241.
Treasure Island, the fourth wall principle in, 85.
"Trick exit" in *Adam and Eva*, 234; in *Cornered*, 235.
Trilby, 112.
Trinity, man as a, 146.
Twelfth Night, hokum in, 240; duke's wig in, 322.
Two Orphans, The, light and shade in, 209.
Type system, 268, 296, 340.

U

Uncle Tom's Cabin, its relation to modern drama, 12; the river of ice in, 356.
Unknown Soldier, The, a curtain in, 424.

V

Vane, Sutton, 236.
Vaudeville, dramatic acts in, 114; the pause in relation to, 129; its nature, 243.
Vibration, 194.
Voice, its use in acting, 147; its registers, 149.

[483]

INDEX